NATIONAL HEALING

NATIONAL HEALING

Race, State, and the Teaching of Composition

CLAUDE HURLBERT

UTAH STATE UNIVERSITY PRESS
Logan

© 2012 by the University Press of Colorado
Published by Utah State University Press
An imprint of University Press of Colorado
5589 Arapahoe Avenue, Suite 206C
Boulder, Colorado 80303

The University Press of Colorado is a proud member of

The Association of American University Presses.

AAUP 1937 2012

The University Press of Colorado is a cooperative publishing enterprise supported, in part, by
Adams State University, Colorado State University, Fort Lewis College, Metropolitan State University
of Denver, Regis University, University of Colorado, University of Northern Colorado, Utah State
University, and Western State Colorado University.

ISBN: 978-0-87421-835-0 (paper)
ISBN: 978-0-87421-836-7 (e-book)

Library of Congress Cataloging-in-Publication Data

Hurlbert, C. Mark.
  National healing : race, state, and the teaching of composition / Claude Hurlbert.
    p. cm.
  ISBN 978-0-87421-835-0 (pbk.) — ISBN 978-0-87421-836-7 (e-book)
1. English language—Rhetoric—Study and teaching—Social aspects—United States. 2. English language—Rhetoric—Study and teaching (Higher)—United States. I. Title.
  PE1405.U6H87 2013
  808'.0420711—dc23
                        2012027782

To and for Roland.

CONTENTS

IV UNCAGED: THE INTERNATIONAL FUTURE OF COMPOSITION

ACKNOWLEDGMENTS

Thank you to Michael Spooner for his editorial contributions to and encouragement for *National Healing*, but also for all he has given and continues to contribute to the profession of composition. Thank you to the anonymous reviewers of my manuscript for their insight, suggestions, and in fact, thank you to everyone with whom I have had contact at Utah State University Press and the University Press of Colorado, including Laura Furney, Beth Anderson, Kelly Neumann, Beth Svinarich, Dan Miller, and Barbara Yale-Read. Thank you, too, to Dan Lowe, Michael Blitz, Harrison Fisher, Derek Owens, Cy Knoblauch, Steve North, Don Byrd, Nancy Mack, Jim Zebroski, Nancy Welch, Elizabeth Boquet, Ann Ott, Dan Collins, Krystia Nora, Cheryl Davis, Carrie Myers, Laila El-Omari, José Vallejo, Donna Singleton, Laura Milner, Nancy Bishop Desommes, Karen McCullough, Muhammed Elgedawy, Karen Sorenson-Lang, Ilham Jan, Lauri Barnes, Kathleen Dudden Rowlands, Maria Rankin-Brown, Janine Rider, Kevin Dvorak, Kimberly Thomas, Amy Lynch-Biniek, Mysti Rudd, Jennifer Johnson, Kathleen Klompien, Julie Peluso-Quinn, Deepak Pant, Dawn Fels, Elizabeth Campbell, Elaine Kelly, Kelli Custer, Heidi Stevenson, Jessica Ganni, Joanna Paull, Peggy Johnson, Stella Sessums Thompson, Ronni Klass-Soffian, Craig Hulst, Kami Day, Michele Eodice, Immaculée Harushimanna, Brian Fotinakes, Melanie Glennon, Anyango Kivuva, and M. G. Gainer. Thanks, as well, to the participants in the advanced seminars in transnationalism (Robin Gallaher, Rachel Goertel, Sarah A. Henderson Lee, Patricia Mathews, Kristene McClure, Jessica Schreyer, Hector M. Serna Dimas, Bashak Tarkan-Blanco, Nicole Warwick, Wan-Ning Yeh) and writing and sustainability (Abdullah F. Al-Badarneh, Ibrahim Ashour, Pisarn Chamcharatsri, Kathleen Foreman, Asuka Iijima, Kyung-Min Kim, Tomoko Odo, Astrid Parrish, John L. Reilly, Laura M. Oliver, Mohammad Shamsuzzaman, Wan-Ning Yeh) that I taught at Indiana University of Pennsylvania in the summer and fall of 2009, also to the participants in the International Sustainable Literacy Project (including Hayat Messekher). Thank you to my colleagues in the Graduate Program in Composition and TESOL at Indiana University of Pennsylvania, especially those who have contributed to my thinking in this project: Gian Pagnucci, David Hanauer, Ben Rafoth, Pat and Resa Crane Bizzaro, Mike Williamson, Sharon Deckert, and Gloria Park, and all my past colleagues, especially Don McAndrew and Pat Hartwell. Special thanks to the continuing inspiration of Jim Berlin and Jim Sledd, Bob Boynton, Peter Stillman and to Geneva Smitherman for standing as a model of integrity and generosity for the entire profession. Last, but not least, a heartfelt thank you to the good people of Project Homecoming in New Orleans and the Shepherd of the Hill Presbyterian Church of Puyallup, Washington, for the lessons in humanity. Each of you helped more than you know in ways you never imagined. My thanks may come late, in most cases, but I offer my gratitude here to tell you all how much I have learned from you and how much you mean to me. Most of all, my sister, Sharon.

NEW ORLEANS: A PRAYER

New Orleans
City of gardens
City of songs
City remembered and city forgotten
City of the dead and dying
City of the living
City of joy and city of pain
City of drowning
City of dancing
City of nations
City, teach us,
Teach us
To rise above.

PART ONE

Cage
The Provincial Composition

LEARNING NEW WAYS #1

It's an early New Orleans Sunday morning. I sit at my usual table in a Marigny coffee shop as a circle of neighbors forms at a table near the front window. They laugh as they talk over each other. One says, "He lives in a different world—that's what I told him."

We are all living in different worlds, and we are all here together. As Jelly Roll Morton once said, "We had all nations in New Orleans." Despite Jelly Roll's propensity for exaggeration, New Orleans had, and still has, people from around the world. And in New Orleans, the people have blended together, kept apart, and through it all—the floods and homicides, the singing and parades—created cultural expressions unique and vital enough to fire a land's imagination for alternatives.

Those of us in this coffee shop, day after day, are connected through conversations about politics, observations about life, and laughter. But, it is New Orleans. An intoxicated man staggers past the window this morning. I have not lived his life, nor the life of the man, "Mr. Okra," selling vegetables from his black pickup truck, covered with the names of fruits and vegetables painted in a rainbow of colors, music blaring from speakers and filling the street, even at this early hour, with funk or his voice, "We got grapes! We got bananas! We got broccoli!" And I have not lived the lives of these other coffee drinkers, nor, despite our connection, the life of the homeless man I met late one night in Jackson Square. He had been a student in the tiny high school where I had once taught in the central tier of New York State. Although I had left high school teaching before he made it to the ninth grade, where I would certainly have had him in class, I knew his grandparents who had raised him. In that rural school district, a teacher knew most families. And now he was here, homeless in New Orleans, in moments angry, in moments in tears, and, by his own description, crazy and broken-hearted.

Nor have I lived my college students' lives back in Pennsylvania.

But I have lived, and I have put together some insights into the meaning and teaching of writing.

Two men sit at the table next to me. They are talking about returning to school, to Delgado Community College here in NOLA, and about their hope. At times, their voices seem tentative, even shaky. But always they speak without pretense in their assessments of themselves, their lives, and their abilities. They talk about their "track records," their "relapses," their desires, and their commitments. One of them says, "We are used to this," as he makes a gesture of shooting up. "Now we have to learn a new way. We have to learn that things take time."

After a pause, the other one says, "There is a beauty in people who have lived."

Sitting at my table, I think—is that it? Is it beauty? Is that what living the hard stuff of life inspires in people? Certainly, there is beauty in making the decision to survive, and dignity. And these two men have each other with whom to share this truth; there is a beauty in that friendship, too. So, yes, maybe it is beauty.

The days pass. People come and go.

At another table on another day, a man and a woman plan a city tour about the history of African American experience in New Orleans. The tour will be for high school students. It will encourage them to learn about the meaning of standing up for one's self and for others. When they take a work break, I ask them about their project and they ask about me.

The students in our college classrooms sometimes write texts about pain and beauty, because they, too, are trying to make a full accounting of having been here in the passing days. And sometimes they write about standing up to wrongs, how to address them, and how to find better ways of living. Our students are trying to learn new ways, even in their every days.

Sitting at my table, I think about my life.

My job as a compositionist is to encourage writers who are engaged in the human project of examining their lives. My goal is to help them use writing to explore the possibility of better lives and ways in a troubled world.

One semester I had a first year writing student come to my office immediately after the first class. She told me that she knew what she was burning to tell the world, in a short book she was going to write for my class. It was about her heroin addiction and how she was battling it. At the same time, she told me that everyone in her high school knew her as an addict. She related how much she had looked forward to going away to college so that she could be around people who did not know her past. She was looking forward to a new start. We discussed the legitimacy of her desire to tell her story, and also the legitimacy of wanting this new beginning for herself. After much talk, she decided to write about the positive role model her mother had always been for her, even though she had not always followed it. Through the several conferences we had during the course of the semester, we developed strategies for her to write her book without giving away information about her addiction. In this way, she learned to tell a story that dramatized the letting go of one part of the past in order to embrace the health of another. She learned a new way.

Take a personal choice such as this student's decision and multiply it to the tens, the hundreds, the thousands, over the course of a thirty-year teaching career. Thousands of students pass through a writing teacher's classroom. We make a difference—in real lives.

MAKING A PAST A PAST AND A
LIFE A LIFE

As compositionists, we have unique contributions to make. We create various schools of composition theory and elaborate profound interpretations of rhetoric. We bring a variety of cultural and ethnic perspectives to our understanding of genre and academic writing. We develop pedagogies that influence teaching in other academic disciplines. My goal is to revisit the history of rhetoric to better understand why we think what we do and do what we do in our classrooms—so that we can make the past the past as we learn new ways.

National Healing is a book about understanding the teaching of writing in the United States. It is an attempt to reorient composition so that it supports, literally, a healthier nation and state, so that the United States might better contribute to the health of the world. And even as I write out my topic, I hear how impossible it all sounds, the outrageous claim upon which my project rests. Perhaps you have heard compositionists say that they write to change the order of things, maybe even to improve the world in some way. Perhaps you have made your own promises, as I have. And perhaps you have been disappointed so many times that you can no longer quite bring yourself to believe such promises. Perhaps you are not sure you will ever believe again. If so, I understand. I have those feelings. I have read and listened. I have studied and written. And I have been discouraged. But, certainly, we also know that we cannot give up. Deep inside we know that not choosing to direct our teaching and writing to the highest challenges of our day will continue to yield its own results. No, we must begin, even if it means that we begin again, and again.

In *National Healing*, I am presenting a vision for an international composition studies, a discipline that investigates composing from various cultural perspectives from around the globe in an attempt to better serve our students—and the world. It is a vision that shifting demographics demands. It is a vision for national healing through international understanding—not to mention cooperation. It is an organic vision in which teachers learn to be conscious of the degree to which local, student-centered instruction and writing is connected to larger, world contexts. To this end, in *National Healing*, I demonstrate how I enact an internationalist perspective in my composition classes, and I explain how internationalism will impact graduate education in composition in the coming years.

I am aware and understand the now commonplace debate over terms in our discipline. Some say that "composition" refers to a course and that the discipline's concerns have grown beyond it, especially in an age where writing programs are splitting off from English departments. The claim is that "writing studies" is a more accurately inclusive term. But I have chosen to stick with the term "composition" in *National Healing* for strategic reasons. "Composition" is still the designation for my discipline, for the major annual conference in my field, and for many key journals. I also adhere to the term "composition" to differentiate international composition studies from didactic writing studies in Europe. While current European studies of writing in the disciplines have much to offer us in composition, they are still, generally speaking, more objectivist and focused on argumentative writing as academic discourse than I would propose. (I wish to add, though, that because I value international dialogue, I would support changing terms as soon as it seems theoretically, historically and materially sound to do so.)

To begin to reach an internationalist perspective, we compositionists must study the nationalist ideology that keeps us tied within provincial concerns and discourses. To accomplish this, we must begin with racism. If we compositionists are to reach the social possibilities that multiculturalism once represented—or, better, reach beyond them—we will need to be honest about the vestiges of racism with which we continue to live and teach. If we are to find the healing we need in order to contribute to the end, finally, of racism, we will need to understand how the personal, political, and pedagogical realms of our lives are inextricably linked. As David Schaasfma and Ruth Vinz (2011, 1) write, "Narratives often reveal what has remained unsaid, what has been unspeakable." It's time to say it—it's past time. And sometimes finding the words and the truth is best done through writing that dramatizes as well as explicates, writing that moves as well as enlightens. Indeed, in composition, theoretical discussions of politics enacted without something approaching artistry can be off-putting, cold, and didactic. The doctrinaire is, in the final analysis, too-easily dismissed; therefore, *National Healing* is a book of pedagogy, poetry, theory, and stories. I employ stories, for instance, because they are epistemic. Stories tell us who we are and who we want to be. They show us what we think and how we do things, and they point to new ways for thinking and doing them. They show us what we know and tell us what we still want to know; sometimes, even what we might wish we did not know—the unspeakable which circles, it sometimes seems, every story. Stories dramatize and illustrate our commitments. They help us see and feel the connections between the local and global scales of human experience. Stories contain history and are contained by history. They reflect and stimulate material reality. As Gian Pagnucci (2004, 1) eloquently writes, some people know—especially healthy people who do not try to project stories onto others—that the lessons they learn from writing, reading, and hearing stories are so necessary and profound that they commit themselves to "choosing stories as a way of life."

I understand that many academics dismiss stories as childish or ancillary or supplemental, as something less than argumentative discourse. I suppose this has something to do with the fact that personal narrative is associated with the mistaken discrediting of expressivism or an allegiance to outmoded hierarchies of discourse. But I suspect that when academics dismiss narrative, it is also often an unconscious decision based in discursive taste (and a strange taste it is when English professors have novels and non-fiction in their offices, homes, and backpacks and on their bedside tables). I wonder sometimes if there isn't more to our commitment to argumentation and denigration of narrative. I understand that some professors feel that they are doing their best for students when they teach argumentation because they see it as serious academic writing. But what of the many, many academics for whom narrative is a necessary genre of academic writing? Perhaps there is another deeper and darker reason for the academic commitment to argumentation. Truth be told, I wonder if many academics do not value narrative because they associate it not only with lesser discourses, but also with lesser cultures: those "ethnic" cultures from elsewhere. Never mind that story telling is the central epistemological mode of so many successful cultures around the world. Never mind that the architecture of a story is as beautiful and graceful as the architecture of any argument. Never mind that the beauty of story takes us beyond ourselves by taking us to the center of ourselves.

The sanctioning of a genre such as argumentative writing is a cultural matter; so is the demotion of a genre. I believe that the dismissing of narrative is just another form of disguised racism, and we need to speak out and get beyond it. The fact is that we need theory to understand composing and writing pedagogy. But the fact is also that we need stories because they achieve what theory cannot. Stories and poetry open up reality in dramatic ways. Indeed, so many scholars and writers have made eloquent claims for the importance and meaning of narrative that I cannot possibly rehearse them all here. As scholars Frankie Condon (2012) and Victor Villaneuva (1993)—to name only two of the numerous compositionists who work in the intersection of story and theory— have demonstrated, narrative helps us understand ourselves and our work and illuminates how we are bound to each other. Telling the stories of who we are sheds light on who we are, and this, in turn, helps us to critique who we are.

In *National Healing*, I include stories and poems, along with history and theory. I do so because stories and poems are as necessary to knowing and understanding, as is argumentative prose. We need every story and every poem as we search for the best in all of us. Indeed, opening composition to the aesthetic realm of experience could be one of the most direct routes to the development of our international discipline. Every culture demonstrates the poetic, whether in verse, song, chant, prayer, dance, or image. These genres open possibilities for recognizing the political realm in our lives. In fact, we should work harder to remember that the poetic and political realms are inseparable. As Ray Misson and Wendy Morgan (2006) remind us in *Critical Literacy and the Aesthetic*, aesthetic needs are also critical needs, just as personal concerns are also political concerns. James Berlin knew this. I remember one night in Cincinnati and the look in his eyes when I told him that I thought his greatest contribution to the profession was his work to reunite rhetoric and poetics. Perhaps if he had lived to continue his work, Berlin might have furthered the relationship for us. Still, he leads the way. In "Rhetoric, Poetic, and Culture," he explains how economics has lead to a deepening of the chasm between rhetoric and poetics in English departments, how "changes in economic and social structures during the eighteenth and nineteenth centuries led to a new conception of the nature of poetic, a conception that defines the aesthetic experience in class terms and isolates it from other spheres of human activity" (1991, 24). We teach lower class writers, in other words, not to compose works of art, but to produce items for consumption; the value of which are measured in capital or, as Berlin asserts, scientific terms. The painful result of teaching in this instrumentalist perspective is the further separation of the imagination from the lives of the people in our classrooms. In civic terms, failing to recognize the imagination in student writing suppresses agency in our students' lifelong imagining of political and cultural alternatives. Berlin was right. We need to reunite rhetoric and poetics.

Lifelong imaginings. Sometimes they begin almost inexplicably in some distant time or place. Sometimes they begin with other people. Sometimes they speak of beginnings themselves, connections that do not make immediate sense. Sometimes they begin in a moment of past pain or love that speaks of present need.

Imagine a past—a past so we can start over. Imagine a distant past—a far away past that is also a cultural source. Imagine Ezra Pound for a moment, incarcerated in the white burning heat of an Italian, mid-August noon in 1945. His voice sounds like an aging teacher's as it reverberates, sometimes muttering, sometimes shouting, across a square, before a villa, maybe, but always from a cage. It is the voice of a grandfather immersed in the corruption of his generation's hatreds—a grandfather never quite delivering on the role model he might have been. His voice is hollow and shrill with the madness of mistakes, of being so wrong and wrong again, of inscribing evil again and again. It is an old, almost familiar voice reaching to shadows that fall across open French doors and the carved folds of ornate arches. It is a voice from darkness: darkness too deep to penetrate, too frightening to bring to light. Searing words twisting in the wind and cutting, sometimes to truth, sometimes to beauty, and sometimes lost to hatred expressed so perfectly. Or maybe dreaming—dreaming the words—and then hoarsely yelling them to the sky; hearing them bounce among the pigeons, once picking, now in direct flight over the nearly endless stones of a white-hot piazza.

But this is wrong. There was no square, no piazza, no ornate arches, except, maybe, in mind or dream or memory. In 1945, when Ezra Pound was arrested in Italy for the treasonous radio broadcasts he made in support of Mussolini and National Socialism, he was taken to the US Army's Disciplinary Training Center (DTC) just north of Pisa. There, yes, he was confined to a cage. But it was in a field, a cage in a row of chain-link cages, all with concrete floors and tin roofs.

Or imagine another past. Christmas Eve, 2009, as I walked through the French Quarter in New Orleans, I found an open courtyard filled with mistaken beliefs and the search for meaning: of a life, of grandparents, and parents—in New Orleans, from Pittsburgh, upstate New York, and back to New Orleans. It was one of those nights in which one recognizes life amidst the remnants of passing scripts. And it was one of those nights in which one realizes what one must do to change.

Pound (n.d.b, 59) wrote sharp, blade-like insights: "A vicious economic system has corrupted every ramification of thought." Such a sentence is a truth, perhaps, but if it is one, it is rooted in the hatred of anti-Semitism. As a sentence, it has a precision amidst exaggeration, but, at the same time, it promotes service to antipathy. It both reaches and falls short. Too often Pound's words simply do not emerge from the best of a life; they lay the hidden bare, but scrape bones as they do.

National Healing is a book of confusions, memories, nightmares, and dreams. It is about trying to figure a personal life's relation to a nation's life, how the two are essentially linked—to comprehend so as to teach for change. It is about a nation's racism and violence; it is about pain. It is about trying to figure out where a self ends and a nation begins, where history ends and a person begins, where they intersect—and maybe where they should not. It is about learning, writing, and teaching to understand a nation's song, the violent strains of nationalism—a nation's failure. It is about making a life of materials too often limited by "-isms," and it is about making a life and freeing it from the love of hate that plagues the homeland. And above all, it is about writing and teaching writing in the course of a life, and the confines of a nation that are both in need of healing.

National Healing is also about listening to a life so you can tell others. It is telling others so you can tell yourself. It is about trying to become new, or, at least, better: a better teacher, a better writer, a better person. Better.

National Healing is about coming to terms with the words of others and translating them into one's life. It is about bringing them as close as possible in order to begin. It is about learning what others teach and how they, too, are finding and listening to beginnings. Their voices and the voices of still others, inseparable. The beginning and end of a sound, or a breath. And always the voices of others. The ones we know. The ones from the past as we select them—and as they select us. The ones we don't. The ones we will never know. This is about choosing to know. This is about choosing a beginning, the beginning of a sound, the beginning of an age. This is about the modern world, the postmodern world that reportedly took its place, and the ever-globalizing and heating world in which we now live and teach composition. And this is the sound of another way of beginning—beginning somewhere else—by choosing a past.

1975

It is a cool, early autumn afternoon in 1975 in upstate New York. I am an undergraduate English secondary education major, and I am sitting in an American literature classroom in a small state college. I am reading Pound's "Mang Tsze: The Ethics of Mencius." In it, Pound (1973, 94) discusses the nature of the ideogram, the difficulty of the translation, the power of the image: "No one with any visual sense can fail to be affected by the way the strokes move in these characters."

Figure 1. Ideogram 8 from "Mang Tsze." 1973. In Ezra Pound, Selected Prose: 1909–1965. (New York: New Directions Press, 81–97.)

I am looking at a single ideogram in the text. Perhaps I did not want to "fail to be affected." Perhaps I simply was. I am studying the movement and angles, the gesture.

Curved and straight lines coming together, a visual representation of how meaning gathers from different places, different sources, different times—a meeting place where the past comes forward for dialogue with the present. A clearing in an American literature classroom where students might suddenly have a sense of what it means to stand in history, to feel, if not yet to understand, the significance of intersections taking shape when layers of meaning touch.

At my desk, I begin to tell myself that I will learn the depth, resonances, and echoes of the ideogram, that I will learn to write the meaning of the shadows and light spreading across my consciousness.

At the same time, as I try to understand Pound's ideogram, it resists. It withholds its content. I cannot translate it. I cannot make literal sense of the design. I have what Pound (1973, 85) says it means, "sincerity" or "the man who stands by his word," but on my own—nothing.

Or maybe something else, I have a desire to understand. Maybe I am simply convincing myself that I will know something of the meaning of this ideogram, or maybe I am sensing that I am who I am because I desire this knowledge, because I seek the knowledge created when cultures fold in on one another and say something new. And maybe I am merely convincing myself, for a moment, despite my own fears and inadequacies—even my own shame in ignorance. What does a beginning in poverty have to do with Ezra Pound? What does China have to do with me, not to mention Chinese? Do I have the right to write if I cannot even understand? I have echoes of Fenollosa (1920, 358) in my head: "We in America, especially, must face it [Chinese culture] across the Pacific, and master it or it will master us. And the only way to master it is to strive with patient sympathy to understand the best, the most hopeful and most human elements in it."

These words, this xenophobic call for mastery, is an odd amalgamate of respect, fear, and threat, concurrent with a rendering exotic the text of the other. I would not have understood this. I should have known—but probably did not—that contradictory emotions and impulses too often lie behind Pound's words as well as Fennellosa's (not to mention so much of life). All I knew were the words on the page, the integration of the desire to teach and write, and the feeling that I was faced with something important.

Ideograms: word becomes picture. Word becomes art. Meaning transformed. And, of course, Pound's translations of the Chinese were as mistaken as they were creative, as self-serving as insightful, as ridiculous as inspiring. That day I saw Pound's ideograms as a beginning, a re-working of texts and meanings in an attempt to compose a world where one imagines the new through writing. For Pound (n.d.a, 57) only "The stupid or provincial judgment of art bases itself on the belief that great art must be like the art it has been reared to respect." Writing was, in this view, about voices coming together to make something new. Confucius as Pound; Pound as Confucius. When the translation is working—opening a space that gathers time and distance, bringing the makers of meaning together—even the reader comes together with Confucius and Pound, stepping forward in the public square of the page to add to the saying, to add to the creation of something new. And it *is* necessary to say something new. It is necessary because there is so much sorrow, so much shame, so much violence, so much war, so much, so much. And so little time to stop the degradation of our planet. It is hard to put it all into words because it is so hard to picture. It is the size of a nation and as small as a human heart.

In 1975, the United States was, in many ways, a country whose spirit had been worn by Vietnam and racial hatred, unrealized promise, a nation of guilt and greed. And we, the students in that literature classroom were left with the task of figuring out (though I am not sure we would have had the words to say so) how to write, teach, think, and live in what some of us thought was the American twilight. But, of course, we were wrong. It was not twilight—though the clock was ticking. It was Modernism's legacy: the stressed dictums of its version of a unified, if mythical, nation-state, the deterioration of some of its creative traditions, and the obvious failure of the American utopia and the golden attainment of history's promise. Lyotard (1984) would later explain that we were enduring the failure of the master narratives, that we were no longer humanism's coherent individuals, that we were becoming selves defined, not solely by our egos, but by the fabric of relationships we were living. Perhaps. But we knew nothing of the fabric. We could only see the tears and feel lost and searching, searching for peace, for hope, for ways to hang onto someone else, each other, and, maybe, even ourselves.

Like so many state college students in the United States, my colleagues and I were studying in a small, isolated town. We were disconnected from the centers of the nation, New York and Berkeley, even if a few of us read *The Village Voice*. For me, 1975 felt like a fabric of failures, if it felt like a fabric at all. I tried to believe that it was still possible to be productively critical of government and ideology and the economic structures that crushed so many Americans. I had demonstrated against the war. I wrote. I argued and dreamed. But nothing changed. I tried to believe that Marxism still offered the best hope for fairness in the world. But nothing changed. I followed a strain of thought which, perhaps, "in the end lost its theoretical standing and was reduced to the status of a 'utopia' or 'hope,' a token protest raised in the name of man or reason or creativity . . ." (Lyotard 1984, 13).

Maybe this was me in a long moment of becoming myself in-folded in the fraying fabric of Modernism's version of elitism and aestheticism— or just my own desire to be in college and enter a higher economic class. I am not sure. Maybe this was just me, or maybe it was a generation trying to tell itself that sometime, in some future, it had to write itself so that "nation" no longer meant us and them, racism and war.

It is probably safe to say that most of the students sitting in the room that day in 1975 did not learn such lessons, but still something took and held. More than one of us went on to become teachers and writers. For myself, I can say that I was, in some sense, in that undergraduate moment, beginning to learn the crafts of teaching and writing. I was learning something essential that would not begin to make sense for many years to come; a truth so real and powerful, so misunderstood and under-taught, so simple and yet so necessary—composing is an international process. It is not the intellectual or artistic inheritance of one nation or group of nations. Its meaning, theories, processes, and effects are not bound by cultural or national boundaries, only by nationalist interests, expediencies, and racist commitments to cultural purity. True, that afternoon I could not have said all that—I did not have the language or knowledge to do so. No, I was rendering the meaning of that ideogram more exotic than actual. But thirty-five years later, as I write this, I know that the ideogram is also about its own composing. It is about composing translation, Pound's poetry, and it is about the grasping of the brush, the flow of black ink across paper. The growing resistance as the paint spreads out behind the bristles—ink left behind, resistance growing in tiny increments. Perhaps an ancient's hand holds the brush, or Pound's bony fingers. My fingertips touching the ideogram on the page. The composing, the image, the words, turning out right or wrong as we try to tell the truths we start with and later recompose.

Somehow the ideogram was opening a door for me, one that allows me to say now, so many years later, that composing is more multinational, larger and more multi-natured, than anyone, not Aristotle, not Edward P.J. Corbett, not anyone, despite their contribution, has written. No one has accounted for the ways of composing any more than one has accounted for the ways of being in the world. Indeed, we teachers of writing have barely begun. Despite our best intentions we are going about the question of composing and the teaching of writing in what, after all, are deficient ways. Composing is not best taught by the teaching of forms. Composing is not best explained as either personal or social. Composing is not merely a cultural or public turn toward activism. There are not, simply, composing processes to answer this or that context. No, composing is a continually changing mix of processes, influenced from here and there, this culture and that, this nation and that, from always, someone or something or somewhere else. To answer, the teaching of writing should be about teaching for international exchange and change. Knowing this alters the ways we have of writing, teaching writing, and even our ways of being in the world.

THE MOST IMPORTANT CLASS

For me, teaching writing means offering each student an opportunity to learn to use language to explore their experiences in relation to the experiences of others. It means offering students the opportunity to change by expanding their composing. It means helping students to learn how and why others make meaning so that they may incorporate, if they wish, some of these meanings, purposes, processes, and techniques into their own writing. Teaching writing means creating a pedagogy in which students explore the critical need for fluency, honesty, beauty, and truth in maintaining world health. At this time, no need presses so firmly on my vision than the need to help students find expression in writing to heal and share healing knowledge. I believe that is the most meaningful response to nationalism and racism that I can inspire.

Currently, though, the teaching of composition is widely defined by a fundamentalist, nationalist, ideology that requires compositionists to teach a truncated view of writing that unites all Americans in normalized forms of meaning and meaning making. We see nationalist ideology in the drive to standardize both writing and teaching practices. Specifically, many compositionists are encouraged, through standardized assessment or boilerplate syllabi, or through administrative practices, such as textbook selection or late course assignments, to teach writing in nearly the same way, semester after semester. For these teachers, sometimes the only difference, semester to semester, is the textbook adopted, the film shown, or some added pedagogical technique, such as peer response groups, journal writing, PowerPoint, MOOS, or Blackboard. Whatever the technique, the thinking behind the course remains the same: we will teach so that all students will come out of our classes at the end of the semester with similar, certifiable, basic literacy and academic skills. If students all leave our classes writing in essentially the same way, meeting standards of grammatical, bibliographic, and argumentative propriety, writing, in other words, with manners sanctioned by the dominant ideology of elite culture, we will have done our part in preparing them to take upper division courses in the disciplines of their choosing. It is our way of guaranteeing our students' academic success. At least, that is the way the thinking goes.

But there is a subtext to this argument, and it goes this way: if we teach all our students to write in the manner we desire and to which we even aspire, they will be further bound to the social identity we support, and even espouse. This thinking is firmly situated in nationalism, and it is what James Berlin warned us about when he wrote concerning the relation of the rise of Anglo-Saxonist ethnocentrism and the centrality of rhetoric's position in the college curriculum in response to the waves of immigration that occurred between the 1890s and 1920s (1996, 22–28).

A nationalist view of composition promotes Western rhetorical forms, particularly argumentation. It is marked by foundational appeals to a blend of Western rhetoric, capitalist consumption models of education, and individualist competition (Hurlbert 1988, 1989). It is marked by a conservative commitment to formalism and a liberal commitment to managed forms of multiculturalism. Its curricular emphasis is on teaching academically sanctioned forms and training writers to control audiences, particularly through the employment of a white, male, liberal voice. In all, it is more dedicated to turning out students who write academically acceptable discourse. Who respect, if not revere, officially sanctioned tradition. Who know how to buy textbooks and compete for grades. And who have at least a sense of how to manipulate an audience, use writing to complete work assignments, and, most importantly, think and write the right things, as determined by academic administrators, textbook companies, and teachers from the right and left and points between.

We want our students to respect learning and to get jobs, and I have even known teachers who sometimes say that the writing and school skills they teach will help students achieve these ends. But it should be sufficiently clear, even from my brief sketch, that this view of composition does not sufficiently expand the processes needed to write for an ever more interdependent world population, where, for instance, propriety in writing and school decorum do not even look or sound the same for one as for another. Yes, many times we do need to persuade others. And sometimes we do need to recognize when we are being led to support unethical courses of action, such as when we are being persuaded of the justification for an unjust war. But just as important is learning how to use language to open up the meaning of self in society, the harmony of one in many, the location of humanity in nature, or to articulate the complex beauty and discord of human being. A nationalist view of composition is not sufficient for teaching writing, or for fostering the intellectual health of a well-developed subjectivity. (No wonder the universal composition course appears expendable to some in higher education!) To put it simply, a nationalist view of composition does not, in and of itself, answer the reasons writers write and so makes a poor, long-term rationale for the universal college writing course.

So how does my vision specifically resist nationalist approaches to the teaching of writing? In the way that teaching often works—in small steps and occasionally something more. And, while I will detail my pedagogy in Part 3, "Key: The Composition Classroom," let me just say, for now, that I ask students to write for the entire semester about whatever is the most important subject matter in their lives, to find or create or learn about and adapt the most useful discursive form or forms in which to do the writing. To find some initiative toward understanding and change— which most often entails health and healing within the project—to share that knowledge in the room or, when appropriate, without, and to learn how each other composes as they do so. This involves a lot of writing, and also a lot of talk and listening. And no single ideologically sanctioned discourse, such as argument, receives transcendental privileging over another.

I have suggested that my education began that warm, autumn day in 1975 in an undergraduate American literature class. I might, no doubt, have picked other days and classes in a lifetime of study. But that day certainly stands out in my memory for how it helped to inspire my search through libraries and bookstores, my browsing and reading, my studying as much as possible in the history of philosophy, rhetoric, and poetics from various cultures. It started me on a journey to learn how composing is addressed in many places and in many ways across time. It started me on a course of study that has led to an understanding of how the one tradition teachers of writing are accustomed to studying— call it the Eurocentric or Classical or Western tradition—is only one part of the story of composition. More crucially, teaching from one, truncated version of the Western tradition of rhetoric shortchanges our students. Teaching the four modes of discourse, or teaching that argument—as important as it is—is the mode for doing well in college and in life, offers only a limited view of what writing is about. This kind of teaching is, indeed, the pale fetish we find in first-year composition textbooks. Because it is based in exercise and teacher-sponsored and teacher-edifying writing, this kind of teaching can drain composing of its multicultural, international, and most human-enriching elements. To begin to develop a more intellectually satisfying and international perspective, writing teachers need to study the rhetorics of the world. They need to do so, not to mandate traditional forms of contrastive rhetorical skills, but to understand the rhetorics that students bring to their composing, and that circulate through lives and cultures; and which writers, to one degree or another, appropriate even if they cannot claim them by cultural or ethnic inheritance. Through this study, the teaching of writing becomes new, becomes a study of the meaning of experience and creation, the meaning of the variety and wakefulness, of options and decisions, the meaning of being human in our equal searches for the meaning of our lives.

1980

In 1980, I began my doctoral work at the State University of New York at Albany. I studied Western rhetoric and philosophy with C. H. Knoblauch. Those days were first and foremost about the process revolution and expressivism in composition. As my fellow graduate students and I studied Classical rhetoric, it was with an eye toward understanding the ways it did, or did not, sanction the contemporary conceptions of composing and teaching we were developing. We wanted to know the Classical tradition because we wanted to know the history—thanks to Cy Knoblauch's student-centeredness—in which the rhetorical revolution in which we felt we were participating was located. With Cy's guidance, we wanted to know what Plato said about ethics and discourse, what Aristotle said about persuasion and process, what Cicero said about the rhetorical training and character of the orator. We were also reading philosophy, especially the works of Ernst Cassirer (1944, 1946, 1955) and Susanne Langer (1942), because we wanted to understand processes of mind, signification, and metaphor in meaning making. We were reading Derrida (1976, 1983) and Foucault (1970, 1982), and we wanted to deconstruct the texts of antiquity in order to articulate how indeterminate textual moments gave free reign to the use and abuse of power. And following what James Berlin (1984, 1987) wrote in his landmark studies, *Writing Instruction in Nineteenth-Century American Colleges* and *Rhetoric and Reality*, we began to question the social and epistemological underpinnings of rhetoric and composition. From him we learned that writing is always a political act, an effect and a response to culture, ideology, and capital. And because any act of writing is infused by poetics as well as rhetoric, we relearned what Ann Berthoff had been telling us for a decade or more, that composing is an act of imagination inspired in dialogue.

In 1986, I had a stroke of life-changing luck. After graduating from SUNY Albany, I landed a teaching position at Indiana University of Pennsylvania. In addition to undergraduate writing classes, I was assigned to teach in a doctoral program that combined the study of composition with the study of TESOL (at the time we called the combination "Rhetoric and Linguistics"). I was assigned to teach EN 731: The Rhetorical Tradition and the Teaching of Writing. This class focused on the Western rhetorical tradition and how the field of composition developed from it. I quickly discovered the course's flaw, the myopic center of vision in its content. A class in the Western tradition of rhetoric and its development into the field of composition did not tell the whole story. The majority of the graduate students who took the class were already teachers or professors from various parts of the world, from countries as diverse as Bangladesh, Costa Rica, Japan, Jordan, Nigeria, China, Nepal, Poland, Puerto Rico, Russia, Saudi Arabia, Senegal, South Korea, Thailand, Taiwan, Togo, the United States, Zambia, and, before the Bush presidencies, Iraq and Yemen. They had learned to write in a variety of ways, and thought about composing from differing perspectives. They had varying approaches to style. In many cases, they saw the aims and purposes of writing differently. Their sense of what language could and should do was textured by the cultures and politics of their home countries. And their composing processes were informed by concerns in many cases different from my own.

In the many sections of the class that I taught in the subsequent years, students talked about how composing was always about living, growing, and even surviving shortages, oppression, migration, and violence—and, even loneliness. Composing was textured by awareness that if one were to look out one's window while writing, one would see a raging Pennsylvania snowstorm, rather than the sun shimmering on palm leaves; by awareness that what one wrote in Pennsylvania could get one sent to the countryside for a second course of re-education back home; awareness that when one wrote, one looked first, with humility, to the rhythms of The Holy Qur-An rather than to Aristotle. And when we talked about the teaching of writing, we talked about how to negotiate the social paralysis brought on by sitting in a circle when a student had never seen one in a classroom in their home country of Japan. Or how to teach writing when one taught in the hot sun of a stadium in Togo, with a class enrollment of three thousand students (and one's gratitude when a resourceful administrator found funding to split the class into two sections). Or how to teach writing from a critical perspective when one's home country's (Egypt's) government could have undercover police posing as students so as to monitor faculty loyalty to the Mubarak government. Or the resistance one would face if one were to teach from an overtly feminist perspective in the restrictive society of one's home (Arab) country. Or the teaching reality for a student who, if they returned to their African home to teach, might very well be identified at the airport and executed by an ethnic cleansing gang.

These graduate classes became dialogues about how composing is always a matter of national constraints and international exchange. No matter how rigid the rhetorical forms and processes of Classical rhetoric sometimes appeared, my students demonstrated again and again that composition is more about interacting with others, developing the self, responding to far-flung places on the globe, and incorporating traditional and contemporary wisdom and avenues for creative expression—more about bringing to bear as many resources as possible to each significant moment of composing, and to each challenging—or dangerous—context for teaching.

We bring our historical inheritances to composing, even as we repeat what we have learned or love, are comfortable with, or have found tedious. Through writing experiences of various kinds, we discover that writing is also about living in a complex world where meeting others or reading their words changes how we go about composing. And that is the growth, and that is at least one reason why it takes so many years to learn to write well. We need time to learn difference so that we can begin to see how a change in practice can lead to new powers to create, so that difference changes how we write, how we make our writing—and ourselves—to the extent that we are able—new.

And so I realized the need to teach a course at Indiana University of Pennsylvania whose rhetorical theory was expanded by the horizons of non-Western rhetorics even as it presented the Western tradition for intensive investigation, and to do both to the best of my ability in one class. There was, at that time, no room in the curriculum for two or more courses in rhetoric. I wanted, as I learned from and with my students, the technical expertise of the Western tradition and the sense of communal meaning making of Afrocentric and many Native American rhetorics. I wanted study of the morality in the philosophy of Plato and the spirituality of Thich Nhat-Hanh. I wanted Lu Ji's commitment to imagination and Gertrude Stein's commitment to experimentation. I wanted to teach a variety of rhetorics because I wanted to encourage students to see that there are a variety of ways to imagine and enact composing, a variety of ways to realize meaning, and a variety of ways to recognize themselves as makers of meaning and health. I wanted students to broaden their understanding of composing so that they would broaden their thinking about what a composition could and should be. I wanted to make a course that gestured toward fairness and healthy meaning making, which respected both the students in my graduate class and the students they would be teaching in their writing classes. I believed, and I still believe, that one of the most healing things I can do is to teach for the widest and deepest exploration of the international nature of composing possible. My lifelong investigation has become this book.

SPEAKING OF LOVE

In her foreword to Duane Roen, Stuart Brown and Theresa Enos's *Living Rhetorics: Stories of the Discipline*, Andrea Lunsford (1999a, xi) asks what are, for me, good questions: "Where were you when you 'fell in love' with the theory and/or practice of rhetoric and composition? What were you doing at the very moment when you claimed the teaching of writing/reading as your way of life?"

I'm not sure. Although I can see a commitment to teaching writing in my 1975 meeting with Pound's ideograms, maybe I am forgetting something else. Or maybe I am not in love. (Indeed, when I see the mechanistic, canned pedagogies enacted in some classrooms or the unwavering commitment to argumentation that is taught in others, I realize that my relation with the field is closer akin to something like love/hate.) But I recognize in Lunsford's words the understanding that when we talk about the profession of composition, we are also talking about people who have made the important commitment to share something deep with their students. When we talk about writing, we are talking about our sacred words and languages, our private voices, our thoughts and fears—our respect for the best of the past and the promise of a future. We are talking about experience and being, about ways of living. We are talking about how we write: paper and computers, notebooks and laptops, in coffee shops (or on buses and trains, in gardens and city parks, under trees or at tables, in hospitals, jails, libraries, shelters, and in homes ravaged by natural or man-made disasters). When we talk about writing, we are talking about our relation to ourselves, to the texts we are writing, to the world in which we live. For some of us, for we lucky ones, we are talking about the glow of the computer screen, the feel of the keys, perhaps the sounds of other people, our favorite music playing overheard or in our minds. We are talking about composing in our anticipations—of a better world, but more to the point of the day-to-day, even, maybe, of the moment in which someone will appear whose face stops our world for joy, or a face which plunges us into our meditations. Writing is one of the most intimate of experiences. It is about our expectations: of ideas, of being loved, of feeling connected to something larger than ourselves. It is the search for something beautiful: a graceful thought, a graceful turn of phrase, a moment of grace leading to the perception of a graceful life in a graceful world. It is our search for places where we get it, get something right, where we love what we have said and love, perhaps, for some of us, for a moment or more, ourselves. And it is always a position, gesture, or call against the politics, the power of those who exploit us and others, the fundamentalisms of those who plan death on an international scale, or, sometimes, even, those who seek to still our voices.

Even when not overtly political, writing is always these things because it is a life impulse, an impulse toward freedom and independence that makes healthy forms of belonging possible. We write to claim our lives, to carve lives out—even for minutes at a time, from the discourses that texture them from without. These moments of writing are where we try to free ourselves, to save ourselves—to the extent that we can—from the unhealthy influences in our cultures, the unhealthy dictates of our nations, from the hunger of capitalist greed that has so successfully eaten its way through our world ecosystem (Foster 2002, 2009; Foster, Clark and York 2010). We write, in other words, to cut ourselves free from the vicious dictates of pain, and also from the limitations on our thinking even as we seek to join with those working for the well-being of us all. We write because we feel the need to write to experience writing again, to be alone with ourselves even as we respond to the words of others (because, after all, responding is also who we are). And we write to change in some way, to be both ourselves and reoriented toward the world at the same time. I know that I write to find something of myself that I want to bring back, to which I want to hang on and to which I want to live up. I write to find new ways.

Many writers have written about how writing has saved their lives. Through writing they find out how to address, redress, do something— to not give up. Some writers write to become someone different from themselves. Some even believe that there is a way to write so that this time the changes they imagine will stick, that they will be healed from wounds large and small, global and local. There is pain enough to go around, and some writers write to address at least *some* of this pain.

Writers use writing as the medium in and through which they change their lives. As Charles Anderson and Marian MacCurdy (2000, 7) put it: "Healing is neither a return to some former state of perfection nor the discovery or restoration of some mythic autonomous self. Healing, as we understand it, is precisely the opposite. It is a change from a singular self, frozen in time by a moment of unspeakable experience, to a more fluid, more narratively able, more socially integrated self." And healing is, among other things, integration freed from racism—one of the most unspeakable experiences. Yet it must be spoken and it must be written—again and again, until it is completely understood, addressed, and replaced with social, political, and economic integration. We must not fail to reach, to anticipate health. Writing is a way of participating. It helps to free us from cultural and ethnic provincialism, especially when combined with a study of international sources. It helps us to realize that the future is about incorporation, not in the economic or fundamentalist political sense, but in the human sense. And the human sense is about opening up the self and opening up the words of the other so that the self is changed; incorporation is saving the self from the insularity, the trap, of hatred, the cage of racism—the death of the soul.

When we teach writing, we teach the deepest epistemological processes, the making of the meaning of a life, a way of participating in the world. We teach writing despite the world's sin of impossible circumstances. We teach in the face of the fact that circumstances make the process and the participating harder for some than for others, and impossible for so many more. And maybe we teach writing in spite of these wounds, or maybe, because of them.

"IT HAD BETTER BE WORTH IT"

The Western tradition of rhetoric offers a powerful conceptual framework and vocabulary for understanding the production and reception of discourse. A categorical system some two thousand years in the making, the Western tradition provides an effective heuristic for identifying and analyzing many aspects of discourse and reception, no matter the culture (though the application of the categories of Western rhetoric on other traditions can raise some serious ethical questions). The Western tradition was, and is, useful for achieving a deep, technical, psychological understanding of the shapes, purposes, and power distributions inherent in certain kinds of discourse. Its categories and structures can probe some of life's daily quandaries, the courses of action we should or should not take. Furthermore, Western rhetorics contain designs that can be aesthetically pleasing. They are complex architectural plans, monuments of the efforts to understand the ways we construct—and shouldn't construct—discourse for others (Hurlbert 1995, 43). Finally, the Western tradition is also the tradition of currency in the profession. It is the tradition that has been most represented at the Conference on College Composition and Communication (though things are changing).

Certainly, some rhetorics are more philosophical than others. These were, and are, for me, the more satisfying moments in the tradition: the humanity of Quintilian as he talks about treating one's pupils with respect, care and moderation; Augustine's (1996) ethical search for truth in *On Christian Doctrine;* George Campbell's (1963) attempt to understand the psychology of discourse in *The Philosophy of Rhetoric;* or Kenneth Burke's career-length emphasis on the centrality of ideology and cultural politics in the study of rhetoric. But it quickly became clear to me, when I began teaching "The Rhetorical Tradition and the Teaching of Writing" at Indiana University of Pennsylvania, that privileging the male, Western tradition was not going to suffice the teaching of writing as it needs to transpire in various classrooms around the world. In the first semesters of my teaching, an educator in my class—who also teaches English writing in a Thai refugee camp—spoke of more immediate concerns than Aristotle's topoi. A Japanese teacher of Buraku students in Japan spoke of more immediate concerns than those found in Erasmus's (1963) *Copia*. A Saudi graduate student teaching English writing in Saudi Arabia explained how he was more concerned about the effects of religious fundamentalism in his classrooms than the literary predilections of the Scottish minister-professors of the Enlightenment. It is true that the Western tradition of rhetoric can serve many writers' and teachers' purposes, but it is also true that it will not serve them all. An undergraduate student seeking to write creative nonfiction in which she dramatizes her experience with alcoholism would certainly not be served, at least not in her immediate writing context, by the judicial concerns of Cicero's (1949) stasis theory.

Jean-Paul Sartre (1965, 325) wrote, "If I am to give myself over to the dead it had better be worth it." The technical nature of the Western tradition can turn rhetoric into an interesting mind-puzzle, striking in its complexity, but still a puzzle. Rhetoric is somehow what, then? A series of manuals, maybe. A series of complex and sometimes magnificent tutorials that contain wonders of design where form can become persuasive in its own right. Certainly, the study of form is a worthy endeavor, and many a writer will extol the virtues of being a quick and nimble manipulator of form in dull writing circumstances. And, of course, form offers its own satisfactions when we seek out moments of well-crafted design, as in the poetry of Donald Petersen (2001). It is just that when we make a fetish of form in the composition classroom, when as teachers our formal expectations become prescriptive requirements, we may do more to shut down the power of fluency than to facilitate discursive innovation and growth in composing strategies. In moments such as these in a pedagogy, the ideological content of form takes precedence over creative and critical thinking, and production can displace the artistry of innovation. This is what Kenneth Burke (1968, 144) called the "disease" of form, the point in a literary or rhetorical movement when form becomes end and meaning in itself.

THE USE AND ABUSE OF HISTORY

The field of composition would benefit from a careful examination of the current, historical context of the teaching of writing, including the ways in which form is a function of ideology. We need greater understanding of how form becomes script for our utterances and our writing. We need greater knowledge about how form becomes an assigned piece of mind, a discursive end in itself. One way to reach that knowledge is by deepening our understanding of the relation of form to merger-terms like "national character" and its reliance on "Classical" sources.

In *The Use and Abuse of History*, Friedrich Nietzsche (1949) explains and critiques the relations that intellectuals maintain with the past. His analysis is rooted in his interpretation of the state of German philosophy, his critique of Bismarck's militarism, and his disdain for the nationalism of the rising German nation-state of the Second Reich of 1871. Nietzsche's text is far too complex to explicate fully here. But in his conclusion, he turns his understanding of history to a critique of education that has value for compositionists and rhetoricians today. The soul of this critique is a call for liberating education from slavish devotion to historical monuments, canons, and imitation of historical forms. Youth, he argues, needs to be freed from the accoutrements of the "*malady of history*" (69), an excessive, uncritical reverence for our national cultures and their sources. This conclusion is based on three orientations to history that Nietzsche sees as both necessary to and limiting of thinking and action in the present—the monumental, the antiquarian, and the critical.

Monumentalists see decay in the contemporary and venerate the past. They take their inspiration from the great men and achievements of history. They believe that people create or perform great works if they adhere to the models provided in a Classical culture. The devotion that monumentalists have for the past, however, makes them susceptible to fanatic forms of nostalgia that require a debilitating servitude to Classical ideals and a stultifying imitation of Classical models. Such imitations, Nietzsche might say, cannot promote present achievement because they are finally only poor metaphors for Classical glory.

Antiquarians study the past and seek to recover and understand it. They revere the past. They are keepers of tradition, and identify with it. They see truth and wisdom in the past and seek to conserve the past for future generations. As with the monumentalists, though with a lower dose of fundamentalism, antiquarians are prone to servitude to the past, reifying past values into strictures that obstruct living in and for the contemporary moment.

Critical historians critique the past because they want to break with it. They see the injustices of history and wish to root them out of contemporary culture. The problem is that their critical focus allows these historians to overlook the deep connections between present practices and past realities. They constantly run the risk of repeating the past's mistakes.

If many compositionists in the present day appear to dedicate their careers to idolizing, venerating, or critiquing the Western tradition of rhetoric and its traditional pieties and hierarchies, many may also be recognized for their dedication to escaping the limitations—though not the value—of traditional thinking. For instance, working within the framework of historical, rhetorical study, Carol S. Lipson (2009, 3) explains in her introduction to *Ancient Non-Greek Rhetorics* that "challenges to the parochial and situated nature of Western paradigms have arisen from various directions: due to the recognition of the global nature of communication in contemporary society, and due as well to the recognition of the heterogeneity of rhetorical frameworks within America itself and the western world more generally." For Lipson, challenges to inherited history are not reasons for dismissing rhetorical scholarship, they are, wisely, occasions for expanding our scholarship.

In "Riding Long Coattails, Subverting Tradition: The Tricky Business of Feminists Teaching Rhetoric(s)," Joy Ritchie and Kate Ronald (1998) describe how two classes they taught, one graduate course in composition and rhetoric and one undergraduate course in the rhetoric of women writers, became struggles with the patriarchy that resides at the heart of the Western tradition. Studying the history of rhetoric, the students in these classes, with their professors' help, articulated projects of recovery and resistance. In the first phase, the students read the works of women rhetoricians who have been neglected, suppressed, or ignored in the Western tradition, or women writers of essays, speeches, and other literature who subverted the conventions of the Western tradition. In the second phase, they voiced their opposition to the patriarchal, argumentative voices of men who seek to silence women. As a

result, the students examined their personal and professional investments in rhetorical studies and negotiated their places in the history of
rhetoric. Viewed in this way, rhetoric is the examination of how models
and categories are imposed in order to silence and exclude, and how
they can be resisted.

In *Living Room*, Nancy Welch (2008) argues that, as it is currently
taught in American colleges and universities, the Western tradition of
rhetoric is a set of discursive practices belonging to and reflective of the
elite styles and values of the economically and politically privileged. As it
is taught, it is essentially a patrician enterprise that does not account for
the resistance rhetorics of the poor and working class, or the disenfran-
chised and excluded. In *Living Room*, Welch reclaims the rhetorical strategies and discursive motives that have been widely used among the working class and mass movement rhetors in, say, union protests. In her work,
Welch makes these neglected rhetorical strategies available for teachers
and students. But Welch's project does not end there. Significantly, she
moves her crucial, historical work into her teaching. Through classroom
and public activities, such as public readings and flyer postings, her students learn to draw on rhetorical practices traditionally excluded from
the college writing classroom to resist the privatization of ethos.

Welch's is one of the most hopeful theoretical positions and pedagogies that I have seen in recent years. In it, students learn their authority
to write, not only to the issues at stake in their experiences, but to injustice in the world beyond their individual experiences. They also explore
what are sometimes closed—to them, at least—venues for speaking, and
in so doing, make both rhetorical occasion and discursive form subjects
for negotiation. Ideology should then follow.

Because Nancy Welch presents a fully drawn vision for the teaching
of writing, one that answers the political and economic realities of our
time, her pedagogy presents a clear plan for creating the changes she
seeks. In this way, Welch's work answers the central question posed by
Kate Ronald and Joy Ritchie in their introduction to *Teaching Rhetorica*,
the "so what?" question. Writing about the teaching they do and how
they encourage students to recover the work of women rhetoricians,
they explain that "As we talk with our students (and with one another)
about these projects, we find ourselves asking, 'so what?' Or, perhaps
more politely, 'That's so interesting. But what will this research tell us
beyond "that's interesting"?' . . . Locally, we insist on exploring what difference reclaiming the emerging canon of women's rhetorics makes to

our teaching of writing and rhetoric" (2006, 2–3). In other words, the study of rhetorical difference is important, but for us educators, the difference it makes is what comes after the study is completed, in the actions we pursue once we close the book.

Let me clarify my position. I am not attempting to dismiss the obvious value of the Classical tradition. Instead, I am arguing that it is a resource to make use of, if we do not let it become—as much by what we don't say as what we do—a monument, in Nietzsche's sense, to the historical sources of the national character of the United States. When compositionists do that, which we do far too often, we support fundamentalist forms of nationalist thinking.

In *Teaching Rhetorica,* Andrea Lunsford and Lisa Ede (2006) ask a powerful question: why don't we compositionists insist on teaching what we love about writing and what we know to work? Their answer to this question is complicated. Their discussion centers around the status of discourse that would be considered "alternative" within the academy. They suggest that if we teach the alternative discursive forms to which we ourselves are drawn, we risk bleeding them of their alternative status. At the same time, Lunsford and Ede recognize that many of the forms and discourses we might call "alternative" have been invented by women and contested by men. To not teach them is to fail to honor the historical and hard won gains of women writers; to not teach them is to fail to make visible the hidden, masculinist ideology that has silenced women in the past—as it would still do today. This conclusion acknowledges and reapplies one of the key conclusions of Jacqueline Jones Royster's powerful history, *Traces of a Stream: Literacy and Social Change Among African American Women*; namely, that by studying the writing of African American women writers and learning to read through the lens of the resistances they articulate, all readers learn some necessary truths about themselves: "With this type of analysis, the ferreting out of actions and achievements in the alternative terrain are instructive for an interrogation of contemporary public discourses, debunking the myth that public discourse is a ground only for institutionally sanctioned voices" (2000, 284). The fact is that the best available means of persuasion may sometimes best be found outside one's customary, cultural, class-based, racial or gendered stream.

A NEW BEGINNING

Rhetoric is not a prison-house. It is a study, as complex and far-reaching as the human quest for meaning. In *Alternative Rhetorics*, Laura Gray-Rosendale and Sybille Gruber (2001, 3) write that the study of rhetoric "cannot be confined within nicely drawn borders. The field is ever-changing, ever-expanding, unconstrained, unconfined, and largely uncharted." According to them, we simply are not obligated to be "satisfied" with "one rhetorical tradition. Instead," they argue, "we want to emphasize multiplicity and fragmentation within and between different rhetorics and different traditions" (5). We need such thinking, we need more of it, and we need it now.

In *The Rhetoric of Racism*, Mark Lawrence McPhail explores how the Western tradition of rhetoric developed hand in hand with the Western model of dichotomizing reason and how that confederation makes the recognition of other philosophical and rhetorical traditions, with their different methods for developing and articulating thinking, nearly impossible. Within the confines of Western, foundational reason, there will always be a choice between one, true rhetoric and one other, alternative rhetoric, whatever rhetoric it may be. All rhetorical choices for compositionists are, then, binary, and as such lead to assessments of quality and non-quality, truth and falsehood, us and them, and all in reference to Western standards. According to McPhail, the result has been a rhetorical failure of mythic proportions:

> If, as scholars across disciplines suggest, the world is *essentially* made up of an indivisable whole, then our reliance upon a language that constructs the world in terms of negative differences can be nothing other than divisive and fragmentary. As scholars, we rely upon a discourse of negative difference—criticism—to generate and reify the essential "truths" upon which we base our understanding of symbolic, social, and material reality. This discourse of negative difference is intimately connected to the foundational principles of reason and logic in Western metaphysics, a metaphysics of truth and falsity, and unfortunately, little in between. (1994, 120)

In this model of reason, rhetoricians have meager resources for dialogue, let alone offering a way past racism. Consequently, the only meaningful alternative we have left is an articulation of a new logic of value with new ways of assessing eloquence and artistry in discourse. As McPhail writes: "Our task is not to *reject* rhetoric as persuasion and argument, but to *reconceptualize* it in a manner which allows for the affirmation of difference" (119). Our task, our necessary project, is to unlock Western rhetoric and literacy instruction, to pull them open—and to do the same with every other rhetorical and educational tradition as well. Our necessary project is to open each to the presence and influences of the other, not merely to encourage respect each for the other, but to open them in respect of what each adds to the others. If we live up to the challenge of this task, if we *truly* live up to the challenge of this task, we will have come a long way toward ridding composition—and culture and nation *and* ourselves—of the vestiges of racism.

But we have a long way to go. Many writing teachers still feel obliged to uphold current-traditional pieties, or to teach modes and graduated themes and assignments as well as a narrowly defined set of academic skills that they think are somehow connected to Classical rhetoric or foundational to academic writing. Many compositionists privilege argumentation in order to fulfill what they believe is their responsibility to colleagues in English departments and other disciplines (even as some privilege argumentation for political reasons). Many compositionists believe that teaching is somehow not dependent on ground-breaking scholarship in the field of composition; they thereby limit their practice to what they have always done or seen. Many compositionists teach what they find in the syllabi that they share as models and the textbooks that are presented by salespeople and required by administrators. And many compositionists teach what they do because they think that to teach otherwise amounts to affiliation with that which is negatively different, and, therefore, unlikely to support the production of responsible citizens. (But, please, let me be clear here: I am not critiquing the practice of adjunct teachers who are assigned at the last minute with inadequate pay and resources. There is no hope in blaming the oppressed.)

We compositionists really do need a new beginning. Of course, the making of formal and somewhat Classical artifacts is an accomplishment, some would say, of high order. But in terms of the first year composition class, many of us know that there just is not enough anticipation in the traditional, hand-me-down rhetorical modes that are actually taught.

When they are ends in themselves, forms, from the modes to the topoi, seem small and mean—little moments of life carved-out of real and important meanings and texts that students might achieve. Finger exercises are small reachings. What they offer a writer is too insubstantial, too fleeting, not worth the commitment and work of opening one's self to the flow of words. When the modes are assigned—and, yes, they are still assigned even if we compositionists would like to think otherwise—it might simply be because they are in the book a teacher has adopted. Or it might be that four writing styles feels like the right number to cover in one semester, just enough variety to fill, comfortably, all the class sessions. Or it might be to cover-up. When a teacher has not spent the time and effort necessary for creating a meaningful vision for the teaching of writing, a vision that does not rely on textbook commodification of meaning making, they may settle on anything to help themselves out.

If we have learned anything in composition studies over the last thirty years, it is that formal exercises do not, largely, encourage student engagement. Of course, there will always be those good students who will do whatever is assigned, with a smile on their faces, and with a degree of quality in the results. And there will always be those gifted teachers who, through force of personality or energy, just seem to make anything work in the classroom. But thirty years of teaching tell me that these students and teachers are not the majority. For the rest of our students there needs to be reason for engaging themselves in the processes of assigned writing. Something in the assignment has to suggest relevance or touch a personal and human need to make meaning. Something has to make an opening—or better—suggest why students should want to participate. Serious classroom writing requires an invitation to students to make the writing theirs. No one, not us and not our students, wants to have our meaning making experiences scripted too closely or the possibilities fixed at the beginning. No, our students must be able to make the assignment and the writing worth it.

THE BABEL EFFECT

Rhetoric is a system of thought for conceptualizing the composing, delivery and reception of discourse. Rhetoric is about work that connects one to another. It is about the composing of the connection. It is also about the claiming of the other's presence (not in possession; rather, in respect of the other). As Daniel Collins (2001) and Michael Spooner (2002) have both shown us, rhetoric is also about the responsibilities of an audience member or reader and how we make meaning of the other's work, the dialogue writer and reader engage in as meaning emerges. The study of rhetoric offers, then, options for composing, for the kinds of texts we could make, and also for the ways we orient ourselves toward the world. Through all of this creating and connecting, rhetoric helps us to address at least some of the limitations of subjectivity.

Philosopher Ram Adhar Mall (2004, 315) claims that "There is no pure own culture as there is no pure other culture. The same is true for philosophy." The same is also true of rhetoric and composition. The Western tradition is certainly and obviously not the only tradition to offer powerful resources for writers and teachers of writing, and there is no reason that we should not be drawing on others. There is no reason for blindly and mistakenly working for a cultural purity in a world of growing interconnection. There is no reason to use our teaching to sanction one, particular, nationalist ideology as if it were universal. Ignorance is little excuse for provincialism when there is so much help available to us when we search for rhetoric's various traditions and the interpreting of the works of individual rhetoricians. For instance, in *Comparative Rhetoric*, George Kennedy (1998) has charted the inception of comparative rhetorical studies. In it he offers chapters dedicated to various rhetorical traditions, from China to India to the rhetoric of indigenous people in the Americas, providing useful examples from each tradition along the way. Robert Oliver's (1971) *Communication and Culture in Ancient India and China* does much the same thing, with a narrower focus and in greater detail. In the 1990s, compositionists and rhetoricians seeking to understand the Eastern rhetorical tradition often turned to the prodigious and insightful works of David L. Hall and Roger T. Ames. Their texts, *Thinking Through Confucius* (Hall 1987), *Anticipating China: Thinking Through the Narratives of Chinese and Western Culture* (Hall and Ames 1995) and *Thinking from the Han: Self, Truth, and Transcendence in Chinese and Western Culture* (Hall and Ames 1998); along with Joel Marks and Roger T. Ames's (1995) edited collection, *Emotions in Asian Thought,* and Roger T. Ames, Wimal Dissanayake and Thomas P. Kasuklis's (1994) collection, *Self as Person in Asian Theory and Practice,* all help one to understand the cultural and philosophical implications of the complex relationships among self, communication and society in Eastern thought and rhetoric. In addition, in *The Dao of Rhetoric,* Steven Combs (2005) explicates ancient Daoist philosophy and then applies the principles he uncovers to the study of contemporary, popular sources, demonstrating, as he does, the possible uses of Daoist philosophy in our work as writing teachers. Xing Lu has explicated how over many centuries ancient Chinese scholars developed a complex understanding of language and philosophy (epistemology and ethics), logic and advising, or ming and bien, literally, naming and argumentation (1998, 4). Her *Rhetoric in Ancient China, Fifth to Third Century B.C.E.* is filled with specific examples of scholars and the development of Chinese rhetoric, a rhetorical tradition that she chronicles in its modern manifestations, as well, in *Rhetoric of the Chinese Cultural Revolution: The Impact on Chinese Thought, Culture, and Communication* (Lu 2004). In *Reading Chinese Fortune Cookie,* LuMing Mao (2006) describes the emergence and significance of Asian American rhetoric for the American scene and the writing classroom. Indeed, in light of the outstanding work of the contributors to LuMing Mao and Morris Young's (2008) *Representations: Doing Asian American Rhetoric,* there can be no mistake that nationalist attempts at cultural purity are bereft of the epistemological vision that is increasingly necessary in writing classrooms: "A deft composer is not truly literate—in fact, remains impoverished—until she has a full understanding of her medium—that is, the local and global contexts of empire that shape the English language and those who use it" (Hattori and Ching 2008, 59). Writing about the research presented by the contributors to the special issue of *College English* that he edited, *Studying Chinese Rhetoric in the Twenty-First Century,* LuMing Mao (2010, 346) acknowledges that rhetoricians "need to move beyond the paradigm of Western rhetoric and to write a different kind of history of rhetoric so that we can open up a space for other ways of knowing and other modes of reasoning—both of which have been ruled in the past as anything but rhetoric." Mao is, of course, correct. It does not serve to limit the possibilities for reasoning or meaning making at this or any time in human history. For this same reason I would add to Mao's extraordinary words and vision what I hope will stand as an important contribution; namely, that we "need to move beyond the paradigm of Western rhetoric and to write a different kind of history of rhetoric so that we can open up a space for other ways of . . ."—composing.

But I have named only a few texts explicating only one tradition. When we consider the rhetorical traditions of the rest of Asia, the Americas, Africa, and the Arab world, we begin to see the vast amount of rhetorical resources that teachers of writing in the United States have to draw on. As Janice W. Fernheimer (2010) and the contibutors to the special issue of *College English,* entitled *Composing Jewish Rhetorics,* demonstrate, these resources stretch across national boundaries and reach back through the millennia. Given our country's changing demographics, given the demands of a society claiming to be democratic, given an ethical view of composition, the study of "other" rhetorical traditions can no longer be considered a luxury—as if it ever was one.

I recently directed a dissertation by Venezuelan researcher, José Vallejo, who points out just how crucial the study of international rhetorics and composition is. In it, Vallejo reports his work in a United States university writing center where he observed tutorials and held follow up interviews with the tutors and tutees. What Vallejo found is disturbing: a series of rhetorical mismatches between well-meaning tutors native to the United States and confused tutees whose national origins were other than the United States. Specifically, because their understanding of writing, rhetoric and even school were different, the tutees in this study expressed frustration with tutors whom they felt did not understand their needs, did not give them the information they sought to make their English writing more effective, and did not even know the answers to questions that the tutees posed to them.

In fact, as Vallejo found out, even when the tutors and tutees were able to get past unproductive, though quite natural, preconceptions about the cultural roles of students and teachers, and even when they were able to negotiate differences in teaching and learning styles, the words, such as "audience," that they used to talk about writing had different sociocultural referents. As Vallejo reports about the tutors and tutees whom he studied, "They engaged in a phonological game; they played by the rules of pronunciation. Yet, they could not avoid misunderstanding.

Even worse, they never knew that the same words they were pronouncing as part of their interactions on global conventions of English had different meanings for them" (2004, 180). According to Vallejo, then, to be effective with tutees of other countries, United States tutors need to be trained in various rhetorics from various nations and cultural groups. The tutors in his study had good will and were hard working, but good intentions do not alone ensure effective teaching and learning.

I have to wonder about compositionists who commit their teaching exclusively to the limited processes and select forms of the Western tradition, at least as it is watered-down and presented in composition textbooks. I also have to wonder about teachers who expect that all students will automatically need to write according to the dictates of Eurocentric argumentation. I believe it is the innate fundamentalism of nationalist ideology that fuels a composition teacher's resistance to rhetorical change (see more on this in Part 2, "Circulations: The Composing of Composition"). Of course, there are other material reasons for entertaining a national centrism. Many overworked and underpaid adjuncts hardly have the resources and time to begin to study diverse rhetorical traditions and composition theories. Overstressed writing program administrators may find themselves unable to procure adequate training for adjuncts assigned to last minute classes, and so they order handbooks and readers that represent the world of rhetoric in simplistic, mechanical and monocultural terms. Professors who feel they are doing the best they can when they devote their first-year composition courses to the teaching of argumentation may simply not see the limitations of their thinking. Professors who know that their students like their classes may see no reason to change. And, of course, there are those complacent professors who simply do not want, for any number of reasons, to do the work anymore, or simply to teach literature and call it the teaching of writing.

And then, there is fear. Some writing teachers fear the deterioration of standards and the loosening of rhetorical values that underwrite composition's gatekeeper function. It is a fear of chaos in the home and in the homeland. Ram Adhar Mall (2004, 319) sees it: "It is a home-made misgiving to believe that intercultural philosophy would deconstruct the concepts of truth, culture, religion, and philosophy. What this misgiving makes evident, though, is the extremely relativistic and totalizing use that was made and is in part still being made of these terms." Mall's words offer insight into why composition teachers might fear an international approach to the study of composition. The fear of the loss of "truth, culture, religion, and philosophy" might lead some writing teachers to worry about the Babel effect, but it is time to tear this mythic and essentialist foundation down.

As stated in the National Council of Teachers of English's "CCCC Guideline on the National Language Policy," students need to learn the forms of wider communication (National Council of Teachers of English 1988, Updated 1992). At the same time, however, we run the risk of short-changing our students of equally necessary rhetorical and compositional skills if we teach only argumentative and other textbook forms. As linguist Suresh Canagarajah writes: "A complex of forces, including the globalization of economy and industry, international communities, the post-Fordist work place, and the Internet, have compelled us to shuttle across linguistic boundaries. . . . In such a context, we readily recognize that teaching literacy in a single language (English) or a single dialect of that language ("standard English") fails to equip our students for the real world" (2003, ix–x). The same may be said of teaching a single rhetoric. Canagarajah is correct, of course. Things are changing. Our students are changing and we need to change with them. We well know that demographics in the United States are going to continue to alter our classroom populations. In addition, many colleges and universities are actively searching overseas for students. In fact, the recruiting of international students has become big business. Some non-profits have gone corporate as they have turned the enrolling of students into profit. Agents working off commissions turn recruitment into lucrative employment. But we need only look at our own colleges and universities to see the extent to which they do or do not assure the academic success and both on and off campus acceptance of all of these new students, some 32 percent more in the United States than a decade ago ("International Student Enrollment" 2012).

So things are changing; indeed, the processes of internationalization can hardly be stopped even if some teachers nurture misguided versions of homegrown purity. For composition instructors, the question is how to support our changing student bodies and the processes of international exchange in ways appropriate to the student-centered writing classroom. The challenge is how to put these processes to use in the development of writing abilities. Perhaps we will develop thinking and initiatives that will be different from what we have done before; perhaps they will be revisions of past practice. Whatever they will be, they will require a necessary advancement over what we have done so far.

For instance, Cristina Kirklighter has argued that because it has elitist, formal properties, the academic essay as traditionally taught in our schools and colleges has contributed to domestic "nation-building" (2002, 135). The essay has been used as a discursive vehicle for excluding those of non-European descent from success in our schools—and beyond. In resistance to conservative prosaics, Kirklighter has called for the development and teaching of personal essay writing that is self-reflective as well as spontaneous and sincere. In her view, a democracy needs writing where the experiences of all are relevant and necessary to an understanding of "we the people." Rather than merely teach for the transmission of elite culture, writing teachers might encourage, in Kirklighter's view, "personal academic discourse" that allows writers to explore their identities and cultural affiliations. Kirklighter's pedagogical vision is tolerant and humane; it is one that would end the anonymity forced on students and academics by the ideology of elite culture and its academic gatekeepers.

Kirklighter's thinking is supported by the research of Terry Myers Zawacki and Anna Sophia Habib. In "'Will Our Stories Help Teachers Understand?': Multilingual Students Talk about Identity, Voice, and Expectations Across Academic Communities," Zawacki and Habib report the findings of research in which, in part, they interviewed international college students studying here in the States. During the course of these interviews, Zawacki and Habib hear from student after student who expresses frustration about the discipline-specific, discursive restrictions imposed on their writing by well-intentioned, but sometimes rhetorically naïve, academics. It is a sad story told by students who claim, sometimes directly, sometimes indirectly, that their national and cultural inheritances, their sources of creativity and originality, are simply not good enough—that their ways of making meaning through writing are not properly academic. The students believe that professors are looking for original work, to be sure, but it must be original within the strict parameters structured by each professor's conception of what academic writing is. Zawacki and Habib offer several ideas designed to alleviate this situation. They call for long-term projects that make disciplinary conventions and expectations clear for multilingual students. They also call on academics to learn World Englishes theory and develop teaching practices that are sensitive to the needs of multilingual students. Theirs is a strong vision. To round their project out, I would suggest adding Kirklighter's insight that academic styles and expectations can be altered and expanded so as to be more inclusive. As one of the students whom Zawacki and Habib interviewed states, "When I speak, my accent reflects who I am and where I come from. Well, I want my writing to reflect me in that way" (2010, 70). Certainly, this is a reasonable expectation for a student or any writer. It is, in Kirklighter's thinking, democracy; moreover, it is critical democracy. As Peter Vandenburg (2006, 558) writes: "As teachers, we might help students more critically examine any claims, including those of multiculturalism, that propose cultural rehabilitation through dominant literacies." To achieve this end, we teachers of writing might begin with our own claims, our own hearts and minds, our classrooms, our own work with other academics, with the public, and all with the goal to open our universities and nation to the voices and rights of others who are already, thankfully, here.

But, even given the emerging realities of the twenty-first century, the study of the world's rhetorics may seem too daunting a proposition for some. It is difficult, after all, to know one tradition well, can I now suggest that we must know several, at least? I can and I do. Freed from the illusion of mastery, however, we might begin this study with the joy of scholarly curiosity, the pleasure of coming to know that which can change us rather than the monotony of selecting yet another textbook to teach because "it looks pretty good." And with true curiosity may come the desire to learn writing deeply and well and in new ways, pushing back our limitations as writing teachers as we do. The fact is that one can devote one's self to the study of various rhetorics for a lifetime and barely scratch the surface of one's ignorance (no standardized testing here—we all fail and get A's at the same time). There will always be other rhetorics to know, other rhetorics known but not translated, other rhetorics to which study is limited by the accessibility of texts and time. But that is not the end of the story.

A QUESTION OF SERVICE

Caring compositionists sometimes ask how students would succeed in college if we did not use our composition classes to teach argumentation and academic discourse. This is a complicated question. The easy answer is that nothing more unfortunate than anything that is happening now would occur. The fact is, of course, that students know how to argue. They do it for most of their lives—if not always well. What is more, while they certainly benefit from learning the protocols of academic arguing, such as open-mindedness, thoroughness, precision, and fair (though invested) research and reporting, we cannot say with certainty and, without, at the very least, considerable institutional research and support, what our students' next professors will expect of them.

In the book, *In Search of Eloquence*, Cornelius Cosgrove and Nancy Barta-Smith explain how they interviewed faculty from various departments at Pennsylvania's Slippery Rock University in an attempt to discover what they hope students will learn in composition. The results of their study are fascinating, if not totally unexpected: outside of desiring grammatical correctness, there is little agreement among faculty about what writing skills they hope students will have when they arrive in their classrooms. As Cosgrove and Barta-Smith report, their colleagues were, in many respects, rhetorically savvy, recognizing that each department works within discipline-specific demands for discourse so that, "We sensed that our colleagues generally regard the learning of what is persuasive in their disciplines as no one's responsibility but their own" (2004, 134). Or, as David R. Russell puts it in his comprehensive study, *Writing in the Disciplines: A Curricular History*:

> Because it is tempting to recall academia's very different past and hope for a very different future, the term *academic community* has powerful spiritual and political connotations, but today academia is a *discourse* community only in a context so broad as to have little meaning in terms of shared linguistic forms, either for the advancement of knowledge (which now goes on in disciplinary communities and subcommunities) or for the initiation of new members (who are initiated into a specific community's discourse). Thus, to speak of

the academic community as if its members shared a single set of linguistic conventions and traditions of inquiry is to make a categorical mistake. In the aggregate of all the tightly knit, turf-conscious disciplines and departments, each of its own discourse community, the modern university consists. Many have wished it otherwise. (2002, 21–22)

To put it simply, we do not largely know what students need to know for their next classes. In addition, we are not likely to know if the information about forms that we impart to students in our composition classes even transfers to the writing situations in which they will find themselves in their next classes (if, and that is a very big "if," they will even do much writing in their next classes). In fact, as Lucille Parkinson McCarthy (1987) reports, early evidence on the transferability of formal instruction is the same as for grammar instruction—there is none. In her study, McCarthy's subject, Dave, found that each class he took in subsequent semesters provided him with unique writing tasks that were in the main scripted by his professors. The teachers of Dave's other classes did not require him to use what he learned in composition. They did require him to write for a wide range of audiences or in a variety forms. The modal and genre practice that Dave performed in his first-year composition class was largely, alas, useless.

Anne Beaufort's (2007) study of her subject, Tim, verifies McCarthy's findings. Following Tim through first-year composition to classes in other disciplines and even through his experiences working in an engineering firm, Beaufort finds that each writing context in which Tim finds himself is unique, requiring adaptation to different writing conditions and prerequisites, different composing processes, genre expectations, different audience expectations, different criteria for appeals and success, etc. Beaufort's solution is to propose the creation of writing programs and courses specifically designed to teach students how to transfer writing expertise from one context to another—certainly a valuable option.

I wonder, though, if it truly is our mission to teach for the next class our students will take and the first job that they will get. Certainly, helping our students to develop metacognitive awareness about the context-specificity of writing is a meaningful educational goal. But I want us as writing teachers to explore and understand the degree to which the higher and deepest motives for writing fall within the purview of the first year composition course and the domain of our expertise. Our mission is not merely to have students practice techniques for the real thinking and writing that they will do elsewhere (and Anne Beaufort would agree, I expect, with me here). If that were so, we would be mere Sophists of a decidedly materialistic sort. (Many English departments of course have actual mission statements that usually claim that one of the chief goals of their introduction to literature course is to inspire students to become lifelong readers. But none that I know explicitly states that the goal of the composition class is to encourage students to become lifelong writers. Instead, they almost always focus on skills. This ought to tell us something.)

There are still other issues to consider. We can teach students how to transfer what they learn in composition classes to other writing contexts, but we cannot alter the prejudices at work in the future writing contexts in which our students will find themselves—at least not without affecting major societal changes first. In the 1980s, sociologist David W. Livingstone (1987) reported that study after study demonstrated that there was a wide gap between a student's aspirations and schooling, and the reality for successful upward mobility for a woman or person of color other than white. Things have not changed. The report of Economic Mobility Project, "Upward Intergenerational Mobility in the United States," tells us that in American society, "Blacks experience dramatically less upward economic mobility than whites," with black women lagging behind black men (Mazumder n.d.). Success at writing any version of modal discourse does not guarantee an African American success in a racist, sexist, business setting. So, while composition teachers still sometimes tell their students that practicing the writing of arguments or other modal exercises will help them later in life, in the next class, or in the workplace, the fact is that we do not really know this for sure.

My suggestion is, then, that we compositionists rewrite any pressure we might feel to teach to the discursive preferences of either workplaces we do not know or a multitude of professors from a multitude of disciplines we probably don't know, either. Instead, we should expand our habitual thinking about writing across the curriculum or writing in the disciplines by following the lead of scholars such as Chris Thaiss and Terry Myers Zawacki who articulate in *Engaged Writers and Dynamic Disciplines: Research on the Academic Writing Life* how intricate and multifaceted the issue of discourse preferences in the academy actually are and how this complexity is worthy of study. Their findings are too extensive to detail here, but it is certainly worth noting that they have found that, while English professors may have expectations about how academics in other disciplines respond to student writing, their prognostications can be mistaken. Despite whatever stereotypes we compositionists hold about, say, scientists and scientific writing, academics from various fields are capable of entertaining views on originality and creativity in writing equal to our own—or at least many of them are. As Thaiss and Zawacki remind us, "The university is not a closed ecology" (2006, 170). Student and faculty populations continue to become more international, and, as they do, they continue to broaden disciplinary understanding of what discourse can and should do. Internationalization breeds discursive tolerance. What is more, as Thaiss and Zawacki argue, the "disciplines are dynamic, responsive to the desires of engaged practitioners, who in turn, convey their vision of the discipline and their goals for writers to the students they teach" (170). The problem we writing teachers face is not necessarily and always what kind of writing is required in other disciplines—though certainly much of that writing can be as stultifying as any some of us sometimes assign in our composition classes—but, rather, what conception of service our courses rest upon. Too often we define "service," and allow colleagues and administrators to define "service," not as service to our students, but as service to the other departments. Too often, as Geoffey Sirc (2002, 8) puts it, our own best impulses and theories lead us to play the "eager lapdogs of the big-ticket disciplines."

I, too, do not believe that compositionists best serve their students when they sign the first-year writing class up for service to literature and the other disciplines. But, I also agree with Thaiss and Zawacki (2006) when they say that that we should celebrate the university's variety by taking it seriously. The challenge is doing so without falling into a pedagogical situation that negates our authority as writing specialists. As Bruce Horner, Kelly Latchaw, Jospeh Lenz, Jody Swilky and David Wolf (2002) warn in their cautionary tale about Drake University, an English department's successful writing across the disciplines program can indeed move some of the responsibility for the teaching of writing to the other disciplines. Unfortunately, that achievement can become all the justification a university administration needs to downsize English by cutting composition faculty, thereby taking the teaching of writing out of the hands of those most expert at teaching it. The challenge is, then, to decide the material wisdom of pursuing WAC or WID programs and to determine how to keep control of the teaching of writing if WAC and WID are truly in the students' best interest. To maintain authority, we will need to have a vision for teaching writing in light of and for variety, multiplicity and difference, as well as similarity and consensus. We will need to be able to articulate a vision that is persuasive and relevant. I argue that responding to the world's growing internationalism is one of the most significant rationales we can offer for our work. Our best service to our students will rest in it; indeed, it already does.

MORE THAN ONE

If compositionists know, now, at this point in the history of our discipline's development, that there is more than one rhetorical tradition in the world, why does the teaching of writing change so little, especially when our students do? It is beyond the scope of this book to pay just attention to the many examples of the work that can be cited as challenges to composition's entrenched order of discourse, but it would certainly be remiss of me not to at least note a few.

For instance, in 1986, Judith and Geoffrey Summerfield published *Texts and Contexts,* a book that encourages students to explore the writing of mixed genre texts of a decidedly postmodern nature. Summerfield and Summerfield did not claim multiculturalism as a rationale for *Texts and Contexts,* but they developed a vision based in a sound reading of postmodern literature and theory. In it, they proposed form breaking, and, by extension, cultural renovation.

In 1995, Lillian Bridwell-Bowles published her article, "Discourse and Diversity: Experimental Writing Within the Academy," in Louise Wetherbee Phelps and Janet Emig's *Feminine Principles and Women's Experience in American Composition and Rhetoric.* In it, Bridwell-Bowles argues for the expanding of thinking about form to include, potentially, new modes of expression. Describing her writing pedagogy, she writes:

> I have invited students to imagine the possibilities for new forms of discourse, new kinds of academic essays. I do this because I believe that writing classes (and the whole field of composition studies) must employ richer visions of texts and composing processes. If we try to invent a truly pluralistic society, we must envision a socially and politically situated view of language and the creation of texts—one that takes into account gender, race, class, sexual preference, and a host of issues that are implied by these and other cultural differences. Our language and our written texts represent our visions of our culture, and we need new processes and forms if we are to express ways of thinking that have been outside the dominant culture. (1995, 43)

Multigenre theory has also stood as a successful challenge to traditional rhetorical conventions. For educators such as Tom Romano

(2000) and Nancy Mack (2002), multigenre writing represents a productive way for exploring the meaning of experience and an effective discursive avenue for encouraging student writing. In 2005's *Revisionary Rhetoric, Feminist Pedagogy, and Multigenre Texts*, Julie Jung articulates a feminist, revisionary rhetoric intended to help students—indeed, all writers—to resist premature, argumentative closure of their thinking when writing about complex social issues. To accomplish inclusive thought, or, at least, a willingness to listen to the ideas of others, Jung would have students embrace writing practices that disrupt and resist the decorum of academic and discipline. Jung teaches her students to "misfit" texts: to blend different kinds of writing, different genres and perspectives to create texts that bridge the personal and the professional. The goal is multiple perspectives, not universalizing discourses, broader vision, not normalizing restrictions.

For Robert L. Davis and Mark F. Shadle, the goal is to encourage multiwriting, which they define as "a practice of composing in which multiple genres, media, disciplines, and cultures are potentially open to use. It differs from an allied term in vogue today—*multi-genre writing*—in that it stresses not the formula of composing in a number of different genres but a more flexible stance, where authors may use any means to compose effectively, reflecting in engaging ways" (2007, 13–14). As they make the theoretical case for multiwriting, Davis and Shadle articulate a methodology, especially evidenced in the intriguing examples of student writing and artistic production that they document in 2007's *Teaching Multiwriting*, for facilitating artistic expression through the blending of various cultural and artistic processes, including various visual media such as sculpture.

In 2002, Christopher Schroeder, Helen Fox, and Patricia Bizzell edited *Alt/Dis: Alternative Discourses and the Academy*. This collection also calls on scholars and teachers to broaden their thinking about discourse. Indeed, the contributors to *Alt/Dis* argue that while academic discourse can be described in general (and Patricia Bizzell [2002] does an especially fine job of this in her essay, "The Intellectual Work of 'Mixed' Forms of Academic Discourse"), it is difficult to characterize in particular because it adheres to many and different commonly held assumptions about what constitutes academic writing, depending on the context in which it is defined. It is, they argue, inclusive of more discursive styles than have hitherto been acknowledged. This fact opens the door, the authors argue, for experimentation in the constitution of scholarship and academic forms.

For instance, in place of traditional, Western thinking, Haixia Lan suggests, in *Alt/Dis,* that we take a Confucian view of the academic/ alternative dichotomy. According to Lan, this would entail complicating the dichotomy by recognizing that "the former/latter cannot be understood without the latter/former—and everything in between" (2002, 74). To understand the academic/alternative dichotomy, we would have to have students reverse the dichotomy so that alternative discourse also becomes primary, and we would have to have students explore the kinds of writing that might be produced between either pole, or, at least, as many kinds of writing as possible. Such Confucian thinking is, Lan argues, more complex and detailed in its vision than relatively simplistic dichotomies. It is collateral, and it is demanding. As Lan writes, "knowledge of a different cultural/discursive practice cannot be thorough without knowledge of one's own culture. In other words, one's sensitivity to the other and to difference cannot be thorough if one is insensitive or ignorant of one's own culture" (78). One must be willing, therefore, to examine one's commitments to and investments in Western and academic discourse practices if one is to understand Eastern discourse practices—and vice versa.

In the same collection, Paul Kei Matsuda correctly points out a serious problem with any project dedicated to the development of alternative discourse, namely that the academy has traditionally been less than gracious in its valuing of discourse by any writer who is not "male, European American, middle- or upper-class" (2002, 192). For Matsuda, then, the study of the academic/alternative dichotomy must entail a reevaluation of whose writing is valued and whose is not, as well as reconsideration of the political and cultural implications of discourse reception. Matsuda's work demonstrates that discussions of alternative discourse are not merely discussions of discursive preferences. They are also attempts at intervening in the ideological regime that controls textual forms.

INTERNATIONAL COMPOSITION #1

There are more informed and productive ways to think about teaching writing than the ones with which we have worked in the past or the ones with which we work in the present. In this regard, I urge us compositionists to consider an international perspective on composition, one informed by international connection, dialogues, and exchanges and that has the possibility to take us beyond the national and cultural boundaries that currently limit our vision and practices.

When I suggest that we turn to an international perspective on the teaching of writing, I mean that we learn how writing is taught around the world, as the contributors to *Writing and Learning in Cross-National Perspective* (Foster and Russell 2002) explicate, and as Xiao-Ming Li (1996) does in *"Good Writing": In Cross-Cultural Context*. And I mean that we investigate how writing has been historically taught around the world, as Xiaoye You (2010) does in *Writing in the Devil's Tongue: A History of English Composition in China*. And I mean that we need to critique the provincialism that marks much of the research in composition studies in the United States, as Christiane Donahue (2009) does in her *College Composition and Communication* article, "'Internationalization' and Composition Studies: Reorienting the Discourse." And I mean that we learn how writing is researched around the world, as we see in collections such as *Traditions of Writing Research* (Bazerman et al. 2010). Indeed, we have barely begun to envision what "writingology" might mean to how we theorize composition (Huijen 2010)—if we have thought about it at all—and we have barely begun to employ the sociological research methodologies and interpretive schemes of French didactics to learn about the material roles of writing in the lives of our students (Delcambre and Reuter 2010). We must use insights such as these, as well from elsewhere, to revise and broaden our own research visions. After all, how can we hope to root out embedded forms of racist and imperialist nationalism in our curricula and pedagogies if we limit our thinking to parochial forms of disciplinarity? We can't. Of course, as we learn about how others perform research and teach writing, we will have our local issues and international disagreements. As we read about educational writing research in, say, European contexts, we may encounter research stances that seem to reduce the complexity of composing to simplifications. But the same can be said of some research in the United States.

The point is that we need to prepare ourselves for international exchange. We compositionists can learn about rhetorical traditions that lie outside the traditional, Western, disciplinary archive of composition. We can learn as much as possible about as many rhetorics and examples of philosophy, poetics and "prosaics" as possible (Kittay and Godzich 1987). We can then bring the wisdom and health they offer to our teaching. Indeed, this work will entail something like a lifestyle change for many of us who teach composition in the United States. To free ourselves of habitual conceptions of composing and teaching as well as ingrained thinking that locks our visions into local, exclusionary, and timeworn interests, we will need to open ourselves to the study of texts that are sometimes outside the purview of our disciplinary study, not to mention our personal, bibliographic comfort zones.

We know that the Western tradition of rhetoric is deeply connected to Western conceptions of rationality. But what would we find if we began looking to other epistemologies for rhetorical sources? In his explication of African epistemology, Mogobe Ramose argues for the centrality of *ubuntu*, which he defines as being-in-the-process-of-becoming, or, specifically, for present purposes, human being in the process of creating harmony through dialogue. According to Ramose, *ubuntu* is a pan-African concept of harmony and wholeness that unifies Africans in their actions in regard to each other, the land, their families, and, significantly, family ancestors. Indeed, as Ramose explains it, the speaking person cannot achieve the harmony of *ubuntu* without the intentional action of one's ancestors (which is why rhetorical acts often begin with appeals to ancestral authority): "The living-dead are important to the upkeep and protection of the family of the living. This is also true with regard to the community at large" (2002b, 237).

Generally speaking, we compositionists teach our students to write to persuade. What if we combined that principle with the idea of writing to remain connected to the harmony of *ubuntu*? What if we asked students, in the beginning, before they start to write a persuasive piece, to compose, say, a justification of their work to their ancestors? What if at some point in the composing process we asked students to write and explain each element of their work to their family, from their research to their reasoning, from their intentions and goals to how they argued their piece? What forms of productive criticism might that give rise to and what sort of harmonizing adjustments? What if students were prepared from the day they enter our classrooms to write in order to enact *ubuntu* as their guiding principle, rather than in order to win an argument, no matter the integrity of the topic? What sort of writing would we see? Yes, one can certainly say that the winning of an argument in terms of re-establishing order is the same as speaking so as to partake of and maintain harmony. I am not saying that these principles are mutually exclusive. I am saying that United States composition classes—with exceptions—do not include presentation of such concepts as *ubuntu* because the reality, let alone the legitimacy, of African epistemology is not recognized, acknowleged, presented, or allowed. What might such work mean to African American students who are not used to seeing the cultures of their ancestors valued in college classrooms? We cannot afford such provincialism. We cannot neglect any access to harmony in our violent world. Despite our best intentions, some of us rob our students of the great knowledge sources of the world—or of the opportunity to share them with us.

We need to explore the rhetorics of the world in the most generous and humble ways possible. The easiest and most ugly thing to do when looking to cultures other than our own for rhetorical inspiration would be to enact a process of reading-as-plundering. In this form of colonialist study, the cultural treasure of the other is read for its extraction value, rather than for the exchanges and changes it can inspire. In "'African Renaissance': A Northbound Gaze," Mogobe Ramose (2002a) warns readers about this danger and the distortions that attend the imposition of social interpretations derived from historical inequities. Epistemological and ontological categories drawn in European philosophy can pollute African philosophy and distort dialogue between Africa and the North. Therefore, we must be vigilant to the dangers that continually threaten to undermine the potential for extraordinary ethical and epistemological growth that international exchange represents. As V. Y. Mudimbe (1988, 175) argues, dialogue between Africa and the rest of the world, exchanges of knowledge and epistemological breakthroughs, can lead, in the long run, to the liberation of humankind. We need this release. In a world of shrinking resources and continuing violence, we need to expand the possibilities for making and replenishing meaning—options for nothing less than our renewal.

NO NEW COLONIALISM, THEN

When we develop an international perspective on composition, we seek to understand the composing of others, to understand what others bring to their composing processes (ideology, religion, material concerns, patterns of social relationships, attitudes and perceptions about writing, etc.). We seek knowledge of how students of other cultures and nations compose so that we might better teach them when they are in our classes. In addition, we seek insights about how others compose so that we may develop our own composing repertoires—to open ourselves to opportunities for learning about linguistic and rhetorical options from our students. Our goal is not to study the rhetoric of the other so as to appropriate it, to study it in the belief that we will write exactly as the other does. And our goal is not to study the rhetoric of another so that we are able to impose our own image upon it. For instance, a rhetorician might decide to construct, say, something called an "Asian American rhetoric," but such a project would be plagued by considerable problems, as LuMing Mao (2004) explains in "Uniqueness or Borderlands?: The Making of Asian American Rhetorics." As Mao points out, in the hands of many Western rhetoricians, an Asian American rhetoric will be constructed in terms of the Classical tradition, rendering primacy to the Western tradition. For Western rhetoricians, the Eurocentric tradition is the lodestone against which all others are tested. Indeed, the Western tradition is technical, so fully defined, so delineated and so documented that its descriptive strength easily becomes prescriptive. The tradition has the quality of a virus. It infects researchers with replicating behaviors so that they see whatever rhetoric with which they come into contact in Western terms. Sadly, sometimes this sort of imposition seems almost inevitable. A rhetorician might attempt an objective description of a Native American rhetoric by cataloging the kinds of ethical appeals and perhaps the number and kinds of topoi available to a Native American speaker or writer. And in doing so, they impose a foreign epistemology, along with its accompanying ideology. Yes, I believe that there are ways, through mediation or creative interpretation, for challenging one's own predispositions and methodologies, even if we cannot fully escape them. Wishes aside, the problem remains.

We need leaders and models. In this regard, Mao's essay is an important example of how to do comparative rhetorical analysis without privileging one rhetoric over another. He does this in two ways, by beginning his analysis with a concept from the Eastern rhetorical tradition, rather than the Western, and by analyzing that concept in both rhetorics and then concluding with an attempt at finding common ground that respects differences between the two.

Mao's project is important, then, for how it teaches about rhetorical theory and tradition and multiple cultures. His project, which he continues in collaboration with Morris Young in *Representations* (2008), demonstrates fairness, thoroughness, respect and compassion in rhetorical studies. After all, why should a researcher expect the rhetorical tradition of another to look or sound like their own? Why would anyone in this day and age who has explored the complexities, depths and meanings of composing expect that there is only one way to theorize it, especially when we continue to develop our knowledge about the world's multitude of cultures? They wouldn't, of course. This is why internationalism in composition must be about learning from the rhetoric of the other in order to develop broader understandings of the self and tolerance of others. It is about teaching for greater fluency by learning to blend the sources of rhetorical performance and expand our meaning making potential.

For teachers, an international composition studies will demand, then, new levels of student-centeredness. As we facilitate our students' exploration of linguistic and rhetorical diversity, we create ever more sophisticated ways of sharing centeredness—in the classroom, and, hopefully, elsewhere as well. When we teach writing, we teach processes that reach to the center of who we are, to our ontological status. The processes of love, desire, pain, and hope, processes of imagined shapes and textures and visions, these largely ineffable processes through which we construct freedom while carrying the weight of our humanity, are our reasons for teaching and writing. We teach writing because we want to make spaces in which students can discover creation with words for themselves. We teach writing to help students reach beyond themselves. We teach writing because in writing and being around others who write we learn to see—for moments—peace, the best in us, our potential for creating the good. We watch other writers and learn strategies for finding our own revelations; we teach writing so that we may better write ourselves. We watch other writers because we want to see how things get completed. It is these moments—and through our change—we are trying to reach.

TRANSCENDING TRANSNATIONALISM?

John Trimbur (2004) makes an articulate case for knowing—and remembering—the realities of history and internationalism in "Keeping the World Safe for Class Struggle: Revolutionary Memory in a Post-Marxist Time." For many reasons, not the least of which is the heartfelt way that it demonstrates how the global is also personal, Trimbur's article stands as a model for compositionists. In it, Trimbur explains how, precisely because it is based in a critical, philosophical tradition, "Marxist revolutionary memory" continues to be a guiding force and persuasive, theoretical construct. Its vision is international and draws on the gains and strength of national and international labor organizing; its tradition is one of activism in response to the material reality of class. Through all the claims of academics whose scholarly work has emerged from the insights of various postmodern theories, Trimbur argues, Marxist thought still sponsors material actions that are based in a coherent model of historical development and goals.

We in English studies have, for the past fifty years, introduced original and complex, literary and rhetorical theories in order to explain culture, politics, and history. In one sense, it is possible to locate the root of one strain of our theoretical practice in deconstruction where literary and then composition theorists first began to exercise our language abilities in decidedly postmodern ways, permutating and twisting every articulation for every nuance of meaning and contradiction. The theorists working in this tradition consequently turned their endlessly differentiating perspective from elegant and complicated critiques of Western reason to the world's state of affairs in general. And as they did so, they maintained, generally speaking and probably quite naturally, given their concern with literary studies: linguistic complication, tropes and nuance.

The 90s brought us the heyday of critical pedagogy and a string of teacher-centered pedagogues for whom teacherly political concerns and reading interests took center-stage in the first-year writing classroom. In fact, over my more than a decade as a member of an English department hiring committee, I witnessed a long run of applicants for composition positions whose letters of application and curriculum vitae spoke of being a cultural, literary, political, queer, or rhetorical theorist first and a teacher of writing second. It always seemed as if the candidates valued their research more than their teaching, that they viewed the teaching of writing as somehow merely a vehicle for their political commitments, which always seemed, in turn, to align these teachers with a renewed commitment to the teaching of persuasive writing. Theory, as in critical pedagogy, then cultural studies, postcolonialism, and the many steps in between, created—and continues to create—a steady stream of rhetoricians who produce brilliant critiques and micro-studies of culture, and dedicate themselves to teaching academic reading and writing as they pursue their chief interests, their political affiliations.

It seems obvious, but bears repeating: theory, divorced from practice, is not the answer for compositionists. For instance, Aijaz Ahmad explains what happens when postcolonial academics do not investigate material, international situations, and specific systems of exploitation. History becomes abstract. When they work without necessary reference to the truths of events, postcolonialists take history in general as their domain, covering the precolonial, colonial, and postcolonial to a, presumably, post-postcolonial end. Lost within the glossing sweep of postcolonialism's comprehensive and abstract perspective, academics can produce multitudes of readings of cultural artifacts in their quest for detail and definition. The postcolonialists' endless search for both specific illustrations of oppression to interpret and accurate global perspectives to promote results in a never-ending production of interpretation. The result is inevitable: linguistically interesting, postmodern, diffuse, and fractional views of history and material reality, without mechanisms for self-examination of the theory's own operations:

"Colonialism" thus becomes a transhistorical thing, always present and always in process of dissolution in one part of the world or another, so that everyone gets the privilege, sooner or later, at one time or another, of being colonizer, colonized and postcolonial—sometimes all at once, in the case of Australia for example. This manner of deploying the term has the effect of leveling out all histories so that we are free to take up any of the thousands of available micro-histories, more or less arbitrarily, since they all amount to the same thing, more or less.

The fundamental effect of constructing this globalized trans-historicity of colonialism is to evacuate the very meaning of the word and disperse that meaning so widely that we can no longer speak of determinate histories of determinate structures such as that of the postcolonial state, the role of this state in reformulating the compact between the imperialist and the national capitals, the new but nationally differentiated labor regimes, legislations, cultural complexes, etcetera. Instead, we have a globalized *condition* of post-coloniality that can be *described* by the 'postcolonial critic,' but never fixed as a determinate structure of power against which determinate forms of struggle may be possible outside the domains of discourse and pedagogy. (Ahmad 1995, 31)

In other words, though we follow liberatory impulses when we either construct literary theories such as postcolonialism or adapt such theories for the field of composition, our investments in the suasory qualities—and maybe capital gains—of these theories distract us from recognizing the necessary study we need to do. Some of this research might include, for compositionists anyway, the relation of specific examples of our curricular contributions to nationalist agendas and international realities.

Postcolonialism and the emerging transnational theory that would subsume it would seem to be the natural choices for composition-ists seeking sources for creating new takes on the teaching of writing. Because writing teachers help students from various ethnic and cultural backgrounds to make the transition to academic life, postcolonialism's intellectual landscape, which includes investigations of race, ethnicity, identity, difference, heterogeneity, hybridity, diaspora, oppression and resistance, authenticity, artistic production, nationalism and imperial-ism, not to mention the linguistic nature of subjectivity, would seem an appropriate source. But literary theory has not always adapted well to composition pedagogy—or theory (with exceptions, of course, for specific instances of theories such as reader-response and feminism). When, for instance, a class focuses on an act of literary resistance, no matter how articulate or aesthetically interesting, the critical analysis of the literary work becomes the pedagogical end. The assignment is often a study that interrogates language and meaning or power relations between oppressor and oppressed, or even the complex, difficult histo-ries and economics of the oppression that gave rise to the literary work in the first place. A shift from having students analyze, say, an example of media indoctrination (as in cultural studies) to a literary story about media indoctrination, written, say, by a Nigerian writer (as in postcolonial pedagogy) is tantamount to a change in objects of study—but neither are, finally, about teaching writing. Neither make the processes or writing of the students in the room the central objects of study. In other words, assigning even a sophisticated, postcolonial study of a literary work does not require postcolonial compositionists to revise the way that they teach writing to any significant degree, including the rhetorical requirements made on the students.

I suppose, then, that like at least some compositionists, I have felt a long ambivalence toward the "post" theories. I learned from the critique of Western rationality found in deconstruction, but its linguistic fireworks and language-induced mystifications proved, at times, more distracting than useful. I deeply valued the turn to politics and critique in the social theories of cultural studies and critical pedagogy, but over time, their teacher-centered pedagogies too often proved incongruent with composition theory. I applauded the global turn of postcolonialism, but over time I have found that it too relies on distracting linguistic fireworks and inspires teacher-centered pedagogy. And so I am at one time supportive of and skeptical about the newest "post" moment: the "transnational" movement.

Transnationalists point to network theory analysis as a key research concern as they seek to help rhetors realize both their locations within networks of relationships and access their power to intervene in oppressive public policies. Following the groundbreaking transnational theory of Inderpal Grewal (2006) and the rhetorical work of Rebecca Dingo (2012), transnational theorists help us to understand the power of networks of "connections" (Hannerz 1996) and "connectivities" (Grewal 2006) and, for working for justice and human rights, "imaginary states" (Hitchcock 2003). They help us to understand how population movements require new thinking about the nature, workings, and locations of identities and allegiances (familial, national, or otherwise). They help us to see oppression and understand forces arrayed against gender and racial rights as well as possibilities for the construction of resisting alternatives. They help us to understand how capitalist globalization employs networks to establish consumerist identities and how capitalist designs have fused conceptions of and perceptions about democracy with consumer choice (Grewal 2006). They illuminate the nature and significance of social media in alliance formation. They explicate how international organizations such as the World Bank Group

employ "megarhetorical" (Dingo and Scott 2012) networks of development discourse to spread Western capitalist control over, particularly,
women, and certainly whatever and whomever is deemed an exploitable
resource. They throw new light on the continuing global blight of patriarchy and violence and illustrate how transnational allegiances exist for
alternative ways of working and being—even that they multiply. We need
the insights of transnational theorists such as Inderpal Grewal (2006) in
order to understand how identity is constructed by transnational consumerism and to resist global patterns of isolation and alienation that
result when the imagination is commodified. We need the insights of
transnational feminist theorists Shu-mei Shih and Francoise Lionnet
(2005) who explain how transnationalism supersedes local/global
dichotomies and contributes to new conceptions of space and time.
Their work helps us to understand how our own classrooms are already
connected to classrooms around the world and to see our classrooms
beyond provincial conceptions of the here and now. We need the work
of Carmina Brittain (2002) to understand the experiences of immigrant
children in school so that we may better understand how teachers might
learn to see immigrant students as bringing cultural additions, rather
than subtractions, to our classrooms.

But I am a compositionist. For me, how the teaching transpires is key.
I agree with Irvin Peckham (2010) who argues in *Going North Thinking
West* that writing teachers face a genuine problem when they allow their
politics to overtake their obligation to teach writing politically—that is,
within the parameters of a student-centered pedagogical and political
configuration. Specifically, and following Peckham's insightful analysis here, I worry about the possibility of teacher-centered, vanguardist
teaching attitudes (Freire 1973, 2000) that may very well arise in transnational pedagogies. These positions could act to dehumanize and distance students from their own needs, concerns, and writing which are
themselves cultural, political, critical, and international (though we
most likely will need to help them see the connections). We compositionists would be foolish indeed if we did not learn from history, especially our own. If the expressivist compositionists of the 1980s taught
us anything, it is that student-centeredness is the crucial component of
sound composition instruction. But when content is added to a composition class, the potential for undermining the purpose and strength of
the composition course is heightened. Compositionists will be watching in the coming years to determine how transnational theory inspires

pedagogy. If transnationalism inspires teacher-centered approaches, it will likely become the newest passing academic answer. If so, it will certainly leave its effects, but these will be traces of the possibility it might have given us—and that will be unfortunate. Some will say that all theories are supposed to come and go as the march of academic knowledge continues. Perhaps so, but the need for political staying power seems acute in a world approaching ecological crises of tragic proportions with resulting political turmoil. (And who cannot at least imagine the possibility of repressive forms of political arrangements developing in a world enduring one ecological crisis after another?)

Of course, rhetoric is not composition any more than literature is composition. Though they overlap to a significant degree, the concerns of these three English disciplines are not identical. But compositionists hear about transnationalism at our conferences and read about it in many of our journals. And when we do, this latest theoretical initiative looks likely to inspire, I fear, a new package of teacher-centered pedagogy. Perhaps it will be different for first-year transnational composition classes. Perhaps pedagogues will learn to facilitate student learning about the World Bank, "megarhetorical" policy networks, and the social networks established by families and activists committed to freedom and resistance. Because I share the political commitments of the transnationalists, I sincerely hope so. But, frankly, I do not expect things to go this way. We compositionists have seen this too many times before to pretend that we do not know the outcome.

Let me put it this way: transnationalism faces two challenges that have shortened the shelf life of all the other "post" literary and rhetoric-based theories, at least for compositionists.

First, transnationalism can too easily be turned, like the literary theoretical "isms" that have gone before it, into product. You can imagine the textbooks for the first-year composition classroom: *Transnational America* or *Topics for a Networked World*, or *The MegaRhetoric Reader*. Any of the above will be complete with excerpts from the web, World Bank documents, writing and literature about cosmopolitanism, examples of film studies' interpretations and readings of visual representations of the subaltern with assignments and descriptions for reading these images and methodologies for sounding something like the new transnational academic. Of course, I am being more than a little facetious here, but because I value the work of the new transnationalists, I want to make as clear as possible the danger that transnationalism faces, namely, the many ways it could be commodified. Product and profit infects the academic (as in "academic capitalism" and vita building [Slaughter and Leslie 1999; Slaughter and Rhoades 2009]); the university (as in give us material that we can force adjuncts to use or give to teachers who don't really want to teach writing but still want to look excellent); and the textbook companies (as in don't be left out in the cold, here is the newest material and methods that you really should be teaching). If transnationalism succumbs to the forces of commodification, it will be multiculturalism and cultural studies and all their textbooks all over again.

Second, if, as it seems they will, transnationalists remain committed to the production of individual rhetorical and literary readings of cultural artifacts such as films or policy documents, and if that fairly traditional methodology inspires them or the pedagogues who come after them to create traditional pedagogies for having students produce facsimiles of transnational scholarship, then transnationalism will not answer the problem of composition's commitment to one cultural strand of rhetoric and so will not, I think, resist the racialized nationalism at the heart of composition. In this regard, transnationalism will help explicate patriarchy and imperialism, but it will not institute, at that point in time, anyway, a pedagogy that resists the idolizing of elite, academic discourse and Western argumentative rhetoric.

In *Global Community: The Role of International Organizations in the Making of the Contemporary World,* Akira Iriye levels a charge against transnationalism that is similar to Aijaz Ahmad's critique of postcolonialism; namely, that it inspires a transcendent, general theory in search of an infinite number of examples. Iriye writes that transnationalism "suggests the building of transnational networks that are based upon a global consciousness, the idea that there is a wider world over and above separate states and national societies, and that individuals and groups, no matter where they are, share certain interests and concerns in that wider world" (1997, 8). Iriye may be over-generalizing here, but he is right in that, at the very least, transnational theory does suggest a transcendental realm of understanding that could turn out to be more of a mystification than a reality. Until the new transnationalists further define what transnational connections are, or consist of, it will be hard to say. But let me speak here as a compositionist.

In her article "Turning the Tables on a Megarhetoric of Women's Empowerment," Rebecca Dingo suggests that teachers can use cultural artifacts such as documentary films to help students understand something about the lives of others from around the world, to inspire emotions and action. The example that Dingo supplies is one where she used a film in a classroom that encouraged feelings of shame in students at their own ignorance of the relative luxury of their lives in relation to factory workers in China. This is a pedagogy designed to help students become more aware of the suffering of others (2012, 190–196). At that point in the pedagogy, one might suppose, students would be asked to write about their new understanding, which is largely one at which the teacher wants them to arrive. My question is whether or not this is the teaching of writing or the teaching of something else such as politics. Of course, the teaching of writing is always political, but teaching politics is not always the teaching of writing. If our students write, for instance, about the shame they feel at the relative luxury of their lives (though so many do come from terribly difficult circumstances), and if they write about why everyone should feel the same, and if they also promise, in these writings, to make some sort of change in their lives as a result, then what has been accomplished? Certainly, the students may have produced smart interpretations of the films they see in class, and these interpretations may contain appropriate rhetorical and political gestures. These readings may also be useful for the awareness they help to concretize; they may even inspire activism. So, I see how well-taught classes in transnationalism might affect students deeply and might even change some of their actions across the span of their lifetimes. But I do not understand how a course in transnationalism, as I envision it being taught after reading transnational theory, would change the composing processes of first-year students (except for the fact that shame and international awareness would be injected into the process—the latter being a pedagogical goal I would myself adopt, the former, probably not). I do not see, in other words, how transnationalism's commitment to teacher-centered, argumentative, academic writing activities would materially alter the teaching of the provincial elements of composing habits and literate behavior; how it would change, through international understanding of writing, the students' parochial views of composing; how it would resist racism in composition.

All of this is not to say, however, that transnational thinking has not produced instructive theory about rhetoric and, by extension, composition. In 2008, composition scholars Wendy Hesford and Eileen Schell edited a special issue of *College English* entitled *Configurations of Transnationality: Locating Feminist Rhetorics*. In their introduction to

the issue, Hesford and Schell explain that feminist, transnational theory "challenges the disciplinary defining of rhetoric and composition
around US-centric narratives of nation, nationalism, and citizenship,
including its focus on feminist and women's rhetorics only within the
borders of the United States or Western Europe, and explores its potential complicity in reproducing institutional hierarchies" (2008, 463).
Hesford and Schell accurately describe how we composition professionals have yet to look much beyond our Eurocentric orientation and
nationalist rhetorical affiliations. We do not know much, they point
out, about how writing is taught in countries around the world, and we
certainly have much work to do if we are to understand the relation of
our rhetorical preferences and pedagogies to the power structures of
international politics. And we need to begin, Hesford and Schell tell
us, with critiquing traditional forms of international thinking that relies
on the nation as a unit of political organization that privileges Western
cultural dominance. Consequently, the contributors to the transnational
feminism issue of *College English*, as Hesford and Schell explain, are committed to expanding the concerns and contents of rhetorical studies to
include feminist rhetorical issues and strategies and to make this new
discipline available for establishing transnational linkages. These linkages would, in turn, connect women around the globe as they merge
domestic and international political movements for the addressing of
women's issues. Feminist transnationalists look, in other words, for liberatory options in the midst of geopolitics and in the interaction of the
global and the local, in how international policy affects domestic locations and, in turn, how local concerns can be articulated in their trans-
border connections.

Any compositionist can learn much, then, from the study of transnationalism. Transnationalists point out the profit-inspired actions of
transnational corporations and how they stress the traditional and leg-
islative integrity of nations. They articulate examples of how the growth
of non-governmental organizations test the relevance of individual
national governments and how the processes of diaspora and migration
challenge certain aspects of provincial planning and other regionalisms.
In their theory, ever-unfolding and developing communication technologies "bring people together" for moments of understanding despite
far-flung geographic locations, and the new knowledge created in these
moments further stress national boundaries. In the connections we can
establish with others who work for justice amidst the pain of life and

the inequalities of unevenly distributed capital, in the moments where the demarcations between global and local interests are transcended, we might, transnational theory tells us, enact alternatives for productive politics. A transnational alliance might enact protest, for instance, when a state uses force against its people and when international governments are reluctant to act. And these alternatives might lead to larger networks of sustainable living. As a theory, then, transnationalism provides ways for developing lines of investigation related to nationalism, internationalism, and globalization, as well as the essential importance of feminist thinking and resistance throughout. It is a theory for studying the structure and directions of existing exchange among peoples of different nations. It is a theory for thinking about innovative, equivalent relations of production. And it is a theory of exchange that might potentially lead to new forms of social connection, consciousness, and creation.

But in "The Locations of Transnationalism," Michael Peter Smith and Luis Eduardo Guarnizo (2008) remind us that if we wish to understand the "alternative world" that transnationalism promises, we will need to analyze it in regard to the specificity of its manifestation. That's a valuable insight that does not seem to have completely taken hold in the world of "trans" studies where scholars still seem to generalize, romanticize, or infinitely create representations of transnational network phenomena without critical self-consciousness. Here, I am thinking specifically, of the "trans" linguistic work of Alastair Pennycook, where his reading of hip-hop's worldwide popularity provides, for him, a view of cultural exchange that is one of "Dionysian excess" and transcendence.

For Pennycook, theories that he calls "transgressive" are, while being postmodern or critical, at the same time about "creating something new" (2007, 37). This "something new" is supposed to be a step beyond postmodernism—a "post" beyond all "post" thinking actually—a time of transgressive politics and social arrangements. In their commitment to continuous skepticism and questioning, Pennycook's "transgressive politics" sound much like the formulations of many other critical schools of thought that preceded him: "On the one hand, it demands that we confront relations of power—dominion, disparity, difference, and desire—while on the other it maintains a constant skepticism, never allowing us to rest on the satisfaction of our own self-conception" (56). On the face of it, Pennycook's formulation sounds great, but as is the case with so many theoretical claims, the devil is in the details. Specifically, it is hard to imagine the concrete operation of Pennycook's thinking. Drawing upon a reference to transgendered, transvestite, and transsexual experi-ence, Pennycook claims that a new time of transgressive politics will be a time in which we would all, one might suppose, learn to be "trans," to "cross over, to transcend the bounded norms of social and cultural dictates" (36). For Pennycook, the time is ripe for moving, as he says, "beyond arguments about homogeneity or heterogeneity, or imperial-ism and nation states, and instead focus on translocal and transcultural flows" (5–6).

I appreciate any theorizing that helps to dislodge the entrenched order of things, and Pennycook's presentation of transgressive politics and transcultural flow is, at the very least, a gesture in the direction of liberation and is to be valued for its contribution. At the same time, I shy away from theories that create mystifications of human experience. I do not believe that Pennycook's "trans" age of cultural flow—what-ever "transcultural flow" even is—is here or about to arrive (indeed, I do not think that his reading, in *Global Englishes and Transcultural Flows*, of hip-hop's popularity accounts for the complexity of hip-hop experience either). Mystifications lead to further mystifications. In the throes of one's own imaginings one can ascribe effect to belief. In such an instance, one is apt, even, to focus on something as impressionistic as "transcultural flow" rather than specific instances of imperial impo-sition and resistance, and all before one has challenged one's own habitual thought patterns and material practices. Such outcomes are dangerous, it seems to me, for one's self, but especially for the victims of imperial designs.

The fact is that we work with too many theoretical mystifications. For instance, we hear many theorists claiming that migrations and transnational organizations put growing pressure on the status of the nation-state. The problem with this statement is that the nation-state, a geographic space where border, ethnicity, culture, and sovereign state system of governance are concurrent, is an anachronism—that is, if a nation-state ever in truth existed. At best, the concept of the nation-state is more of an ideological mechanism for inspiring unity than any political configuration for representing reality. Yes, the status of both the nation and the state have come under considerable scrutiny and pressure in our time (but that is a different consideration). Many people of the world are, in lavish comfort or out of necessity, in move-ment; and states, governments, and economies do continue to endure crisis and alteration that can, in some cases, stress national affiliations.

Exchange causes change. The constitutional integrity of discrete demographic entities seems less and less identifiable when migrations, immigrations and dual-citizenships challenge the self-images of traditional populations (though these were often not historically homogeneous to begin with). Indeed, we can question whether the parochialism of any single, national perspective can survive in a world where international exchange and awareness are ever more prevalent and seem to threaten the sovereign power of a state as activists call for international alliances. But none of these phenomena in and of themselves mean that the power of the nation or the state as either categories of human organization or sets of cooperative or coercive practices are in immediate or serious jeopardy. States continue to prove their vitality in any number of ways, from declaring war, to nationalizing, in part, control of various banks and economic interests, often in competition with other states, as we saw in the economic crisis of 2008, not to mention its continuing aftermath (though, certainly, globalized economic-political ties complicate the meaning of autonomy for national or state governments). Politicians continue to appeal to national allegiance, telling stories—mostly quite flimsy stories—of the nation, of who we are, in order to be elected. What is more, the continuing birth, fervor, and growth of nationalist movements around the world stand as proof of the continuing relevance and strength of the idea of nationhood. People die every day for the rights of breakaway republics—or for the establishment of homelands or for the sovereignty of their nation. The fact that people cross national and state borders, whether legally or illegally, does not mean that protectionism is subsiding in the halls of government. Border walls may be cracking, but they are not failing. Armed guards are still checking papers; they are not putting down their guns and going home. (Indeed, statements about the porous nature of national boundaries and discourses that glorify border crossing might even seem, in some instances, as the height of presumption. When does border crossing, one might ask, become transgression or infiltration rather than liberation? When so many oppressed, indigenous nations are trying to maintain national membership and sovereignty, the question is how can political compositionists both claim to honor indigenous cultures at the same time they further a border crossing mentality? No one I know has written about these matters for compositionists with greater insight than Scott Richard Lyons.)

As Ian Tyrrell (2007) argues in *Transnational Nation: United States History in Global Perspective Since 1789*, modern nations have been constructed by processes and forces of cohesion from within but, also, from the time of their institution, by processes and forces from without, whether from migration, commerce, or threat. Nationalism is not a static ideology; it evolves to include new rationale and policies. It changes with the times and accommodates new social phenomena, such as the presence of people of many languages in any one nation. Nationalism has this kind of flexibility. It welcomes minority populations into the fold of its population even as it holds elite segments of that population, along with their cultural artifacts, including discourse, up for emulation and reward. No, contemporary geo-ethno-political circumstances do not indicate that the modern state is in danger of falling or that nationalism is a failing ideology. Nationalism is too resilient and able to induce newcomers to allegiance. Nations have demonstrated an impressive ability for responding to change, even if they seem slow to do so. In fact, the truth of the matter is that, rather than failing, developing ecological crises will likely fuel nationalist sentiments and movements as capitalists manipulate international struggles for scarce resources such as oil and water. And while this new eco-nationalism will continue to be stressed and fragmented as the poorest peoples of the earth bear the full brunt of the effects of global heating, the world situation will likely still inspire the "us against them" mentality that benefits the wealthy of each nation for quite some time to come. At least, that is the future I fear, unless we begin to act now.

Where does this leave us? In *The New Transnationalism*, Sidney Tarrow writes that as long as states exist, so will international state relations. Transnational activists will, therefore, "continue to lobby and protest, encounter others like themselves, identify friendly states, and, from time to time put together successful global-national coalitions" (2005, 219). And transnationalists will perform their activism in a variety of ways because there "is no single core process leading to a global civil society or anything resembling one, but—as in politics in general—a set of identifiable processes and mechanisms that intersect with domestic politics to produce new and differentiated paths of political change" (9). As we explore these specific processes and paths, and as we learn from the insightful and caring work of transnational theorists, I would remind my colleagues in the profession to remember to foreground in their work the fact that people are oppressed in material ways and that, consequently, the paths of redress will also, finally, be material. We will develop new paths for change, and while I do not pretend to be seer enough to know these in advance, I am sure that we will develop new paths toward health because we humans are imaginative creatures, but also because people around the world are suffering. We need each and every initiative and need to support each new gesture toward genuine hope.

In fact, the discipline of composition is large enough to accommodate many approaches to the teaching of writing, and many writing programs are large enough to contain a variety of writing classes. Just as our students come in a multitude of varieties, so might our pedagogies. I may feel that the best way of teaching writing for change is to help our students understand and honor various cultural contributions to the development of meaning in a troubled world. And I may want them to learn processes for meaning making with others so that their dialogues may lead to wider circles of cooperation. But I am also aware of how, in *The University in Ruins,* Bill Reddings (1997) explicated the importance and power of dissensus. Perhaps my response to the theory and rhetoric of transnationalism and how it may inspire another teacher-centered pedagogy is best situated in a dissensual model where different approaches to the same political end can be located in dialogue. My only caveat is that, as we compositionists talk about political ends, we remember that we should first be talking about students. If, again, transnationalism inspires a pedagogy in which students face the "literacy demand" (Blitz and Hurlbert 1989) of reconstituting, in high academic and argumentative fashion, a teacher's reading of a World Bank policy or a documentary film, the result would be valuable because the analysis would be instructive in its own right. It would not, however, be different from the reconstitution of a literature professor's required interpretation of a literary text in the form of argumentative critical analysis. Again, the production of such reports and analysis is instructive in the context of literature classrooms, but they are not as meaningful in the context of a student-centered composition pedagogy. And it is, as always, again and again in the teaching of writing, a question of student-centeredness.

For now, I chose internationalism for my configuring, and I do so because the concept signifies, despite the world's long history of violence and oppression, an equally long history of activism, alliance, and cultural pluralism (Iriye 1997). While it is true that the history of international relations among nations has been rife with conflict and exploitation, it is also true that internationalism has given rise to thinking and action that runs counter to cross-border exploitation. Non-governmental organizations have worked to alleviate poverty worldwide and to improve and promote agriculture, the arts, economics, health, women's rights, the peace movement, etc., and the number of these organizations is growing as they serve a greater number of the world's population (though surely history also teaches us that NGOs are not sufficient to addressing problems as large as world poverty). As a theoretical construct, internationalism recognizes the existing power of nation and state, calls on us to learn and understand and then resist or respect that power when appropriate, even as it reminds us to respect the sovereignty of nations and states. It helps to recall and draw on the continuing promise and relevance of revolutionary memory. It helps us to recognize the many ways that meaning making, as well as politics, is inspired and textured by international stimulation. And in and through the study of it all, we may also learn that composition—composing—is not the domain or resource of any one nation, state, or culture. And, as a last word, within an international construct, I offer no product (as you will find in Part 3, "Key: The Composition Classroom"). No one, as far as I can see, can use my work here to produce a handbook or reader for the first-year composition class (though I suppose one should never underestimate the machines of capital). At any rate, let me condemn, in advance, any attempt to "merch" my work.

INTERNATIONAL COMPOSITION #2

An international view of composition promotes rhetorical diversity. In an internationalist composition classroom, students are asked to learn about each other's writing processes. For instance, when students from other countries take our classes, they are encouraged to talk about their home cultures and home languages, of course, but they are also asked to share how they write: what do they think about as they write, what are their resources, what are their inspirations? And when students from other countries do not take our classes, we have the same discussions. Difference does not need a passport. An internationalist composition classroom is developed with, and in respect to, what writers and teachers know about composing and in relation to what can be learned through dialogue with others, beginning with the person sitting in the next desk. And, finally, in an international perspective, the rhetorical canon remains open to international, class, gender, racial, and sexual orientation influences. In it, ancient and contemporary texts and texts from every country can potentially influence how we write—sometimes with dramatic consequence.

In *Avarice and the Avaricious,* eighth-century Arab writer and philosopher, Abu 'Utham al-Jahiz, includes a letter from one Ibu Tau'am, about whom little is known. The letter offers writers of any age and place a necessary warning about how the power of persuasive writing can corrupt the soul of the writer who uses it for immoral purposes:

> . . . what about the poets and demagogues who learn rhetoric simply to line their own pockets? Nothing would please them more than for the rich to neglect security and leave their money unguarded and vulnerable. Beware of such people. Do not be deceived by appearances, for vagrants have more integrity. Do not be fooled by their carriages, for vagrants are more content. They may dress in the costumes of princes but, in truth, they are untitled rogues. They may have the bearing of royalty but, at heart, they are common knaves. Their demands and their methods may differ but each has the soul of a scoundrel. One may ask for finery, another one beg for rags, one may look for thousands, another one for small change but all have one aim and their

tricks are the same. They differ in the amounts they ask for, in proportion to their craft and cunning.

Be careful of their charm, watch out for their traps and keep your fortune secure from their guile. Remember that their wizardry can dazzle your wits and rob you of your judgment. The Prophet said, "Eloquence is a form of witchcraft." (1999, 167–168)

While the writing teachers and poets I know surely did not choose these professions out of greed nor "dress in the costumes of princes," the warning is clear: persuasion is a dangerous skill both for the rhetor and the audience because it can corrupt absolutely. The lesson for writers is also clear: look to one's heart and be sure that one's intentions are ethical and healthy—a worthy discussion for any classroom or any writer's inner dialogue. But how often do we ask our students to examine their writing in light of the words of, say, the Prophet Muhammed? What might it mean to our Muslim students—to all our students—if we did? That, of course, is a rhetorical question. Writing from a different cultural perspective, Bernadette M. Calafell (2010, 109) testifies to her own search for Latina culture in academe, a place that continues to privilege "the norm of the space as white, male, and heterosexual, essentially universalizing this experience and perspective." Indeed, Calafell's "Rhetorics of Possibility" ought to be required reading for how it teaches us about honoring all our students' cultures.

A contemporary source, Saddeka Arebi's *Women and Words in Saudi Arabia: The Politics of Literary Discourse*, offers a profound model of anthropological and rhetorical research. In it, Arebi presents writing by several Saudi women writers and intellectuals, analyzes the literary, cultural, and ideological import of the work and, significantly, presents insights from her interviews with the writers about the writing, their lives, and the continuing social situation.

For instance, there are the words of educator and writer Najwa Hashim's fictional character, Samia, a divorced woman writing a letter about the personal and public pain of being divorced by her husband:

The shared language, which is what usually brings two people together, I have never known . . . All I have known is a life with a bitter taste . . . I tried to finish school, but couldn't . . . I did not try to seek help from anyone . . . I had to decide for myself . . . Only I could change the situation . . . To seek help from another person would prevent me from establishing my own identity . . . From now on I will take refuge in myself . . . the greatest asylum in the history of humanity . . . I will take refuge in truth . . . it is the only virtue . . . I will take refuge in the remnants of hope that were left within me . . . To take refuge in the warmth of words is fantastic. To choose silence as a defensive means is even more terrific! (Arebi 1994, 148)

Hashim's use of ellipses is a study in the value of slowing a text down in order to deepen meaning by heightening the resonance and impact of one's words. Hashim's ellipses teach any writer how to construct a text so as to let the unsaid—be it the materiality of abusive patriarchal practice, the death of love, or the absence of human touch—speak from behind the words on the page. This is writing for the absent as well as the present, the unsaid as well as the said. This is writing for what is missing from one person's life, as well as the lives of many. It is writing for what is powerfully present and for what is painfully withheld or withdrawn. Reading Hashim's evocative text, one can feel the need for change in a world where the right to identity is infringed upon by traditional and oppressive ideology and discourse. In fact, reading Hashim's text, one can come to believe in the power of writing to bring about transformation, even if it is, for now, to be confined to one human heart, or written out for one other.

Any writer might also learn much about rhetoric and the state of citizenship for women from a phone call, by a married woman who tells columnist Fatna Shaker, in another piece in the same collection, about literacy and marriage: "I wish I could read, and do other things, in front of him. I wished an idea here or there would bring us together and renew our life together. But he drove me, intentionally or ignorantly, to practice my hobby secretly and away from him. For me citizenship is the right not to exercise my humanity in the dark" (211). Texts—even fictional testimonies such as this—can help writers to escape provincial conceptions about writing, cultures, citizenship, and ignorance by creating commonalities of understanding and purpose. And texts such as this one can make a reader remember to be thankful when and if they get to exercise their humanity in the light.

AND TO GO BEYOND THE WORDS

We know next to nothing about Lao Tzu, the contemporary of Confucius who wrote the great guide to Taoist living, the *Tao Te Ching*. In it, Lao calls on readers to follow the Tao, or Way, the entering of the process of letting go of desires and negative impulses in order to enter into harmony with nature and life. According to the *Tao*, to live effectively is to live ethically, aware, without harming, without the need to control.

One does not have to read very far in Taoist literature, of course, to see the difference between Western rhetoric with its emphasis on persuasion and eloquence and Taoism, with its emphasis on letting go and simplicity. According to Lao Tzu:

> True words aren't eloquent;
> eloquent words aren't true.
> Wise men don't need to prove their point;
> men who need to prove their point aren't wise. (1988, 81)

The decision to speak is, or should be, taken seriously. Hadrat 'Ali, one of the first followers and son-in-law of the Prophet Muhammed, fourth and last Caliph following the Prophet's death, and honored Shi'ah teacher, left important writings about spiritual and civic issues, including the uses and abuses of speech and rhetoric. Many times, throughout the course of *Living and Dying with Grace,* and no doubt in response to the turmoil of the times in which he led his people, 'Ali warns that he who "habitually engages in disputation will not see the dawn of his night" (1995, 68). Speech is a dangerous weapon: "Many a spoken word is more piercing than an attack" (60); consequently, it is better to seek truth and to use language judiciously, including in the service of God, because "The tongue is a wild beast; when it is let loose it wounds" (8).

How different our classrooms would be if our pedagogies and actions were based in principles such as these! Imagine if writing and speaking were so valued in US society that we practiced performing them only when we had considered them, only when we were certain of our intention to do necessary work, to do good for the communities we would like to join. Imagine if writing and speaking were so valued in our classrooms that we practiced only asking for them when we thought that sharing would contribute to genuine harmony—not uniformity. What if, as a nation, we valued peace and significance as much or more than acknowledgment and prestige? I suspect that we academics would teach differently, not to mention behave differently in faculty meetings and at professional conferences. In our classrooms, we would simplify our pedagogies: clear away the clutter of exercises and assignment rubrics and composition textbooks. We would not assign weekly essays on teacher-sponsored topics or work that stifles a university and a student's life with bureaucratic noise, the stuff of mechanical evaluation. We would, instead, ask our students to complete assignments that are at and in the moment, absolutely crucial. We would not ask students to write that which demonstrates allegiance to our political commitments, our activisms, or our public positions. We would ask students to write and explore their allegiance to their own political commitments, their own activisms (if they have them, and if not, why not), and their own beliefs (private and public).

When one reads in the Taoist tradition, in a book such as Tony Barnstone and Chou Ping's *The Art of Writing* (1996), a collection of poetry and prose from Taoist writers who lived in China during the first three hundred years of the Christian era, one sees insights into the nature of writing that are far different from those of the rhetoricians working in the West at the same time. This can be seen, for instance, in the writing of Lu Ji, a nobleman and military leader originally from the delta of the Yangtze River whose fortunes rose and fell with changes in the political winds, until his execution.

Lu Ji lived from 261 to 303 C.E., between the time of Quintilian, 35–96 C.E., and Augustine, 354–430 C.E. After the time when Quintilian was writing about the training of a rhetorician and the means of persuasion available to a rhetorician, and before the time that Augustine was explaining matters of faith, study and discourse, Lu was exploring the ineffability and beauty of composing. For Lu (1996, 17), writing is an art, and an "art can't be captured by the finest words." For Lu, writing is a spiritual, epistemological, and ontological endeavor. It is mysterious, sometimes tortuous, and sometimes magical. It cannot be mastered; it must be experienced and developed. It cannot be codified into a set of prescriptions; it must be lived, practiced in all its complexity, and it must be understood in all its mystery:

A writer makes new life in the void,
knocks on silence to make a sound,
binds space and time on a sheet of silk,
and pours out a river from an inch-sized heart. (10)

What is it about writing that keeps some of us coming back to it, out-side the confines of classrooms and jobs? The answer to this question is simple and complex. We write to answer our needs. We write because it feels good to put words together and to move them around in pursuit of the meaning of our lives. Writing feels good because it leads us to the more profound understandings of existence, including the meaning of our relationships with each other, with our gods and beliefs, with all the emotional and physical contours of existence. That's the point: writing feels good, or it can when it becomes, as T. R. Johnson explains, our music—our healing. And writing feels so good when it is working that we hang in there even when we are struggling. We keep trying, or take breaks, or stare at the wall because we have the knowledge or belief or hope that we can do it. That's what we need to teach students. As Lu Ji reminds us:

There is no absolute standard for anything,
And since things keep changing all the time
How to nail down the perfect description?
Control of language shows an author's skills;
Craftsmanship comes when rhetoric pays concept's bill.
Writing is a struggle between presence and absence. (1996, 11)

We write to be here, to be present, and to ward off absence.

In the *Art of Writing*, Lu Ji provides a poetics. At the same time, he is working well within a rhetorician's intention to categorize styles. And though, certainly, he endorses the need to practice writing, to exercise particular skills and styles so as to master them, he never loses sight of the fact that when writers compose, they are involved in the most pro-found of human activities. For Lu, the primary use of writing can be found in the exploration of the spiritual realm, rather than in winning one's case in a court of law. Lu seeks to let go of the desire to control or lead through writing; instead, he conveys a sense of observation, of being present, of trying simply to witness, in the face of beauty, things larger than the self. Indeed, for Lu, it would seem, writing completes its purpose when it guides readers to a place where they, too, apprehend the process of being, beauty, or nature, and let go of controlling desire. In this moment, writing is complimentary to meditation, the articulation of our simplicity, our place within nature, and our complexity, our unity with being. By embarking on the Way, Lu Ji claims, "each day the word is new" (1996, 20). Each day our writing offers access to the knowledge that filters into and through our texts, making them living moments in the consciousness of others. Our texts, appropriately quiet or noisy, graceful or livingly awkward, smoothly wild or roughly peaceful are most meaningful when they are both personally and socially significant.

Barnstone and Ping's *The Art of Writing* also includes excerpts from later writings in the Taoist tradition, including from *Poets' Jade Splinters,* which was edited by Wei Qingzhi, a scholar and poet of the Fujian Province of whom little is known, and was finished sometime around 1200 C.E. *Poets' Jade Splinters* is a collection of aphorisms and stories from different poets and writers, which, like Lu Ji's *Art of Writing,* offers a spiritual orientation toward practical issues of textuality. Their Taoist goal of letting go of the will to control can be seen in advice, such as that given by Shi Ling, that "The heart of the poet's secret is right here. Those who try too hard don't understand" (Wei 1996, 60). To understand, then, requires less control. In a classroom, for me at least, this advice supports the value of not scripting every moment of class time with drills or exercises. It means engaging students in long-term writing projects that hold their attention, that call on students to give themselves over to the writing. In another selection from *Poet's Jade Splinters,* Song Dynasty poet Su Dongpo explains, "The secret of writing lies in reading more and writing more (Wei 1996, 61). Practice and letting go. Learning how to remain open to the possibility of writing and the understanding that comes with it, remaining open so that writing will arrive in the first place; this is the way of writing.

In *Reclaiming The Tacit Tradition,* George Kalamaras (1994, 164) describes meditation as an attentiveness that brings us to a "powerful manifestation of the divine experience," a sense of "immensity." Kalamaras writes of the "consciousness of consciousness" that arises in meditation and how it is "a deepening of experience" (194). True, the act of writing is not the same as meditation, but attentiveness is central to both. Writing can be an opening of the self through mindful engagement. It is a path for thinking that must be prepared for, lived as a way of life that allows words to come. Or as another eleventh-century Daoist poet who appears in Wei's *Poet's Jade Splinters,* Shan Gu, writes: "Poetry cannot be forced. It hits you when mood, time and place converge" (Wei 1996, 51). Teachers can set the mood—most days, anyway—for working in a time and place. They can teach for the important convergences, where being present to work reflects openness to the multidimensionality of self: where the personal and the public, the aesthetic and the political, all come to bear on the work, to produce the crucial writing.

In her proto-postprocess article, "Uses of the Unconscious in Composing," Janet Emig (1983) calls on writing teachers to make room for the creative power of the unconscious. A student's unconscious may not be moved by a teacher's argument for the importance of exercise assignments, or for the schedule by which students are supposed to complete a writing process and turn in their essays. The best teaching is directly tied to finding ways for preparing students for convergences, for making the absent present. Readiness must be practiced. We must be ready for writing on the run, on a slip of paper while waiting for a bus or walking across a field. Or, as Carrie Myers describes her writing experience as a mother tending to her child in "Writing in the Dark: Composition and Motherhood," writing can be scribbled when one is lying in the dark next to one's child. It is writing with a crayon in a coloring book, when one's child finally falls asleep (1996, 81–82). Carrie Myers's work represents just one of the many material realities of writing about which we need to read and teach, one of the practices of love that help us to work to lessen the material burdens that can be part of these realities.

The Chinese poets of the Taoist tradition write about the necessity of freeing one's self from the containments of counterproductive desire when one writes—a necessary step if one wishes to achieve that state in the writing process where one truly feels in touch with something larger than one's self. I am talking about that moment in writing that we sometimes call "flow," that moment when language seems to move through us, nearly unfettered, that moment of openness where resistance to the flow of language is at its lowest, or, as one of my undergraduates once put it, "Yeah, I know that! I like it—it's a rush." Yes, it is. At the same time, there is no hurry-up in the ancient Taoist poets. Their work is about listening and attending. This is where their insights converge with my student's words. His giving over to the writing is different from Lu Ji's, but it is a giving over nonetheless. It is about the moment of making something; it is about the moment of its arrival; it is about the surprise in it, the feeling of finding the heart of something. It is a process of becoming, finding originality, knowledge, and hope for the future. It is, again, about convergences, of coming to voice by giving one's self over to the work, over to directions outside of the self, toward others, toward the ways that others make meaning.

In *Being and Nothingness,* Jean-Paul Sartre (n.d.) argues that as we enter into complex relations with others, we come to know them and ourselves, but only in moments, in glimpses. We never know, as they say, "it all." We are always pulled out of the connections we are making and back to the limitations and containments of our selves. And within the limits of our subjectivities, our knowledge is necessarily incomplete. But as we have apprehended that which we pursue—the other, knowledge of the other, or that which we have not said before—we imagine our always next attempt at understanding. This reaching and pulling back—both movements—inspire us to recreate ourselves, to prepare ourselves for our next attempt at writing.

One possible outcome of these composing events is a feeling of being new, a feeling of being someone who makes things, rather than being someone who continually consumes them. (Derek Owens [2001] might have called this a developing of "sustainable consciousness" in his *Composition and Sustainability.*) Writing, in other words, may be an event through which we can better ourselves. This writing lesson is larger and more meaningful than "Questions for Further Discussion," at the end of textbook reading selections and more useful than drills in the arbitrary breaking of paragraphs.

THE STYLES

Because it is reminiscent of Aristotelian attempts at inclusive rhetorical categorization, readers will find echoes of the Western, Classical, rhetorical tradition in the writing of Taoist poet Sikong Tu (837–908 C.E.). In his Tang dynasty treatise, *The Twenty-Four Styles of Poetry*, Sikong catalogs style, from the "The Masculine and Vital Style" with its "potency and masculine strength" (1996, 25), to "The Flowing Style" which "takes in like a water mill / and turns like a pearl marble" (38).

But because Sikong's text combines a categorical study of poetics with a philosophy of composing and living, Western readers will also find themselves surprised and enlightened by the *Twenty-Four Styles*. This unique blending of perspectives on writing causes one to be reoriented by this ancient text. The book has the power to retune one to think about composing in new ways. It is in the Taoism, in the firm standing in the belief that the letting go of egos makes successful creation possible, that one can see new possibilities for writing.

For instance, to achieve realism and a faithful rendering of reality in one's writing, "The Actual Scene Style," Siking tells us: "Use very straight speech / Without design or deep calculation." Fair enough. That is instruction any writer should follow. But quickly Sikong follows this advice with Taoist mysticism and interiority:

> Chancing upon a hermit
> Is seeing the heart of the Tao.
> . . .
> Go where your temperament leads.
> Not seeking makes it splendid.
> With luck you will stumble on
> this rare and crystalline sound. (35)

In *The Twenty-Four Styles*—indeed, everywhere one looks in the *Styles*— the characteristics and experience of style are expressed in imaginative, spirited terms. For instance, in "The Implicit Style" the experience of implicitness is presented as much or more than any definition:

This style's like straining full-bodied wine
or like a flower near bloom retreating into bud.
It is dust in timeless open space,
is flowing, foaming sea spume,
shallow or deep, cohering, dispersing.
One out of a thousand contains all thousand. (31)

How far from Western epistemology is Sikong's poetics. How far from the rhetorics of the West where the goal is persuasion and where the focus is on controlling the appearance of the self and the actions of another. In Sikong's poetics, to achieve a natural style, you

Go with the Tao
and what you write is fine as spring.
It's like meeting flowers in bloom,
like seeing the year renew.
Once given to you it cannot be stolen,
but gain it by force and soon you're poor again. (30–31)

It is easy to see what is often missing in composition studies. By permitting the poetic realm of writing to remain the intellectual property of creative writing, literary criticism, and, sometimes, literary theory, rather than claiming it as an essential concern of rhetoric and composition, we in composition continue to give up our claim to the heart and soul of writing. One is not likely to find much of this kind of imaginative exploration of style in classically-oriented Western rhetoric. This situation has, over the historical long-haul, contributed to the maintenance of instrumentalist views of writing, where writing is used to complete an exercise or job, to win a case by influencing the feelings of others. In this view, writing is a tool for achieving manageable ends: getting a good grade, finishing a report, etc. Indeed these are important, perhaps even decisive ends, depending on the context of the writer. But writing is also a complex set of processes that contribute to the ongoing creation of the meaning of the world. Yes, writing is an instrument for persuading, but it is also a means by which we make order out of chaos, bring the past to light and imagine possible or necessary, and sometimes beautiful, alternatives for the future. True, these too can be matters for persuasion. As compositionists such as Amy J. Devitt (2004) and Anis Bawarshi and Mary Jo Reiff (2010) have told us, our genres are no less complex, complicated or interrelated than our needs and intentions. But by focusing on the material ends and quick gains, we can miss the deeper reasons for writing. A grocery list can speak of the love of family ties; a lab report can speak of a student's respect for parental sacrifices to pay for a college education. Writing should be taught in all its complexities, and even its contradictions. It is all a matter of the vision from which you start when you teach. Do you agree with Quintilian that in writing instruction you need to start with minute skills and work up to discourse, or do you believe that you start by encouraging students to open themselves to deeper meanings and others' writing, needs, and practices and working from there?

Of course, Aristotle's cultural understanding and categorical impulses led him to separate poetics and rhetoric, and poetics (tragedy) from comedy, and such separations have favored, for rhetoric, technique over the immensity of "timeless open space" (Sikong 1996, 31). The result has been a two millennial perspective suggesting that the majority of people who study rhetoric do so in order to participate in legislatures and courts of law—or the academy. It is a perspective that does not recognize the local, artistic, and deeply personal and human purposes that writing also serves. The little rhetorical history I offer here does not account, of course, for the imaginative elements in epideictic rhetoric or for the spiritual, metaphysical, and personal component—no matter how stylized—of the Christian tradition of rhetoric as seen in Saint Augustine's *Confessions* (1961). Still, it reminds us how the instrumental and categorical separation of imaginative discourse from rhetorical discourse runs deeply in Western tradition.

More and more I know that it is spirit that we need more of in composition. Look around composition studies and you will see what I mean. It's in the work of the early leaders in our field. We can find it in Bob Boynton's vision and energy and Peter Stillman's commitment for using publishing to create a discipline in order to better the human condition. In James Berlin's work, it is the unflagging desire for fairness and justice. In James Sledd's work, it is the fire of truth. In Geneva Smitherman's work, it is the courage to forge paths in thought, justice, and voice for the rest of us to follow. In Ann Berthoff's work, it is the vision and strength to reclaim the power of the human imagination. In Janet Emig's work, it is the return to processes of the unconscious and student-centered teaching. In all, it is about the spirit of the work that remains and replenishes; its humanity; the joining of the creative and the critical. And it is in the work of countless others, so many others. Yes, there is still much hope. There is still hope because so many people are still trying.

We remember the feeling of composing when we return from writing, and it is the composing we remember when we return from reading Lu Ji's text. We remember that "Writing is joy / But if you fail to make it new / you can only repeat the past" (1996, 14).

RHETORICAL BOUNDARIES
AND AGENCY

The study of rhetoric inspires inner debates about one's preparation and abilities. What does one need to study or know to approach the Confucian tradition? What can one know of the Arabic tradition of rhetoric? What if one does not read Arabic? Do we need to know the language of the other in order to understand its rhetoric? In one sense the answer to this last question is an easy "yes, we do." After all, how can we hope to know another's rhetoric without fully understanding their language, without knowing the historical and semantic nuances that inform authorial choices in text production, as well as the choices audiences make in reception?

But where is the time to learn the various languages I need to know: Egyptian Arabic, Classical Arabic, Modern Arabic, Taiwanese, (the dialects of) Chinese, etc., etc., etc.? Our students will be in class Monday morning, new ones next semester. Ever more and more faces, languages, and rhetorics. Yet, there is only so much time.

Problematic or not, working with translation is, obviously, not a new phenomenon. And neither is the process of transposing the meaning and significance of a text from one cultural context or time period to another. As philosopher Ram Adhar Mall puts it:

> It is undisputed that the process of transposing is a troublesome thing, and never succeeds in producing total congruences, be it on the inter- or intracultural level. Nevertheless, this is generally the case irrespective of whether we translate the Greek *logos* as the Latin *ratio,* as the Christian God-Father, as the German *Vernunft,* as the English *reason,* or in expressions of other languages. To be sure, a similar translation is even more difficult and problematic in the intercultural field because of the greater differences of the language- and culture-spheres. Yet, the differences between the towns of Athens, Rome, and Jerusalem were no less considerable in the beginning. (2004, 321)

The challenge is to continue to build after and with the other's words, with their art, as carefully, honestly, and ethically as possible. This process entails precision and a dedication to getting the meanings right, an absolute commitment to being true to our better selves and the best of the culture of the other, to the other's absolute right to selfhood and his or her own meanings and, when we have a sense of them, the other's meaning-making processes. Of course, linguists know that we can never experience the language of the other as the other experiences it. The bilingual never masters a second language to the extent of a native speaker. The same is true for rhetoric. We study other rhetorics to achieve the level of expertise that the study affords us. We work against and accept, with humility, the limits of our knowledge. So, yes, we must begin by reminding ourselves that the problem of understanding is part of the human condition. We proceed from there with the tools we have available to us—or we go get the tools or help we need.

As linguist and language educator Michael Byram reminds us in his book, *Cultural Studies in Foreign Language Education,* even people who speak the same language do not always understand each other. Factors such as dialect interference and highly contextualized semantic content can complicate communication and understanding. These are the barriers, and we overcome them, work with them, or walk away to return another day. The point is that "a substitute for unconscious cultural, and linguistic, competence can be provided through conscious learning, accompanied by an imaginative willingness to abandon temporarily the semantics of [one's] own language and culture" (1989, 91). This willingness to let go so as to understand the linguistically unfamiliar requires that we make an "imaginative leap" (87). As Byram explains it, this leap may take us to new knowledge even as it supplies meanings that are closer to the experience of the interpreter than to the other. But the dialectic of understanding and misinterpretation is the hermeneutic problem with which we are all faced everyday. To greater or lesser extents, we are always making imaginative leaps in our communications. Understanding another—not to mention one's self—is the central problem of our lives.

I believe that a similar "imaginative willingness" to learn about another's composing processes, when accompanied by a willingness to open one's self to meaning making processes from elsewhere, can likewise provide a meaningful analog to first-rhetoric composition. In fact, Byram is actually writing about a form of engaged living. It is a desire to escape the limitations on living, to escape provincialism and to expand our composings. It is a struggle mediated by the will to understand and the power of the imagination.

PART OF THE STORY

I grew up in Johnstown, a small, depressed, mill town between the Mohawk Valley and the Adirondack Mountains in upstate New York. Sixty years ago, it was filled with thriving leather mills and glove shops. Now, after years of economic erosion and cheaper labor costs overseas—NAFTA—only a few remain, and only a very few, more modern, smaller ones have begun production.

The class structure was always remarkably visible in Johnstown and its twin town, Gloversville, the setting of many of Richard Russo's novels. The rich and the poor lived, after all, only a few blocks from each other. The houses of the wealthy were large, meticulously kept, and surrounded by high fences. The houses of the poor were mostly small, in need of repair, and crowded together. The rich had hedges and sculptures in the yard; the poor had rats and other predators in the yard at night. The neighborhoods of the rich were quiet and green. The neighborhoods of the poor—my neighborhood—were loud and hot. One of the most frequently heard topics of conversation around the dinner table, yard, or in the diner or neighborhood bar was how "The rich bastards are screwing us, getting rich while we die of cancer." And many did—my own family included. They died of cancer from breathing and handling industrial chemicals, toxins poured as untreated sewage into the Cayadetta Creek, which ran through the heart of town and once caught fire. Then the talk would immediately turn to the fact that "We are the lucky ones. Did you hear how so and so just got laid off and is on unemployment? Poor bastard, no one is hiring."

I grew up in what seemed to me, by the time I was a senior in high school, an environment custom-made for the raising of a sufficient amount of class consciousness to stand up to the mill owners—for, I came to believe, a revolution. I still own the copy of Charles A. Reich's *The Greening of America* I bought when I was eighteen in 1977. I remember sitting on the stoop of my family's house reading it, feeling excitement. I was not alone in my anger at the travesty of fairness and democracy and health that America had become. *The Greening of America* connected me, a teenager in little Johnstown, New York, to a movement, something large and national, a communal desire to make a better future.

If I had been a little older and a lot wiser, I might have seen how wrong I was. But I was young, and I trusted what I perceived to be the academic truth of Charles A. Reich of Yale University Law School:

> There is a revolution coming. It will not be like revolutions of the past. It will originate with the individual and with culture, and it will change the political structure only as its final act. It will not require violence to succeed, and it cannot be successfully resisted by violence. It is now spreading with amazing rapidity, and already our laws, institutions and social structure are changing in consequence. It promises a higher reason, a more human community, and a new and liberated individual. It's ultimate creation will be a new and enduring wholeness and beauty—a renewed relationship of man to himself, to other men, to society, to nature, and to the land.
>
> This is the revolution of the new generation. Their protest and rebellion, their culture, clothes, music, drugs, ways of thought, and liberated life-style are not a passing fad or a form of dissent and refusal, nor are they in any sense irrational. The whole emerging pattern, from ideals to campus demonstrations to beads and bell bottoms to the Woodstock Festival, makes sense and is part of a consistent philosophy. It is both necessary and inevitable, and in time it will include not only youth, but all people in America. (1970, 2)

As I read these words, I felt a responsibility. I wanted to get every detail right, to find the right courses of action in life that would push the revolution forward, that would bring the dawn of the world utopia. I believed that becoming a teacher was one of the best ways for me to proceed.

So, I went to college to become a teacher.

I sat in my poetry and few writing-oriented literature classes (the ones taught by writers), and I began, with my limited ability, to think about writing, teaching, and, well, life, and I naturally took my limitations to my first high school teaching position, to my mostly white graduate programs, and to my first college teaching position. My limitations. My inherited ignorance, fueled by my family's poverty. But no matter what childish, revolutionary thoughts I was nurturing, I knew few of anyone but European Americans throughout the whole of my elementary and high school years. My small town was mostly white and my idea of social, political, and economic change was limited by my experiences.

I understand that I am saying that the pedagogy, the questions we take up through our teaching, the books we choose, the methods we employ, answer, to a degree, the issues of our autobiographies. And, of course, I am not the first to suggest that teachers' pedagogies are autobiographical. The writers in Jane Gallop's *Pedagogy* (1995) recognize that identity is at the heart of teaching: how teachers perform their identities, how the students perform theirs, and how identity becomes the writing, are all at the heart of teaching. This vision is, of course, also part of the story. If there is one thing any sentient person knows, it is that human identity comes fraught with issues as well as beauty.

In *Making Meaning of Whiteness*, Alice McIntyre reports a study she conducted with thirteen white, undergraduate student teachers and how they avoided, when the subject of race came up during pedagogy discussion sessions, any of their own identity issues related to whiteness. Trying to appear considerate and kind, or feeling susceptible to blame, these teachers enacted avoidance behaviors that are all-too-typical of caring, white people: "derailing the conversation, evading questions, dismissing counterarguments, withdrawing from the discussion, remaining silent, interrupting speakers and topics, and colluding with each other in creating a 'culture of niceness' that made it very difficult to 'read the white world'" (1997, 46).

McIntyre's work is instructive for several reasons. She blends directness and concern in her exposition so that her readers will follow her to an understanding of how whiteness operates in the processes of identity. In this, her study is a model of critical vision and caring representation. McIntyre does not vilify her subjects, even as she helps us see how racism works. She demonstrates how some white people employ specialized language behavior when they are trying not to not hurt anyone's feelings by talking about racism and "how the language of white talk actively subverts the language white people need to decenter whiteness as a dominant ideology" (47). McIntyre's work thus demonstrates how applied linguistics can take us in composition, not only to new understandings of our practice, but to insights into who we are as teachers, as people. As McIntyre's study shows, whiteness functions in largely invisible ways in curricula and pedagogies and in the lives of teachers. Or, as the teachers in McIntyre's study admit, after many false starts, white people are "the group who 'sets the standards' for everyone else" (84). The question, of course, is what white people are willing to do about it.

White people have options. One is to shut up, to be separate, and to not call attention to the privilege. Being white entitles one to the advantages automatically bestowed through participation in class inaction.

It's a pact, a silent contract, and one of its clauses says, "Accept who you are and be silent. It will be worth it. Be quiet and let the others pay. Just be quiet so you don't screw things up for the rest of us." These words produce a self-corrosion that leaves the failure of a weakened, twisted soul in its wake. It is a corruption and a spiritual ending that is only prevented by taking a cure. The cure is honesty, confronting the self and the culture and working for health in the home and nation.

In one of the finest studies of white privilege and composition that I have seen, Nancy Dessommes writes with a clarity and a precision that can only encourage readers to identify the workings of racism in their own lives. Writing of her teenage years in Atlanta, Georgia, in the 1960s, Dessommes models the truth-telling to which compositionists need to be dedicated if we truly wish to dismantle the systematic avoidance we know to be white silence, and especially if we wish to encourage students to join with us in this cause:

> I remember cheering for the Atlanta Crackers with my daddy in the stands of the old Ponce de Leon ball park, completely unaware of who was sitting in the level above us and out of sight. Not until I was almost forty did I see in a historic picture displayed in *Atlanta Magazine* the "White Only" sign posted at the gate of this section I once occupied in 1962, the year the photograph was labeled.
>
> Although I was oblivious to the injustices evident around me in all of these situations, I was no less complicit in the oppression of black people at that time than I was the day the first small group of black teenaged boys showed up at "our" local hangout, the neighborhood public swimming pool. These dark, athletic bodies in swimming trunks were a sight I'd never seen or imagined before, black people existing generally outside my consciousness. My experiences with "the Negroes," as they were politely referred to, had been limited to a few glimpses of poor black children in the grocery store, children that I perceived were "staring at me" from the edges of the aisles. But *these* young men were invading our space, strolling confidently along the hot pavement and acting as though they had as much right to swim as we had; and now *we* were staring at *them.* As the black boys lined up for a turn on the high dive, every swimmer—all whites of course—made for the sides of the pool. I sat there with the rest of my friends, legs dangling in the water (probably a Salem dangling from my mouth) and gawked with the others as the boys took several dives into the empty deep end, then grabbed their towels and headed out the gate. Only after their departure did the white kids go back in the pool, ending the stillness and silence that accompanied the previous

performance. Much murmuring commenced in the next few minutes: "What were those Niggers doing coming here and putting on that show?" "Don't they know where their nasty bodies belong?" "Well, this pool will never be the same again." "I'm going to go home and tell my parents they have to do something about whatever the shit is happening here."

Whether I participated in this chatter I've chosen not to remember, but the question of what was happening to "our lives" in white suburban Atlanta came into focus the night of April 4, 1968, when the assassination of Martin Luther King, Jr. caused fear on neighborhood streets not felt since the Cuban missile crisis of 1962. Race was clearly an issue then; it was not a good time to be black . . . or white. When I think of the racial injustices I've witnessed and the inhuman, explosive answer to the call for non-violent change, I feel the discomfort of wearing a white skin. (2006, ix–x)

So often academics hide the truth of their lives behind the comfortable veneer of academic collegiality. We tell our students to investigate, call to light, and respond to all matter of personal, social, cultural, political, and economic problems while we maintain our comfortable distance from the kinds of necessary disclosures that make our critiques stick. But Nancy Dessommes works differently, with the power and authority that only the truth can offer. That an academic tells this story is important. But what makes this story vital beyond even its historical significance, more than its status as a moment of truth-telling or a venting of self-consciousness and pain, is the fact that it is characteristic of a pedagogy of honesty, the necessary forerunner of hope. As Dessommes demonstrates:

As my black writing students have pointed out, white people don't know much about the culture of African Americans—and don't want to know. Whites, according to these students, want to keep themselves personally insulated, as well as keep institutions (and neighborhoods) of whiteness, white. My story seems to validate their point.

Naturally, I prefer not to relate my own coming-of-racial-age experiences to my writing students because race is, after all, a delicate subject, one that we "don't like to talk about." But if I expect student writers—especially white student writers—to "come clean" before they can critically assess their own possibility in the context of race relations, then I must be willing to take that risk myself.

After thirty years . . . I have finally broken my silence. This past spring, when I opened up to my students about my racist past, yes, I received stunned looks. But I had to let our writing community know that I have had my own experiences with racial identity issues and have only recently begun to examine my own whiteness. How else could I ask them to question theirs? (xii)

Nancy Dessommes leads the way for teachers, in her honesty, through her research, and in the generous way in which she shares resources and information to better the lives of others. Her work is a beginning in which we can all take hope because it is the labor of a person in the process of improving a life. And, as compositionist Laura Milner (2005, 230) writes, "one person's healing or hurting is never just his or her own, for no matter how isolated or hidden an action may be, its consequences reverberate outward in immeasurable ways."

Some write to heal. Some write to say it and to save themselves. Some write to change everything. And some write to, this time, get it—something—right.

For me, one of the finest moments among many fine moments in the collection, *Race, Rhetoric, and Composition,* occurs in "Racing (Erasing) White Privilege in Teacher/Research Writing about Race," where Amy Goodburn questions the ways in which her own dissertation in composition research is racialized. Goodburn writes how, in her qualitative dissertation, she represented talk in a mixed-race classroom: ". . . in describing 'my own fascination with how the discussion became polarized as soon as racial difference became an issue,' I did not feel compelled to justify *why* I found it fascinating or how this fascination was perhaps tied to my own position as a white researcher invested in examining issues of difference" (1999, 77). It is one thing for a white teacher or researcher to say that whiteness needs to be interrogated so that we do not end up "inside a bankrupt race-relations model" of thought and action, and it is quite another to do it. And it is yet another thing to do the interrogating in public without falling into self-satisfaction for one's honesty. Goodburn's model is rich in meaning and possibility in this regard.

But how often, really, are white compositionists prepared to interrogate white privilege in the classroom? This is a complicated question. A compositionist's willingness to do this important work depends on their understanding of and stances in relation to identity, culture, ideology, language, nation, rhetoric, and, of course, teaching. And it depends on one's ability to change. This means that white compositionists must listen to their hearts, minds, souls, and to the voices of others. They must be open to the just, moral, and healthy doubts that tell them that their teaching, when it is based exclusively in white, Eurocentric rhetoric is unnatural, unhealthy, unjust, and immoral. I believe these doubts are out there. The better teachers of writing I know continue to question; they remain open to the idea that there are still better ways of teaching writing than the ones they have so far discovered. And the better teachers of writing I know act with the insight of John Dewey (1916, 98) who wrote in *Democracy and Education*: "The secondary and provisional character of national sovereignty in respect to the fuller, freer, and more fruitful association and intercourse of all human beings with one another must be instilled as a working disposition of mind." This "disposition of mind" is courageous. It does not fear ideology, the censures of fundamentalist forms of patriotism, or the coerciveness of neoliberal forms of the national identity. To put it simply, it privileges people and communication over the "-isms" that divide and control through prejudice and greed.

RHETORICAL TRADITIONS: A STATEMENT ABOUT METHODOLOGY

I have revised EN 731: The Rhetorical Tradition and the Teaching of Writing many times during the course of my years of teaching at IUP. I call the newest version of the course "Rhetorical Traditions." In keeping with the purpose of the graduate program in which I teach, I design the class for teacher-scholars. I structure the course around the idea that teachers of writing can meaningfully study rhetoric and its histories from various cultural perspectives in order to enlarge and deepen our sense of what a tradition of rhetoric is, how it is made, what it contains, and what it means to compose within it. The idea of the course is that if we stop thinking about writing in truncated, textbook ways, ways in which we make idols of forms, we teach writing as composing—in the broadest and deepest senses of the word. Or, to put this another way, the idea of the course is to help graduate students employ theory to become better teachers and researchers of writing.

I have drawn on various sources over the years as I have revised my Rhetorical Traditions class. I have employed insights and ideas from comparative rhetorical studies, and, indeed, there are exceptional discussions of methodology for doing comparative rhetoric by scholars such as George Kennedy, Carol Lipson and Scott Stroud. But I am working in a different domain, specifically, in composition rather than comparative studies. As I read, I certainly look for understandings about rhetorical theory as it has been articulated in various times and places, though not with the intent of becoming a Classical or comparative rhetorician in the traditional sense. Instead, I primarily look for insights into writing—its nature, processes, history, the economics and politics surrounding it, its material and spiritual realities, its social potential, history in general, and insights into the roles it might play in the making of possible futures.

For instance, like countless others who are interested in Eastern thought, I sometimes carry those little Shambala pocket-books with me. I had *The Teachings of the Buddha* with me last fall when I was riding my bike here or there. Whenever I had an appointment or needed a stop, it was there. The heart of Rhetorical Traditions is also there. So many lines in that little book seem like they should be internalized by writers and writing teachers alike:

> With our thoughts we make the world.
> Speak or act with an impure mind
> And trouble will follow you . . . (Kornfield 1993, 4)

These three lines inspire so many questions. What is the relationship of thought to world? Thought to action? To what extent do our thoughts contribute to the world? How do they do so? What is the relationship of purity to the discourse one makes? Closer to the classroom, to what extent should teachers of writing be concerned for the ethics of the writers in the room? Are we teaching students to use writing to whatever end they wish? Even ends that hurt or oppress others? Even more important, perhaps, what is purity of mind? How does anyone achieve it? Can we ever achieve the purity of mind necessary to write in such a way that trouble does not follow us? To what extent should we worry about trouble, to what extent are we, ourselves, troubled—or trouble? And to what extent should we situate this single moment of the Buddha's teaching in Eastern conceptions of public propriety, rather than Western individuality and responsibility?

Some of these questions could easily fall into the realm of rhetorical studies, and some could be dismissed, I suppose, as irrelevant to first-year composition students (though I would disagree with the latter position). For me, many of these questions are crucial for a first-year writing classroom, depending on the students and the context. In fact, I have posed some of these questions to writing students, though I usually do so in individual writing conferences (it is hardly reasonable to expect all of our students to be at the same places in their lives, open to all such questions at the same moment. Still, sometimes we all need to hear questions before we are ready for them. Sometimes the meaning does not become clear until much later). For me, personally, some of these questions have become haunting questions, and so I go on looking for answers.

When I started teaching The Rhetorical Tradition and the Teaching of Writing as a multicultural project in 1987, I could only name six or so rhetoricians or compositionists in the United States who were teaching rhetoric to graduate students from the same perspective. The number has grown since then, and there is much hope in that. Still, I am willing to bet that the number is still relatively small in relation to all the courses in rhetoric that are taught in the United States each year. Perhaps this is attributable to the fact that so few have written at length about how to pursue this study, though there are exceptions. In *Bootstraps*, Victor Villaneuva writes about the focus of his graduate course in rhetoric. As he describes it in that book, his approach is to have students explore the ways in which rhetoric moves, blends, how it has "traveled with the conquerors" (1993, 88). He writes about the movement of Classical rhetoric east, across northern Africa with Arabs who brought it to Spain, creating the unique rhetorical blend that came to the New World with conquistadors and priests. Susan Romano (2004) brilliantly illuminates that in Mexico, the teaching of rhetoric-composition was rich with ethno-recovery methodology of indigenous literacy and texts rife with institutional allegiances. In *Rhetorics of the Americas 3114 BCE to 2012 CE* Damián Baca and Victor Villanueva (2010) collect essays by researchers who tell the story of colonization and the continuing importance, resilience and contribution of indigenous rhetorics, work the spirit of which can also be found in the research of such cultural theorists as Angel Rama, in the writings of such compositionists as Resa Crane Bizzaro and Ellen Cushman, and in indigenous press collections such as the Jerry D. Blanche's *Native American Reader: Stories, Speeches, and Poems* (1990). In addition, in *Latina/o Discourses in Vernacular Spaces: Somos de Una Voz?* Michelle A. Holling and Bernadete M. Calafell (2011) collect research that teaches us how multiple, strong, and beautiful voices arise in and from each and every cultural tradition. From books such as these we learn the power of respect, community, historical awareness, sustainability, and resistance to oppression. We need as much knowledge as we can create from all of America's rhetorics; even the ones we cannot claim by birthright. It is only by learning from the other that we come to learn ourselves. We need, therefore, to share our thinking about international rhetorical studies, how rhetoric should be studied at this time in history so that it informs international composition studies. We need to talk about method so as to throw light into dark places.

Let's suppose that one is teaching a graduate course in the history of rhetoric. One might pick Bizzell and Herzberg's *The Rhetorical Tradition: Readings from Classical Times to the Present* (2001) to present excerpts from some canonical rhetorical texts in the Western tradition, with some few examples of feminist rhetorical writings. There are other texts one might use such as Benson and Prosser's *Readings in Classical Rhetoric* (1988), a slight collection of writings from the tradition, including, again, the usual Classical rhetoricans. Or, one can choose a book about Western rhetoric, such as in James J. Murphy, Richard A. Katula, Forbes I. Hill, and Donovan J. Ochs's *A Synoptic History of Classical Rhetoric* (2003). One can even take a selective, representative approach, where whole texts, rather than selections from readers, are picked for reading with more complete study and analysis. One might choose Plato's *Phaedrus* (2005), Aristotle's *Rhetoric* (1932), Quintilian's *Institutio Oratoria* (1922), maybe *The Rhetoric of Blair, Campbell and Whately* (Golden and Corbett 1968), and maybe a text by Kenneth Burke, or Perelman and Olbrechts-Tyteca's *The New Rhetoric* (1969).

But what does one do if one understands that there are other traditions of rhetoric in the world that we in the United States can no longer ignore or deny? There is no Bizzell and Herzberg anthology of other rhetorical traditions. Perhaps one day an editor or editors will use their knowledge of rhetoric, philosophy and poetics to create a collection for compositionists that illustrates the international history of thought about discourse. In the meantime, what do you do? For one thing, you begin by reorienting yourself in relation to texts and disciplinary scholarship. You construct a new mental filter with which to navigate bookstores. You orient yourself in such a way as to look for tradition. Confucius, for instance, was not concerned with offering the world a rhetoric, but his philosophy includes many moments in which he speaks about communication and opens doors for thinking about rhetoric. As he says in *The Analects,* one's speech marks one's character, how one is living, how one is proceeding on the Way. As the Master explains, one speaks, or writes, to accomplish one's work, one's life tasks, but also to promote harmony and truth in society: "Staunchness, stamina, simplicity, and reticence are close to humanity" (1997 13.26, 138). These are the root values. One must have the forthrightness to stand by one's words, to speak honestly and to know when to remain silent. And when one does speak, one should "Keep wholehearted sincerity and truthfulness" as their guiding principles (9.25, 106). The Master eschewed artifice and inappropriate ornamentation as examples of pride. For him, "As long as speech conveys the idea, it suffices (15.41, 158). Being persuasive, in other words, is far less important than being virtuous—a lesson for any writer.

Not that persuasion did not play a part, of course, in the Chinese tradition of rhetoric. When one reads Han Fei Tzu, a philospher who lived circa 280 B.C.E. to 233 B.C.E., approximately one hundred years after

Aristotle and one hundred and seventy-five years before Cicero, one finds descriptions of the role of persuasion and manners at court and advice to rulers about how to maintain order in the state. As a writer in the Legalist tradition of Chinese philosophy, Han did not explore the moral issues facing individuals and society as Confucius and the Taoist writers did. Instead, he was interested in the health of the state and the strength of the ruler. His writings are filled with admonitions to the ruler to maintain control and order: encourage agriculture, suppress turmoil and itinerancy by restricting the movements of artisans and merchants, and maintain a strong military. In "The Difficulties of Persuasion," Han (1964) explores some of the principles of persuasion, such as learning how to present the character of the other that one seeks to portray in words, how to watch for danger at court, and how to make one's ethos pleasing to the king.

Han did, on occasion, investigate epistemological issues. In "Eminence in Learning" (1964), he discusses the problem of interpreting Confucius's philosophy when Confucianism had given rise, by Han's era, to eight separate strands of Confucian thought. But even here, Han's conclusion is to advise the king to follow his common sense when deciding which actions to take when matters of state stability are issues of prime importance. Instability could mean catastrophe, of course: conquest, famine, and massacre, so harmony and social order necessarily come before all other considerations.

I mention these two philosophers from among so many to remind readers how rhetorics from various places and times look and sound different from one another. We can expect to have to do some creative and critical work, looking for rhetorical principles in places where we might not automatically expect to find them. And, once we do find them, we may have to do some creative and critical translating as we seek to understand principles and transpose them into current contexts, always with respect to the historical and cultural contexts from which they come.

FOR INSTANCE, A MINDFUL RHETORIC

In his introduction to Buddhism for social action, *Interbeing: Fourteen Guidelines for Engaged Buddhism,* Thich Nhat Hanh presents a series of mindfulness trainings anyone might practice in order to understand the ways that we inspire anger and cause suffering with our words and learn, as a result, ways for enacting and encouraging ethical living. Specifically, Hanh explores how communication can inspire happiness when we engage in caring dialogue with one another.

In *Interbeing,* Hanh also describes how our attachments to beliefs can lead to fanaticism. When this happens, we use language to resist or persuade others to our viewpoint. This causes anger and leads to suffering. As Hanh points out, desires, intentions, and actions can motivate even the most benevolent of us to attempt to exert inappropriate levels of force in order to persuade others to our thinking. The result is anger that blocks communication and results in suffering.

Hanh encourages us to adopt nonattachment in order to let go of intolerance and the desire to control others through coercive discourse. Imagine for a moment, if you will, the classroom where a teacher asks students to consider their writing in terms of the First Mindfulness Training, in which we are asked to become: "*Aware of the suffering created by fanaticsm and intolerance,* we are determined not to be idolatrous about and bound to any doctrine, theory, or ideology, even Buddhist ones. Buddhist teachings are guiding means to help us to learn to look deeply and to develop our understanding and compassion. They are not doctrines to fight, kill, or die for" (1998, 17). Imagine if we asked students to think of their writing in terms that momentous. Imagine how deeply they would learn to think if even their and our religions or patriotism were open issues and available for questioning. Imagine the new, rich, and meaningful pedagogies we could construct.

Or, imagine, for a moment, if we taught writing in light of Hanh's Third Mindfulness Training, that we become: "*Aware of the suffering brought about when we impose our views on others,* we are committed not to force others, even our children, by any means whatsoever—such as threat, money, propaganda, or indoctrination—to adopt our views" (17).

How would this mindfulness training be enacted if it were to become a rhetorical and pedagogical principle? Lunsford and Lunsford (2008) write that the number of composition courses dedicated to the topical study of persuasion is increasing in the United States. How would this mindfulness training lead us to reflect on that trend? Perhaps that is one of the reasons that *Interbeing* speaks to me: it articulates the necessary— though most difficult—terms of the commitment we need to make. Specifically, in a world where international cooperation is ever more necessary for our mutual survival, we need to develop the metacritical filters that will enable us to become more conscious of the effects of our words on others and the world. In Hanh's terms, we need to become: "*Aware that words can create suffering or happiness,* we are committed to learning to speak truthfully and constructively, using only words that inspire hope and confidence" (20).

Imagine for a moment if rhetoric were not the study of persuasion. Imagine if it were, first and foremost, the study of how to use words to "inspire hope and confidence" as epideictic rhetoric can sometimes do; or what if it were both persuasion *and* hope and confidence? More than any of the other mindfulness trainings, this one speaks to me in my role as a teacher of writing. It leads me to ask students again and again about how they see their writing is affecting the world, right down to their choice of a word in an individual sentence. It means that when they write about a personal event, that they take into account the feelings of the people of whom they make characters. It means that they consider the power they exert as writers when they create characters of and for people. In turn, it means that I ask students about what they believe and how that belief contributes to the world, even the parts of the world that they may reasonably expect never to see. Again, Hanh describes the personal investment any of us must make if we want our teaching to inspire change: "The way to prevent war is to make peace. We accomplish this first in our daily life by combating fanaticism and attachment to views, and working for social justice. We have to work vigorously against the political and economic ambitions of any country, including our own. If important issues like these are not debated on national and international levels, we will never be able to prevent societal violence" (48).

As a teacher of writing—not to mention as a man—I have seen how national and international debates transpire in the individual mind. Certainly, we sometimes learn what we think by interacting with others, but just as often, we make decisions about our commitments in our own hearts and souls. What teacher would not wish for at least a modicum of purity—and health—in the words and allegiances we choose?

VOICES FROM THE DARK; VOICES FROM THE LIGHT

The Russian psychologist, Fyodor Vasilyuk, explains how the conflicts that each of us faces in our lives can counteract the creative nature of our experience. We can lose, the "psychological possibility" (1988, 195) to act in a world that overwhelms us with either difficulty or ease (95–172). In either case, we may fail to face that which makes a situation "critical," that is, the factors that require our creative efforts toward a solution. When that happens, Vasilyuk argues, we fail, as peculiar as it sounds, to experience life fully. We fail to work for solutions to mundane and world problems, and we fail to construct the "new selves" necessary for life in the new circumstances or worlds we imagine and for which we work (164). Conversely, when the psychological possibility for action is restored, experience leads us to produce futures rather than to repeat the past or endure the present. We can write for health, when we realize the possibility for bringing health to thinking and living that is confused, contradictory, or disconnected (Hurlbert 1991, 146).

To experience fully and creatively takes all the resources at our command. The process is so critical, so essential, and so necessarily creative that it requires our openness to nothing less than change. I, a Western writer, search for these resources in the East as well as the West, North and South, as I attempt to deepen the possibilities for composing and teaching writing, and to enrich the experience of the processes of both. I cannot tell you how many times during the writing of this book I have had to sit back, here, in the moment of composing, before putting fingers to keys, to reach a place of "not trying deeply" (Sikong 1996, 26), not trying deeply because it is the only way I know to open myself to the words to say and the way to say them. It is the only way I know, today, to get them right. Reading Sikong, I find the reminder I need to remain open to the words, open so that the words will come, that state of mind where I can entertain the critical in creative ways.

Poet Pierre Joris has formulated what he calls a "nomad poetics." A nomad poetics is a dynamic theory for unfixing, in distinctly international terms, our conceptions of what a poem can look like, how it can sound, and what it can contain and mean. It is a poetics of movement; it is a declaration of intent against static formalisms. It is a theory that is "always on the move, always changing, morphing, moving through languages, cultures, terrains, time without stopping" (2003, 26). It is a poetics designed to make inroads against the entrenched universe of discourse, not to mention the entrenched economic order that supports it. As the epigram that begins the essay, "The Millenium Will Be Nomadic or It Will Not: Notes Toward a Nomad Poetics (1996–2002)," says, in part: "The days of anything static, form, content, state are over" (25). A nomad poetics resists provincial and exclusionary thinking about first and second languages, and it provides a rationale for why we should resist discursive residence in our native rhetorics. Why? Because, again, according to Joris's epigram, "The past century has shown that anything not involved in continuous transformation hardens and dies" (25). Transformation is life itself. And life requires us to draw upon all the options for meaning making that we can discover even as various nationalisms would consolidate power for use at home and against other states.

In "The Millenium Will Be Nomadic or It Will Not," Joris gathers ideas and insights, some written and published by critic Brian Massumi in another text and inserted, with permission, by Joris into his own. Some of these insertions are crucial for understanding the relation of nationalism to composition. For instance, "The State-form is not a form. It is an abstract process: a drive to 'unity'" and "[a]ny drive to unity is necessarily a drive to dominion, and necessarily fails" (27). The unity is the unity of the nation, of course, the consolidation of state power, certainly, but also the unity of the people into one discourse (despite the accommodation of difference in the form of acceptable experiments of state-sponsored discourse). The value? According to Massumi, "Unless the people are made one, there is no way to make them attain their desire. Therefore, they are made one; as a result of this unification, their strength is consolidated. . . . A country that knows how to produce strength . . . can make the people do what they hate in order to reach what they desire" (28). The hope is in a nomad poetics that teaches us not to love unity more than difference. The hope is in a nomad poetics that understands persuasion and its power to unify by means of coercion, whether through direct or hidden means. The hope is in a nomadic poetics with its many ways for constructing human relationships and situating people in union.

For instance, in *The Afrocentric Idea*, Molefi Kete Asante critiques Eurocentric ideology and colonialist perspectives in cultural theory and develops an Afrocentric metatheory and rhetoric that draws on Afrocentric oratory. The goal is a union of speaker and audience through the effects of language and performance invested with the power of spirituality and magic (*nommo*). It is a rhetoric that valorizes circularity of form, indirection in structure. Its language is lyrical and epistemic: "Rhetoric, in an Afrocentric sense, is the productive thrust of language into the unknown in the attempt to create harmony and balance in the midst of disharmony and indecision" (1998, 46). Of course, you do not see Afrocentric forms of rhetoric being taught in most composition classes in US colleges, and usually it is only the special case where a student is "allowed" to do something creative, like writing a rap or creating characters that speak in the dialect of their homes. In this regard, Kermit Campbell tells us why as he questions his own teaching: "These days, in fact, I wonder about pedagogical approaches (mine included) that center on the use of African American vernacular discourses as a bridge to mainstream academic discourses, because the concept behind the approach still implies the deficiency of the former vis-a-vis the latter. When all is said and done, our pedagogy (not to mention our theory) still privileges elite discourses, or put more bluntly, discourses that reflect and sustain white hegemony" (2005, 143). Even when students study with a sympathetic basic writing teacher, Campbell continues, who values the rhetoric of another as much as they value their own, the students will go to another teacher the following semester who more than likely will not. But that teacher, whoever they may be, and as Campbell makes clear, is no excuse for failing our students by locking our curricula—not to mention our subjectivities—into subject matters closer to our own interests than our students'" (143–144). We have to be better and do better than that.

Geneva Smitherman threw light on the racism at the heart of composition in her 1977 *Talkin and Testifyin*. In it, she describes what she calls the "four black modes of discourse": call-response, signification, tonal semantics, and narrative sequencing. When Smitherman wrote *Talkin and Testifyin*, compositionists and linguists were not likely to question the primacy of Western, Eurocentric rhetoric for the making of meaning. The truth today is as bitter as it was then: you won't find the black modes of discourse in composition textbooks. You won't find them being assigned for practice in very many composition classrooms. In fact, you will barely hear them talked about at all in the vast majority of composition classes in this country. They are absent because they are black. And, all our students suffer the results. In 1994, Smitherman published "'The Blacker the Berry, the Sweeter the Juice': African American Student Writers." In it she uses empirical methodology to demonstrate that students versed in African American narrative techniques score higher on the standardized test, the National Assessment of Educational Progress (NAEP) than those who are not. As Smitherman writes: "As cultural norms focus from 'book' English to 'human' English, the narrativizing, dynamic quality of the African American Verbal Tradition will help students produce lively, image-filled, concrete, readable essays, regardless of rhetorical modality—persuasive, informative, comparison-contrast, and so forth" (1994, 95). Revolutions of thought begin with findings such as these. In this case, as in all of Geneva Smitherman's work, it is a healing revolution for all.

African American rhetoric is brought to class by students who live the rhetoric (though the low statistics of representation are still a shame for the nation and the state). It is brought to class by the students who listen and see and watch and learn from black artists. It is present, always present, in every classroom whether acknowledged by the teacher or not. The absence of African American rhetoric in our curricula, however, should wake us to the whispers and shouts in our hearts and souls. The voices come from the shadow places in which fear lives and the bright places where outrage at injustice rises. After all, we composition teachers must know that despite all our best efforts and talk about multiculturalism and all the multicultural readers we adopt for our classes, we have not in reality committed our classrooms to a multicultural agenda. We must know that we have to date failed the dream of multiculturalism. The fear we must be feeling in the face of this is based in truth and experience. All we have to do is ask ourselves: do we teach the black modes of discourse? Do our colleagues? Do we teach the brown ones? The red ones? The yellow ones? Do we even know what they are? Do we ask what this color scheme means? Do we want to change?

Elaine Richardson has written as well as anyone about the rhetorical and cultural assumptions that lie at the heart of the contemporary English department and its curricula: "One of the major roots of African American literacy underachievement is the ideology of White Supremacist and capitalistic-based literacy practices that undergird curriculum construction and reproduce stratified education and a stratified society, that reproduce the trend of African American literacy under-achievement" (2003, 8). What we teach is essentially connected to our racial, cultural, and class-based assumptions. Despite our best efforts on our students' behalf, we compositionists provide the conduits, our class-rooms, through which the structural inequalities are maintained. We employ the terminology of cultural or postcolonial studies in our schol-arship and in our classrooms, but the truth remains. When we adopt corporate textbook pedagogies, whether from print textbooks or online media, or commit our classrooms to other monocentric content such as "academic writing," traditional rationales and foundations, we are about the business of the white, nationalist ideology that scripts so much of American education at all levels.

Responding to our field from an indigenous perspective, Malea Powell turns to the scholarship we produce and consume, the discourse that teaches us and prepares us for the teaching we will do in our col-lege classrooms. As she does so, Powell points to the heart of the field of rhetoric and composition as the source of the problem:

> I believe that rhetoric as a discipline has been and continues to be complicit with the imperial project of scholarship in the United States. I believe that rhetoric as a discipline does not see the foundation of blood and bodies upon which it constitutes itself. I believe that many of us who work within this discipline participate daily in the un-seeing, in denying, and, in doing so, perpetuate the myth of the empty continent. I believe that scholarship in America can never be set forth on neutral ground. I believe that even as the marginalized and radical "anti-disciplinary" and /or "cross-disciplinary" discipline, rhetoric takes for granted its originary relation to Greece and Europe—its fundamental relationship to imperialism—and gives little critical thought at all to the geographical space in which it now exists. I believe that rhetoric, as a discipline and as it is enacted by its scholars/teachers, merely tolerates "other" discourses at its margins. (1999, 11)

Year after year, many of us compositionists go to the Conference on Composition and Communication and hear panels (when we tear our-selves from the textbook stalls and corporate-sponsored parties) on including alternatives: alternative rhetorics, alternative discourses, and alternative writers. But when we return to our home institutions, do we change our pedagogies or do we go back to practicing business as usual? It is fine, the textbooks seem to tell us, to include a piece of indigenous literature, but there is no place for students to practice indigenous discourse patterns, conventions, or language in our learning and writing classrooms. Inclusion matters as long as the included minds its manners and fits comfortably with the skills we in composition agree are the heart of our mission (a pointed word, in this context, yes?).

We teachers of writing are clear, in other words, in what we tell students. It is simple: we have rules about what can be said and how it can be said. These rules extend beyond the parameters of our assignments and have to be learned. These rules are cultural, and they are racial, and they tell students who they are and who they should want to be:

> We enforce these neo-formalist rules. we align ourselves up with that. our talk about giving students access to academic discourse is our secret LIE. this is just the postmodern description for college grammar skill-drills and instruction in the formal, surface aspects of writing. we never ask the questions: what the hell students writin'? for whom? and for what? There is no interrogation here of social consciousness and change, just form over substance. Seem like only a fool would see this lie as radical revolutionary when it really just the same ole, same ole.
>
> And here's another of our lies: the notion of w(h)id(t)er communication . . . [which] direct[s] students to write for a white, middle-class, consuming audience. If they succeed, they win the prize of being the one good, moral voice who intervenes in the humanity of whites . . . while preparing and serving dinner like the black maid (Old Delie) in William Faulkner's *The Sound and the Fury*. Again, this is not about social transformation but about accepting a prescribed subordinate role. (kynard 2002, 34–35)

There are, thankfully, alternatives, and many teachers know this. As carmen kynard later shows in her essay, enacting a student-centered pedagogy means, as a start, students selecting and bringing in the texts they want to study, the words and language they need to hear and share, and the ideas they need to entertain and resist. It makes room for the students to study the realities of their lives, academic and other, and so to learn what engagement in culture, world, and growth offers. It makes academic study relevant, and also necessary.

MUSEUM PIECES

Rhetorical study is, in the constricted sense of what it means to do rhetorical study, formulaic. You begin by learning the various means— formulas—for persuasion: the kinds of speakers, audience, and discourses, and the ways for crafting persuasive confluences among the three. Rhetoric has formalism at its roots. And so, here's my fear. It is clear that we compositionists could·turn an interest in international composition studies into a search for new formalisms to apply to our classroom pedagogies. We could make various international rhetorical handbooks for what we might call African American rhetoric and writing, Asian American rhetoric and writing, or Arab or Buddhist rhetoric and writing—or even the all-in-one, the big handbook for "dealing with" difference. We might, in some future time, persuade the textbook companies to publish these books, and we could take them into our first year composition classrooms and assign the modes of African American rhetoric or the styles of Buddhist rhetoric to our students. We could then have the students process their exercises and develop them for their portfolios of multicultural awareness. We might then tell ourselves that we are teaching for multicultural harmony and world peace. We might even turn these good feelings into justifications for our composition curricula.

There is, of course, nothing wrong with constructing our classrooms as centers for genuine cultural study. But I suggest that among all the unproductive results that could emerge from an international composition studies, the worst would be the emergence of new and ever-more critically resistant strains of formalism.

In *The American Poetry Wax Museum,* Jed Rasula argues that poetry anthologies are lifeless representations of the dynamics of complex texts and composing processes. They are, Rasula tells us, museums, dedicated to commemorating that which we already know. They are "Arnoldian shrine[s]" dedicated to maintaining the canon of the "dignified" (1996, 4). They exist to display culture as we want it to be. "[D]riven by the inventory, the taxonomic compulsion to sort and measure" (12), museums tell us how to see and what to look for in our lives. By doing so, museums produce culture: "The museum, like the factory, is not merely a 'mode' of production but also a site prompting membership" (13). The museum reminds us, in other words, of our individuality, our always growing connoisseurship, but also of our membership, our allegiance to the nation, the collective universal called America. Furthermore, the collective universal is presented as the realization of national benevolence: the museum collects, rehabilitates, and exhibits. Never mind the censoring impulse operating behind the walls of display: "Driven by a taste for novelty, Americans seem intent on celebrating as sublimely original only those achievements that are servile imitations" (9).

Poetry cannot thrive under such conditions. It requires tradition, but it needs to exist in its own terms, spaces, impulses, and intentions. Poets need their own ways with words, latitudes for originality and agency, for saying that which has not been said but what needs to be said. Poets need an original geography, not repeatable except in metaphoric terms. Many of them need to write that which should not be fixed with museum note cards, voice-over discourse explaining the words and telling us what to say in response. Poets must say who they are and who we are so that we will know ourselves. They must have space to be undignified, to sound the disharmonies, and to construct new ones so that we can face difference in the disharmonies of malady when they materialize in ourselves. Poetry does not need intellectual benevolence, though it requires largeness of thought. Poetry requires no membership, and indeed, often resists it, but it does require freedom from servility. In a free work space, or as free as any work space ever is, we may also hear, through our poetry, the sounds of who we are so that we may know them, and ourselves, and sometimes for the first time.

Of course, Rasula's analysis of poetry anthologies can also be applied to our composition readers. They, too, are driven by the same American repetition compulsion. It is the same cultural neurosis displayed in the design of our cars, the reproductions of the world's cities in Las Vegas, the vapid utterances of our politicians, and the comfortable familiarity of our academic and other industrial conventions, where we go to feel, among other things, at home and away from home at the same time. In the same emotional vein, our readers are dedicated to displaying the dignified, collectable essay. As a crucial part of the collection, readers also present the new and novel, the unique, where, as long as it also passes for appropriate, it is promoted as an object of imitation. Students read the collected specimen and produce their own, imitating style, content, impact, and intentions. They replicate crucial results and moments of culture, creating specimens that satisfy our discipline's objectivist and ethnographic inclinations, which they then prepare for portfolio display and critical assessment.

Collected works can be analyzed as well as imitated. Students can answer questions at the end of essays, again and again, in the form of mini-imitations of scholarly essays. And through accomplishment comes membership, of a sort, in the club of those who imitate the voices of the cultural elite, the academic community. In all of this, and there is so much of it, readers support pedagogies of "harmlessness" (Rasula 1996, 4). The readers assure that assigned writing will be acceptable, to one degree or another, and anything not acceptable can either be fixed or dumbed down through evaluation.

Geoffrey Sirc says it: we need to make composition happen again, to restore the intensity and necessity of our processes. We need to look to art, not the collectors of art, for the best of what it is we do in our composition classrooms. Ann Berthoff (1981, 1984) said it first: we need to "reclaim the imagination." We need to make it all matter, beyond the limits of the national plan. We need to, that is, if we wish to break the cycle of replication and do more than or different from what we have done before.

OH, MULTICULTURAL AMERICA

There aren't many textbook rhetorics presenting themselves as multicultural; Robert Cullen's *Rhetoric for a Multicultural America* (1999) is one of them. We can say that Cullen deserves praise for his attempt to bring multiculturalism to rhetorical study and the composition classroom. But the problem is that even in this text Western rhetoric is the default rhetoric, the foundational rhetoric posited as the one that serves all. The result is that the text both homogenizes a people for cultural unity at the same time that it stresses the value of diversity.

And throughout, the impetus toward conformity is everywhere evident. For instance, Cullen notes, at one point, that Henry Louis Gates's spelling of the word "signifyin" is "unusual" (1988, 132). Unusual. In another instance, Cullen offers what is certainly meant to be positive encouragement to student writers. It is the assumption from which Cullen writes, however, that is the problem: "If you are lucky enough to be bilingual, bicultural, or bidialectal (fluent in two dialects of English), you may occasionally have the opportunity to educate the rest of us concerning important words or concepts that don't translate easily into English" (11). Assumptions are made, in statements such as this one, about who the rest of us are. (I suppose that Cullen means native speakers of an acceptable variety of English.) Given the racism inherent in the teaching of writing and the nation at large, it may be time to get past assumptions about the "rest of us" and the responsibility of the "you" to educate this "rest of us." It is past time the rest of us took responsibility for ourselves.

To be fair, instead of arch, Cullen's textbook does offer multiculturalism as an important knowledge for students to have, but the problem is that it is not for first-year composition students. Knowledge of multicultural choices in writing is something additional, supplemental, something for afterwards, after one has learned the basics of Western rhetoric. Or, as Cullen writes, "In my experience, cultural disagreements about how to organize writing have surfaced more often in advanced work like a master's thesis than in introductory courses, where options are more limited and the assignments more specific" (86). How sad it is to think that the first year composition course is so terribly limited. Perhaps it is time to ratchet up the content of our classes.

There is, I think I can safely say, a level of careful conservativism in Cullen's book that is consistent with textbook rhetoric. It is what Geoffrey Sirc (2002) calls "Post-Happening," devoid of the spirit of the improvisation and change. Teaching for change needs to be more dramatic than that which any current textbook company will package. Multiculturalism is a failed project precisely because it has been enacted as a nationalist add-on to academic thinking. It is, in this sense, just one more educational fad. Instead, I want it to be the one educational initiative (the other is Derek Owens's [2001] sustainable pedagogy) we dare not fail to get right. Too much is at stake. The health of all of us depends on it.

Maybe I am a more impatient man than Cullen, and maybe I am not above writing impatient things, even if I do not want to cause suffering. I have my limitations, but I do not want to read an assertion such as "Naturally signifyin(g) is not taught in schools" (134) without screaming, "There's nothing natural about it!—and what's with the 'g' in parentheses anyway?" What *is* natural in Cullen's text is the Western rhetorical tradition, and while the Western tradition is of course worthy of serious study, its centrality in a text entitled *Rhetoric for a Multicultural America* is a problem. In his chapter on Classical rhetoric, Cullen writes: "This chapter offers a quick overview of the history of rhetoric—a history that has strongly influenced your education and that has helped shape our most important institutions, including Congress, the courts, the media, and many religious organizations" (167–168). Exactly. Rhetoric is the vehicle of our nationalism, and European American culture clearly has primacy. Here, as throughout this text, white American culture is the foundational point of departure for the students' investigation of rhetoric.

Some of Cullen's assignments also assume the same cultural starting points. For instance, consider the following: "Write a detailed analysis of a short piece of writing that aims to *persuade*" (169). It seems to me that for a fair and productive multicultural rhetoric to be written, it would, by necessity, not look or sound like this. It would not ask for such mechanical work and writing. It might very well not begin with persuasion. It probably would not look or sound like anything we have ever seen.

This cannot work forever. We compositionists may soon outlive our relevancy. There are more calls all the time, from administrators and from compositionists themselves, to do away with the universal composition course or to move the teaching of writing to the other disciplines. I believe that either option does our students a terrible and tragic disservice. Still, who can blame those who make such calls when we compositionists teach canned, monocentric, nationalistic, and ever more irrelevant pedagogies? We have to start to learn beyond our comfort zones. We have to start to learn about the world. No, this cannot go on forever. As historian Anthony Smith writes in *Nationalism and Modernism*: "Nationalists can sometimes use the 'ethnic past' for their own ends, but not in the long run: they soon find themselves locked in to its framework and sequences, and the assumptions that underlie the interpretations of successive generations" (1998, 43). And so we become museum pieces.

A RECENT HISTORY, A DECENT FUTURE

In the eighties, while we in composition were developing new pedagogical practices under the general categories of process and student-
centeredness, our colleagues in literature were developing the theoretical implications of the ideas they were importing from Europe. They
began the process of deconstructing the canon of received literature
and critiquing its white, liberal, middle class, patriarchal nature. They
theorized inherited models and, thinking about the author, interpretive practices and ideological texturing of the literary. They developed
breakthrough methodologies for studying cultural objects that lay outside the traditional purview of literary studies. In other words, as we in
composition turned our attention to developing new pedagogies, our
colleagues in literature were developing their theories and, particularly
for present purposes, exploring the possibilities and meaning of multiculturalism. In a significant turn, in the early nineties, NCTE published
Practicing Theory (Cahalan and Downing 1991) and *Changing Classroom
Practices* (Downing 1994), two texts that marked how our colleagues in
literature began to investigate the pedagogical implications of their new
and suggestive theorizing—though this work has not developed as much
as it should have since. To put this another way, canon reformation led
to new formulations for the teaching of literature. At the same time this
turn occurred in literature, we in composition were borrowing insights
from literary theorists. Compositionists such as David Bartholomae
(1986), Jasper Neel (1988), Elizabeth Flynn (1988), John Schilb (1996),
and Cy and Lil Brannon (1984), to name just a few, were developing
ways for us to understand the theoretical underpinnings of our practices. We in composition did not, however, make a crucial turn. We did
not begin—with the exception of Elizabeth Flynn's landmark essay,
"Composing as a Woman" which called on all of us to rethink, dramatically, composition's forms and processes—the necessary work of recon-
ceiving and, most importantly, expanding the received canon of forms
and thought embodied in what the handbooks tell us is the Western
tradition of rhetoric. This is true of even the more sophisticated Neo-
Aristotelian handbooks of Corbett (1971) and Crowley (2008).

Indeed, composition studies has witnessed over thirty years of feminist work that explores the nature, forms, strategies, and concerns of women's rhetoric. Feminists have critiqued the nationalist ideology that scripts women's marginality, but we do not yet see the discourses of feminist rhetorics centrally situated in composition textbooks and classrooms, with the exception, perhaps, of journal writing (Gannett 1992). We do not see feminist rhetorics, generally speaking, acknowledged in composition classrooms for the essential contributions that they make. The critique of nationalist patriarchy goes on, and the recovery of women's writing and rhetoric goes on, but the study of writing continues in decidedly patriarchal and white ways that are, again, sanctioned by the Western tradition of elite culture and the nationalism that underwrites its privilege.

Not that some compositionists haven't made arguments that could be seen to anticipate the development of rhetoric in other and even internationalist perspectives. For instance, in 1990, Derek Owens wrote one of the most crucial, most overlooked and under-cited articles in the history of composition, "Beyond Eurocentric Discourse" (work he later revised and expanded in *Resisting Writings*). In it, he argued for progressive curricula in multiculturalism and writing that are still, twenty years later and counting, being reinvented by other compositionists (including Sharon Crowley [1998] in *Composition in the University*). Imagine an English curriculum, Owens suggested, that includes writing courses that students could take throughout their entire undergraduate careers. Students would begin with an introductory class and then choose from various other courses in much the same way they take period and genre courses in literature now:

Introduction to Philosophies of Composition

Aristotelian Argumentation

Personal/Expressionist Expository Prose

Understanding Modes of Scientific Discourse

Writing for Accounting (or Business, or Computer Science, etc.) Major

Arabic Rhetorical Strategies

Japanese Expository Prose

The Poetics of Chinese Composing Practices

Native American Performative Discourse

Afrocentric Rhetoric

Theories of Latin American Communication

Writing the Postmodern Essay

"Feminine" Composition and *l'ecriture feminine*

Composing with the Avante-Garde

Algorithmic Composition in the French Oulipo Movement
(1990, 97)

To put it simply, Derek Owens was twenty years ahead of his time in this work. Such a program for English or writing majors would provide significant opportunity for studying various cultural perspectives in composing and rhetoric. Combined with options for writing and workshop exchanges between first and second language writers, or TESOL and composition team teaching, or making symposium presentations, in the mode of Gerald Graff's (1992) teaching the conflicts, the possibilities for growth would be endless.

To fail to take advantage of this time in history would be a shame. In *The Decent Society*, Avashai Margalit (1996) writes that a society is indecent if its institutions humiliate people. I wonder about the degree to which, despite our best intentions and effort, our schools and universities, or, more directly, our curricula and our teaching, are indecent. I wonder about the cultural wounds we in composition perpetuate. Specifically, I am concerned about the sorts of humiliations our composition curricula inspire when we privilege white rhetorical forms and discursive possibilities in our classrooms. When we regulate rhetorical possibilities in our classroom along racial lines, we limit the discourses brought to class by those who are not white, male, and upper or middle class. Such decisions ration the subjectivities that students are allowed to share and develop in our classrooms. As a result, I fear that we cause students to endure alienation and, consequently, humiliation. I think that we need to take new responsibility for ourselves and our pedagogies.

I hope that we will take it as our responsibility to remember that, as teachers of writing, we can teach for international understanding, health, and peace. I hope that we will say that in our attempts, as contingent and as contextually limited as they will necessarily be, that we will commit ourselves to creating decency. That is a profound beginning. There is considerable life in it.

WHAT WILL THE YARD SALES SAY?

My late colleague, Patrick Hartwell, liked to acquire old composition textbooks. As he visited country rummage and yard sales and flea markets, he found great, old texts. From John Franklin Genung's (1891) and Fred Newton Scott and Joseph Villiers Denney's textbooks (1897, 1909), to rhetorics, such as Alexander Bain's (1890), Pat collected history.

In *Writing and Reality*, James Berlin (1987) wrote that one can tell a lot about a society, including its history, by studying its rhetorics. Pat Hartwell knew this, too.

Now imagine a scenario in which a rhetorician of the future goes about the task of searching out and collecting composition textbooks from our time. I hate to think what the yard sales of the future will say about us. I fear that they will tell the story of a nation that valorized one rhetoric, a study in which the teachers of writing in our time were neglectful of the existence of rhetorical traditions other than the dominant one. Worse, they will say that to be so ignorant, or, in some sense, arrogant at this late date in human history was folly at best, racist at worst, destructive in total. How is it possible to think otherwise?

We still have a chance to intervene in this future. We compositionists can find ways to break down the doors of the cages of nationalism that have kept us locked in our provincialism—and racism. We need to learn what holds us back; we do not yet know what is possible; we need to figure out what we still could write.

PART TWO

Circulations
The Composing of Composition

WHY EZRA?

In *The Making of Meaning: Metaphors, Models, and Maxims for Writing Teachers,* Ann Berthoff (1981) employs the work of critic I. A. Richards as a source for her epistemic, hermeneutic approach to rhetoric, and Charles Sanders Pierce for her understanding of signification and the pragmatics of interpretation. And in *Reason To Believe: Romanticism, Pragmatism, and the Teaching of Writing,* Hepzibah Roskelly and Kate Ronald demonstrate the value of claiming the uniquely American Philosophies—transcendentalism, and pragmatics—as sources for contemporary composition pedagogies. Doing so, they explain, rejuvenates our understanding of the relation of language to thought and action. Doing so can return the field of composition to "the sense of hope, mission, and passion that has been one of its hallmarks during the last thirty years—the belief in the power of language and in students' abilities to produce it" (1998, 1).

We pick our sources, or, somehow, they seem to they pick us. Sometimes the source is one we honor; sometimes it is one we wish we didn't. Sometimes the source is someone who stands as a model for us, a person of whom we speak with great respect, as Krista Ratcliffe (2006, 32) does Adrienne Rich: "People sometimes ask why I still focus on Rich instead of more current theorists, such as psychoanalytic and postmodern feminists. My answer is that Rich's texts still speak to me—with clarity, with dignity, with ethics, with wisdom. She is no more irrelevant today in rhetoric and composition studies than is Aristotle's thought." Poet Juliana Spahr expresses equal reverence for the influence of Gertrude Stein on her work. In her book, *Everybody's Autonomy: Connective Reading and Collective Identity,* Spahr writes about how Gertrude Stein's *Tender Buttons* so affected her in her youth that, in fact, *Everybody's Autonomy* marks her continuing effort to come to terms with it. *Everybody's Autonomy* is, as Spahr says, "an attempt to figure out my own story, to understand what happened when I was in high school and found Stein in an anthology of twentieth-century writing and everything that I thought I knew about reading changed" (2001, 14–15). Spahr is right, of course. Certain texts do change us in ways that both inspire—and, sometimes, require—creative, scholarly response.

Using the historical figure of Ezra Pound as an organizing and met-
aphorical figure in this book may seem an unexpected, odd choice,
and, in fact, even as I rely on him, I readily admit that unlike either
Ratcliffe's response to Rich or Spahr's to Stein, I do not find Pound to
be a particularly attractive character. In fact, if I could go back in time
and meet him, I doubt that the occasion would unfold without considerable ambivalence for me and even more for him, that is, if Pound would
even meet the likes of me. At the same time, I cannot deny his influence
on my work and thinking when I bracket off his malevolence. (And isn't
this many times the way with cultural inheritances? They are often not as
clean and univocal as we might like them to be.) Consequently, I would
like to mention just a few of the reasons that I have chosen Ezra Pound
as a focus for a book entitled *National Healing*.

First, Pound was a poet who was deeply interested in education. He
spoke to English teachers in the pages of *English Journal* in ways no other
of the greats of modernist literature could, or bothered, to do (Hurlbert
2005). He told us to design original and creative curricula, to stop rely-
ing on textbooks, and to bring the realities of writing to the teaching of
writing—lessons still worth learning.

Second, as I believe this book will make abundantly clear, Pound's
Cantos (1970) resonate in my psyche in ways that I can hardly understand. Perhaps because of modernism's continuing hold on the aesthetics that guide my composing, or perhaps because of the personal pains
and responsibilities that dwell within any thinking human being at this
time in history, I feel what Sondra Perl (2004) calls a "felt sense," a need
to address the reverberations in my heart and mind. In other words, I
use Pound as a figure for foregrounding the connections among person and nation and state, and, ultimately, between person and world.
By demonstrating the depth and exploring the meaning of these connections, I hope to articulate some useful insights into the persuasive
mechanisms of nationalism.

But, of course, our time is not Pound's time. We eschew the horrors of fascism. Still, it is certainly possible today, to find fundamentalist
examples of what look and feel like nostalgia for complete unification
of ideology and affiliation. A loyalty to a group that may counter one's
loyalty to another or to one's self, nationalism is an odd phenomenon.
It seems to affect where you are looking and where you are not looking (even our classrooms). And then it seems a set of controls set up by
others, but put in ever-accelerating motion by choices you did not even

know you were making. And if you discover them, you may feel you are staring at the end of the world, at the end of time, or just at an end. And when you get there, what you hear and see is the cause of pain and sorrow, even, of war. And sometimes, nationalism will seem a curse—the one where nothing seems to matter because your life has come home to haunt you, to tell you that it never belonged to you.

In all, I employ the figure of Pound to enact tensions—even tensions that perhaps or probably he never knew—by which, I have to admit, I am troubled as I try to understand the meaning of living in the United States and teaching writing in ways that answer material realities. These tensions cut close to the bone and can only be reached through image and language. I use Pound because he represents meaningful, writerly desires to create truth in art even as he embodies the worst of a human writer. (His anti-Semitic sentiments and writings are disgusting to any person of conscience.) Pound stands, then, as a model for artistic achievement and a lesson for the continuing need to work through the dreck of cultural inheritance, the work that we, all people, need to do if we are ever to enact our higher motives.

Ezra Pound's *Cantos* are a hauntingly beautiful series of poems, yet they are both the screams of a mind in times of failure and pain and, perhaps, one kind of music a soul makes when it reaches beyond itself. They are testaments to the grace of language and the eloquence of breaking form. They contain cultural resources stitched together, artfully, as in a tapestry, or suddenly, with difficult joints, as in one's first attempt at homemade furniture. Or, as Charles Bernstein (1992, 126) writes in "Pounding Fascism": "When we read *The Cantos* with the incredulity it demands, as a text field with systematic self-delusions and fragmentary illuminations, with magnificent gleanings and indulgencies, we will find not the mastertext of modernism but the wreck of Enlightenment rationalism: scarred remnants of a struggle among the divine, the satanic, and the ordinary—a text made beautiful by its damages and ugly by its claims." Enlightenment rationalism, modernist master-text, postmodernist proto-text, "the struggle among the divine, the satanic and the ordinary," any writing with such sweep, such emotion, such strength and weakness, such breadth and depth of living and thought, deserves the attention of compositionists—of anyone.

Consider this, too. In "The Contemporary of Grandchildren: Pound's Influence," literary critic Marjorie Perloff (1985, 206) reports that Allen Ginsberg thought Ezra Pound's experiments in meter, his syncopation,

amounted to: "no less than the whole alteration of human consciousness." We who follow in the footsteps of the expressivists and cognitiv-
ists and take the relationship of mind to discourse as a crucial avenue of
inquiry know the importance of a writer such as Pound. In *The Cantos,*
he constructed a representation of the processes of a mind. He provided
a record of thinking, of a mind forming meaning, crafting it, weaving
sources together into shapes and statement. *The Cantos* are, perhaps, in
this regard, the most artful writing protocol ever created. Pound didn't
just write *about* the processes of mind, he *wrote* the processes of mind
out for readers to see: a large, at times eloquent, at times seemingly
inchoate map of thought, synthesizing, arranging, interpreting, composing, insight, and darkness. *The Cantos* are a record of a man collecting
sources and scenes, dialogues and words and works of wisdom, in time
and in order (of a sort). *The Cantos* are a portrait of a man attempting
to amass images and scraps of cultural, historical, and political artifacts
that comprise the whole of a nation, the course of culture, the span of a
era, a complete life—a fool's beautiful and terrible errand, in resonant
semantic bits, in broken syntactic pieces:

> Tho' my errors and wrecks lie about me.
> And I am not a demigod.
> I cannot make it cohere.
> If love be not in the house there is nothing. (1970, 794)

In *The Pisan Cantos,* one sees images of incarceration, slavery, and
execution, and in the late *Cantos,* one sees a writer whose strength is
sapped by what he has seen, lived, and written, and by his continuing
desire for coherence. The late *Cantos* display the deterioration of the
comforting textual turns and the surviving desire for meaning in a life's
work, all shown in the light of its author's ridiculous and all-too-male-
and-human hubris:

> M'amour, m'amour
>   what do I love and
>   where are you?
> That I lost my center
>   fighting the world.
> The dreams clash
>   and are shattered—

and that I tried to make a paradiso
terrestre. (1970, 802)

Pound tried to say it all—literally, everything that mattered—to set it before us. He exhibited words from literary works, and he recorded his mental collapse around them; he wrote out his aspirations and his shortcomings. Through all, *The Cantos* demonstrate that philosophy, thinking, learning, observing, reading, and writing are inseparable from the pain, joy, and beauty of living.

True, you do not need to know Pound to live in the world, to know what it means when the guards walk the fences, all the while cheered on by voices proclaiming the joys of homeland security and jobs for us. You do not need Pound to know that we are evermore in touch with each other and evermore, it seems at times, alone and at odds. You do not need to read *The Cantos* to know love and pain and dissolution and loss and betrayal (of self as well as other). And you do not need Pound to break things to within an inch of your life, to take the parts and put them someplace else, in some other order. And you do not need to read Pound to want to know at least a better way to live, at least a way you can admire for its health, admire because you have chosen it, chosen it as a better way, to participate with others in the making of what one has not known before. You do not need Pound, in other words, to work with others who are here or not here except in their texts. But reading Pound can help because beauty and eloquence are still meaningful qualities even in a force-fed homogeny and super-heating eco-scape. Reading Pound helps because in his words you can find and better understand, perhaps, wrong and right, hatred and love, indifference and caring, and even the preposterous and the sublime. In fact, reading Pound helps one to learn the compressed and critical nature of the in-between that is living.

Third, I have chosen to use Ezra Pound as a figure in *National Healing* because Pound stands as a cultural marker, signifying both the continuing consolidation and decay of modernist ideology, a source ideology for composition studies to this day, despite the many postmodern influences that compositionists have entertained and even incorporated in theory and practice. Part of the modernist aesthetic is the two-pronged development of a national culture and a coincidental turn to other nations and cultures for corrective thought and artistic development. And make no mistake: although postmodernists have employed difference, fragmentation, and repetition as necessary correctives to modernist ideology, we have not, as yet, left the modernist aesthetic behind. On this, I agree with literary scholar Matei Calinescu (1987). As long as we define our era in terms of—or against—modernist principles of self, time, art, and culture, and, I would add, nation, we are working out modernist influences and their sources. As long as we invoke measurements of novelty, innovation, futurism, and decadence in order to position our artistic and literary productions, we are still very modern indeed. In fact, we who inhabit this late-modernist age of alienation and change pressed ever more firmly into capitalism's measurements of cost and consumption. We who struggle to maintain a sense of self and liberatory affiliation—both within and across national borders, even as our governments erode our freedoms and corporations track our every move and purchase—know all too well that modernist forms of fundamentalism—and fascism—lurk around the next corner and the next flag raising. We still live in modern nations that refer to sometimes mythologized classical origins and Enlightenment thinking. We inhabit the logic of modern economic forms and processes that, though they often seem to evolve at hyper-speeds, nonetheless rest in modern class structures. Indeed, I believe that there is good warning about capitalism to be found in Pound's work, illuminations that must be turned away from their anti-Semitism and toward their critical impulses, turned from their hoodoo economics and toward serious study of transnational capitalism and international exploitation, turned from personal ugliness to social potential.

Even a cursory reading of contemporary poetry demonstrates that Pound's poetics remain, with a vision of international cultural exchange, a source for creative response to international difference. The number of writers and poets that have been influenced by Pound in this regard is far too great to be covered here. Still, it would be remiss of me not to at least mention Nicaragua's national poet, Ernesto Cardenal, who has argued the importance of conserving the revolutionary impulses in Pound's work (Dawes 1993).

Cardenal is a Catholic priest, a Sandanista (until party corruption deterred him), a mystic, and a poet. As a young man, Cardenal came to the United States to enroll at Columbia University where he studied American modernist poetry and was deeply influenced by Pound's writing. In her introduction to Cardenal's *The Doubtful Straight,* Tamara Williams (1995) writes how Cardenal was intrigued by Pound's formal, imagistic, and rhythmic experiments in *The Cantos*. Perhaps, to some degree and in response to Pound's *Cantos*, Cardenal has continued, throughout his adult life, to develop his own poetic form in a long documentary poem, *Cosmic Canticle*. In it, Cardenal records his country's history, from the beginning of time, from the formation of the universe, to the birth and torment of Nicaragua. A national poet, he bears witness to Samosa's atrocities: the torture and murder of women and children, the bombing of villages and slaughter of peasants, the butchering of freedom fighters and the rape of the land, all to feed Samosa's capitalist appetites and the greedy interests of Samosa's sponsors in the United States.

Cardenal has recorded the love of Nicaragua's people for each other, the drive of a nation, of life, of the cosmos to change and evolve. Cardenal, a poet of a revolution, flew over Nicaragua after the Sandanista victory and wrote:

> In the little round window, everything is blue,
> earth bluish, blue-green, blue
>   everything is blue
> blue lake and lagoons
>   blue volcanoes
> the more distant the earth the bluer
>   blue islands in blue lake
> This is the face of the liberated land.
> And where all the people fought, I think:
>   for love!
> To live without the hatred
>   of exploitation.
> (1993, 162)

In his love of people and the earth, indeed, in many ways, Ernesto Cardenal has been an example for other writers to follow—including in his criticism where he has certainly been right about Pound. Many times we do need to save the work of another from the contamination of the hatreds of the heart, or in Pound's particular case, his fascism and anti-Semitism (Dawes 1993). We must liberate the liberating impulses in good work—in Pound's, in everyone's (though it may not be possible in all cases to do so). And Cardenal's work has needed liberating, too, not from anti-Semitism, but from the grip of partriarchy (Cook 2005).

In *Winter Epigrams to Ernesto Cardenal in Defense of Claudia*, poet Dionne Brand speaks back to Cardenal through one of his own poetic characters, Claudia, whom he wrote about in *Apocalypse and Other Poems* (1977). In Brand's poetry, Claudia teaches Cardenal about the manner in which he represents her, through the distortions of machismo:

> Have you ever noticed
> that when men write love poems
> they're always about virgins or whores
> or earth mothers?
> How feint-hearted. (1984, 29)

As Brand makes clear in writing about Cardenal, and as critic Méira Cook makes clear in writing about Brand, we all need liberating—and healing. My argument is that in performing such beneficial work, we compositionists might learn ways for dislodging the liberatory elements of composition from the nationalism and cultural centrism that currently holds sway in the profession of our discipline and in much of the university's curriculum.

Finally, I invoke the figure of Ezra Pound in *National Healing* because his interest in Chinese culture, teaching, and writing is an important and original model for us in composition and rhetoric as we begin to do the necessary, international broadening of the intellectual domain of our discipline. Pound's desire to work through American provincialism by expanding his own horizons can stand as a paradigm for how to get beyond imposed national and cultural limits on thought and speech. Pound argued for multiplicity before it was called that and for the necessity of an international orientation toward the world. As he wrote, "For those who read only English, I have done what I can. I have translated the TA HIO so that they can learn to start THINKING" (1934, 58).

A short though suggestive text on the need to advance the self in order to improve the world, Confucius's *Ta Hio: The Great Learning* begins in the need for meditation, for thought in pursuit of reason and moral purpose. The fruit of this meditation is insight, the ability to form a judgment about the essence of things, especially about one's purpose and duty to improve the self so as to contribute to the stability of family and state. With the attainment of order in one's personal life, one helps to ensure that "the world enjoys peace and harmony" (1928, 9). In this view, each level of one's life—from the personal to the social—is organically linked. To lose sight of this is to contribute to disorder in both the self and the world—a lesson, to be sure, for those in composition studies who still try to pit expressivist against constructionist, cognitivist against critical activist.

Of course, no matter what the message of the *Ta Hio*—or any other text with Pound's name attached—some will simply give up on the old, mad, fascist poet. And many times I have done so myself. But I come back. Despite the blindness and hatreds that led him down his darkest paths, Pound was an astute observer of American culture. His critiques of US devotion to its military strength are as valid today as the day he wrote them. Some will dismiss Pound's rants as those of an aesthete living the life of a naïve or lunatic bohemian. And, yes, there is truth in that critique. But Pound was more than his cosmopolitanism. He was a student as well as a taster of culture, and he was determined to bring the best of Eastern thought to the West:

> The sum of human wisdom is not contained in any one language, and no single language is CAPABLE of expressing all forms and degrees of human comprehension.
>
> This is a very unpalatable and bitter doctrine. But I cannot omit it.
>
> People occasionally develop almost fanaticism in combating the ideas "fixed" in a single language. These are generally speaking "the prejudices of the nation" (any nation). (Pound 1934, 34–35)

It is tragic that Pound's words are as necessary in our time as they were in his own. Yes, some will say that, today, we well-know that "no single language is CAPABLE of expressing all forms and degrees of human comprehension," even that such a statement is obvious. But knowing that does not change the fact that we can find these "prejudices of the nation," when we look for them, in our profession, in our colleges and departments, in our rhetorics and literary sources, in our curricula, and elsewhere as well: in the prejudices of family, friends, and, yes, ourselves. They lie at the heart of values and choices, informing some of the worst parts of our cultures. When we look for them, we can see the prejudices of the nation in the willingness of the United States to use military violence to achieve the end of ill-begotten foreign policies and in the actions of those who value power over creation, the exporting of arms over art, and the terrible results: "But if we are ever to communicate with the orient, or cohabit a planet rapidly becoming more quickly circumnavigable, had we not better try to find the proportions, try

perhaps to collect some of our own better writers (of the ages) to present to our oriental contemporaries, rather than offer them an unmixed
export of grossness, barbarities, stove pipes and machine guns?"
(Pound 1973, 95). Machine guns indeed, weapons grade e-technology,
super-sized McDonald's meals, gas-guzzling status symbols, Post-Fordist
entrepreneurial business practices, and maverick, free-market greed.
Exportation for exploitation. The times change and the greed grows in
proportion to the spoils. Our success is our tragedy.

· NATIONALISM

Change begins at home. If we educators are to teach for a world free of racism, a world where all nations cooperate to solve problems such as the climate crisis we face, we will need to learn how our teaching serves—or fails to serve—our nation, the state, and its citizens. Along the way, we will need to question some of our deepest held beliefs about the teaching of writing, and we may discover that what once stood as the sources and rationales for our teaching have become traps from which we now need to escape.

A healthier nation. A healthier world. Question our deepest held beliefs. These are tall orders, especially when so many of us composition instructors often teach so many sections of our subject each semester. These are tall orders for we who feel so isolated and besieged in hostile departments and colleges, and often for such little remuneration. But we must teach for the health of our nation and world, no matter how great the material demands and how much realities are stacked against us. I understand that some readers may stop short, saying that national and global concerns are not the appropriate content of writing instruction. They will argue that we have enough to do just reading all the papers so that we prepare students for the writing that they might do in their next classes. As sympathetic as I am to the heavy workloads that compositionists carry, I still believe that no matter how locked we feel into our own circumstances and subject matter, once we understand the relation between how we teach writing and the state of our nation, we see just how responsible we are for both. It is an eye-opening, sometimes unnerving, sometimes even shocking, lesson.

You see, it is all in the glue that connects our teaching to the policies and actions of our country. Nationalism is the feeling of affiliation that binds a people within and to a nation and its identity. It is a feeling of belonging, of being a part, of identity in its relation to land and border and neighbors, even when the neighbors may be of different ethnicities. Nationalism leads a varied citizenry to work to maintain the political independence of a nation by motivating the public to meet the responsibilities of citizenship as they are enumerated in discourses of loyalty and patriotism. Nationalism draws its power from the strength of tradition, the shared cultural values that are identified as sources of prosperity and the inhibiting of those identified as destructive to the social fabric, including expressions of subversive minority cultural affiliation. Consolidated and transferred, in part, by means of capitalist production and consumption of print and media (Anderson 1983), nationalism is the ideology of citizenship, and, in large part, it orchestrates the suppression of minority languages and structures the content of education. Language and education—these are our domains. Because we compositionists are responsible for literacy, we contribute to the maintenance of nationalist ideology. We play our part in supporting the majority language, the forms of majority discourses—to the detriment of others—and the health of the nation. It is a role we hardly acknowledge, let alone comprehend. It is time for understanding.

An influential historian and theorist of nationhood, Anthony D. Smith points out that the concept of nationalism has a long and complicated history. In fact, he claims that there are as many definitions of nationalism as there are historians to define it. So, naturally, Smith offers his own. Nationalism is, he writes, an ideology for "attaining and maintaining autonomy, unity and identity on behalf of a population deemed by some of its members to constitute an actual or potential nation" (1971, 171). This definition is important for a number of reasons. It tells us that nationalism works at the level of belief, that it calls for the maintaining of affiliation and trust in the value of unity, and that it informs the identity of those people included in the common good, the national membership. At the same time, this definition also reminds us that, precisely because nationalism is an ideology, *some* citizens are exerting authority—or power—to maintain the "unity and identity on behalf" of a nation's population.

Nationalism depends on a complex of governmental policies, judgments and controls, laws and rewards, and statements of values and interests, all interacting to unite a people, even a people that would otherwise be divided by race, religion, or other ethnocentric or civil factors. Indeed, in the right political and economic circumstances, nationalism can even be deployed in such a way that those institutions that have historically divided people, such as religion, can be mobilized to dampen criticism of state actions taken in the name of nationalist sentiments. As such, and by popular demand, then, nationalism is seldom critiqued in any systematic or widespread way.

But the results of quiet acquiescence, no matter the payoff, are, of course, serious. In "Racism and Nationalism," French political scholar Étienne Balibar explains that nationalism never acts alone, that it is always attended by other "-isms" that pass low on the radar of our consciousness. As Balibar describes it, nationalism is a centripetal force, pulling together and bringing to bear such complex and various "-isms" as "civic spirit, patriotism, populism, ethnicism, ethnocentrism, xenophobia, chauvinism, imperialism, [and] jingoism" (2000, 46) in a common, national identity to which people swear allegiance. In this identity, we see reflected our desired version of our homeland, the one in which our cultural traditions are honored and our cultural values are promoted and propagated. Exclusion is not an issue under the rule of a nationalist ideology because we the people feel that our cultural standards are essential and universal; our history is privileged; we are the enfranchised ones, the lucky ones, the in-group to which everyone aspires, the "good" people (Anderson 1998, 360–368) whose American core values accommodates all who meet the requirements of citizenship. To put this another way, nationalism is the ideology of "us" and how we do things. It is a way of thinking that sanctions how "we" live, what we know and believe, even whom we love, and directly to the point of composition studies, how we communicate with each other. Nationalism operates in and through our everyday practices, including our institutional and professional practice. Balibar explains it this way: "Nationalism is the organic ideology that corresponds to the national institution, and this institution rests upon the formulation of a *rule of exclusion, of visible or invisible "borders,"* materialized in laws and practices. Exclusion—or at least unequal ("preferential") access to particular goods or rights depending on whether one is a national or a foreigner, or belongs to the community or not—is thus the very essence of the nation-form" (2004, 23).

Of course, Balibar tells us, nationalism and racism are not exactly equivalent terms. It is possible for a patriot to resist racism. But the effort will seem Sisyphusean because "[r]acism is constantly emerging out of nationalism" (2000, 53). After all, the story of the nation is the story of the founders, and those who come after them, looking and sounding like them, even if the similarities are a mirage. Nationalism is deeply embedded in historical protections and rationalizations for membership and its privileges, even as it, in the United States, argues for national equality and fairness. According to Balibar, "The overlapping of the two [nationalism and racism] goes back to the circumstances in which the nation states, established upon historically contested *territories*, have striven to control *population* movements, and to the very production of the 'people' as a political community taking precedence over class divisions" (48). It is not hard to see the same overlap at work today. Some of our controls are more overt than others, as in the hawkish rhetoric about safe borders we hear coming from Washington, D.C. or states such as Arizona. And some are more covert and unconscious, as in the value judgments at work in the privileging of sanctioned, homeland, rhetorical styles and forms over those from what we determine to be unacceptably from without.

IS IT PATRIOTISM OR IS IT NATIONALISM?

Anthony Smith draws a sharp distinction between nationalism, the ideology held by those trying to attain or maintain statehood, and feelings of "national sentiment," or patriotism, that are shared by those who live in a country that has already achieved independent statehood (1971, 174–175). I value Smith's distinction between a population that lives in an established state and a population that struggles to achieve and preserve statehood. Among other things, this delineation helps us to remember the difference between patriotism, in the sense of putting a flag on the lawn in front of one's house, and revolutionary fervor, in the sense of putting one's life on the line for national independence (not that citizens of an already established nation do not also, at times, put their lives on the line in defense of their nation, ample examples of which can be seen in the continuing "Arab Spring"). In other words, Smith's distinction encourages us to remember that some peoples of the world have national homes (even if they often forget that the integrity of their nations has to be maintained through critical thought and action), while the oppressed of the world struggle to establish nations of their own, often in resistance to other nations that seek to subjugate them. Smith's distinction also reminds us that nationalism runs in deeper channels than fleeting moments of patriotic sentiment. It reminds us that patriotism is a feeling and nationalism is an ideology.

So, in *National Healing* I am working with the view more generally held by historians, including Smith, that nationalism is an ideology that holds people in affiliation within a national identity. In other words, nationalism is a set of related beliefs and values that maintains a national identity and, specifically, sustains a population's participation in or allegiance to the project of statehood.

I realize, at this point, that some readers might be saying, "So, what's wrong with loving one's country? What's wrong with nationalism, for that matter?" In and of themselves, there is nothing wrong with either of these concepts or feelings. Patriotism, or love of one's country, is a valid emotion. It becomes a problem only when the emotion runs unrestrained by respect for others. Nationalism is one root of patriotism. It is a necessary ideology, at this moment in history, anyway, for the peaceful development of modern geographic and demographic territories, a tragically ironic fact given its relationship to racism. In addition, nationalism can also too easily lead to a belief in a state's right to invade another country, a state's right to oppress regional factionalism, and even a state's right to cleanse its ethnicity. As an ideology, nationalism has the ability to circulate unchecked, scripting our everyday actions and suppressing, in the name of unity, individual choice and agency, often without us even realizing it. This is true at all times, and especially true, perhaps, in times of national stress, such as a war, when nationalistic allegiance can call forth the emotion of patriotism in order to quiet dissent and silence those who would try to elucidate the tragedy of war and warn the future against it.

I call this book *National Healing* because my country is damaged by a nationalism that has inspired a dangerous national identity that is largely blind to its own proclivity for racism and perpetrating international violence. It is an identity that is largely loath to examine the "-isms" upon which its character rests, specifically and most dangerously in the context of this study, racism. It is, largely, an intellectually lazy identity, one that revels in proclaiming for freedom while failing to use that freedom to articulate widespread and systematic critiques of the forces that limit that very same freedom. It is an identity that serves imperialist designs, a war-like persona and set of foreign policies that the United States has enacted in various places around the world for over two hundred years. And it is an identity scripted into a tragic story, ending in violence, again and again, the way imperialism always does. I would like to say that the current level of US nationalism is unique in our time, that it is simply an accoutrement of the military adventurism enacted by recent administrations. But that would not be the whole story. We and the educators who have come before us, many of whom we laud as pioneers in the development of our profession, have long taught us to think beyond the present and easy conclusions that tempt us with platitudes instead of wisdom. If recent history has taught us, the citizens of the United States, anything, it is that times of national stress are when we most need critical thinking. In fact, if recent history has taught us anything, it is that we need critical thinking every day.

Let me offer a hypothetical example. Many compositionists teach the first-year, college writing course as a class in argumentation because we feel that doing so offers students the best preparation for fulfilling the demands and responsibilities of citizenship. When we act—or teach— in this way, we act with responsibility and patriotism. But when we do so without examining the belief that a first-year, college writing course in argumentation actually is the best writing training for the academy and citizenship, or when we fail to study what other meaningful content is also available for us to teach in composition, we may be acting in the interest of nationalist ideology rather than in the best interest of our students. The point is that ideology operates in the unconscious, as well as the conscious, level of decision-making; it is not easily identified or studied. It can pose as good common sense and even as discipline-grade thinking. It can even lead compositionists to create curricula, pedagogy, and assessment procedures in the interest of nationalist concerns without even realizing it. We need to understand the nature and power of nationalism if we are to understand fully our teaching and our alternatives.

So, let me be clear: I am not saying that I think teachers—or anyone—should reject all manner of love for their nation or state. I am saying that love, even love of one's country, can be, when it goes unexamined, a blindness. And when we are talking about the lives of nations, the results of such love can be devastating. I am speaking of the obvious, namely war, but also the not so obvious, for instance the way that nationalism prevents our government from forming liberating alliances with people from other nations to achieve creative objectives that would help us to heal a divided, conflicted planet and damaged biosphere.

CRITICAL LITERACY

In his landmark study, *Nations and Nationalism,* historian Ernest Gellner outlines the features he feels are necessary for the rise and maintenance of a modern nation. These essentials include power, which some in a nation's population will have and some will not, and a shared culture, which is transmitted in several ways, not the least of which is through a system of education. Gellner describes education's role in the circulation of culture this way:

> The next element in the model is access to education or to a viable modern high culture (the two being treated as equivalent). The notion of education or a viable modern high culture is once again very loose but nonetheless useful. It refers to that complex of skills which makes a man competent to occupy most of the ordinary positions in modern society, and which makes him, so to speak, able to swim with ease in this kind of cultural medium. It is a syndrome rather than a strict list: no single item in it is, perhaps, absolutely indispensable. Literacy is no doubt central to it. (1983, 89)

Literacy is a chief vehicle, in this perspective, for bonding an individual to a society and unifying a nation through the values attached to it by the society it serves. Literacy values perpetuate the integrity as well as the boundaries of the social fabric. They are nationalist in intent and effect. Of course, that is not the whole story of literacy. If it were, there would be no divisions within national populations, no resistances. Indeed, in the 1950s and 1960s, the Soviet Union legislated the teaching of the Russian language to the citizens of its various republics. The objective was to foster national cohesion through a taught love of Russian culture. (Indeed, the English-only movement in the United States is an Anglo-Saxon version of the same nationalist motivation.) The Soviet attempt at homogenization failed because it did not recognize the value of diversity and because it underestimated the cultural commitments of its citizens; the US movement is doomed to similar failure.

Still, we educators in the United States have longed understood that our curricula inculcate capitalist values in our students. We have listened to critical theorists, such as Louis Althusser (2009), who have explicated how the educational system acts as a state ideological apparatus, calling—or "interpellating"—students into the ideology of the nation. Sociologists of education, such as Samuel Bowles and Herbert Gintis (1976), have described how school systems exist to produce compliant workers for American industry. Critical educators, such as Paulo Freire (1972, 2000), Henry Giroux (2000, 2001), Ira Shor (1992), and Kathleen Weiler (1988, 1992) have articulated the ways in which teacher-centered education trains students to be passive receptors for knowledge and ideology. And educational researchers, such as Paul Willis (1977), have told us how working class children learn attitudes and work habits at school that script their places in the workforce as menial laborers. In addition, linguists and literacy researchers, such as Basil Bernstein (1971, 1973, 1990), have taught us that the literacy styles that students bring to school mark them for success or struggle, and that, too often, schools respond to these styles by tracking, by prohibiting home styles, or simply by marking disempowered students down. In the same vein, Jean Anyon (1980, 1981, 1997) has argued that the literacy practices that students bring to school track them for success or failure. Shirley Brice Heath (1983) has demonstrated, perhaps more clearly than anyone, how home literacy works for or against, depending on the student's home, the educational opportunities and successes students will likely have. Patrick Finn (1999) has explained that our challenge is to help working class students and parents realize their right to claim critical or "powerful" literacy instruction for themselves. And Irvin Peckham (2010) has argued that we need to do some serious thinking about how we use writing to sort people— and take some serious action to democratize our pedagogies once we do.

I barely scratch the surface here of the many wake-up calls we have had, and I have not done service to the ones I have listed. But one thing is clear from reading the work of these researchers: schools, colleges and universities are ideological state apparatuses that enforce, through ideological indoctrination, the capitalist economic system of the United States (and this is true of curricula offered and pedagogies implemented by many critical, cultural and leftist pedagogues). As Bill Readings (1977, 45) writes in *The University in Ruins*, the university is "the primary institution outside the nuclear family for the training of subjects of the modern nation-state." We compositionists play a central role, and we play it well.

I begin in this understanding, but I follow a different direction from the one usually articulated by the left in critical pedagogy. The

structural, Marxist, and ethnographic studies from which compositionists have benefited do not, for the most part, speak directly to composition theory and pedagogy. Critical pedagogues claim literacy as their
area of concern, but they do not move, largely, outside of a concern for
ideology, economics, educational policy, and even literary theory. As
important as these subject matters are to our understanding of writing
instruction, they do not help us to discover and critique the precise and
specific ways in which nationalism inspires a racism that is perpetuated
in and through the teaching of writing, despite our best efforts to teach
composition for democracy and multicultural understanding.

As Ernest Gellner points out, among the many lessons we educators
are responsible for establishing are the lessons of "[h]omogeneity, literacy, and anonymity" (138). According to Gellner, it is our job to teach
nationalism by teaching the "cultural style" of the empowered, with
promise of reward for those who would fit in and remain (more or less)
anonymous as they do (138). And make no mistake about it. Attempting
to adopt the "cultural style" of a society's elite, no matter how one
botches the job, is about attempting to fit in by practicing anonymity as
a discursive, behavioral posture. We compositionists see it so often in the
depersonalized, strictly mannered style of the academic discourses that
are valued in our universities and colleges. (I am thinking of an incident in one of my recent composition classes where a student was com-
plaining about how her biology professor had given her a low grade on
a report even though she had put a lot of effort into writing it. Another
student in the class claimed that she also knew the professor and advised
her colleague to simply write her next report "as quickly as possible," to
not use the word "I," and to try "to sound like a man." Two weeks later
the first student happily reported to the whole class that she had followed the advice and that she had gotten an A on her next report. And
while I cannot say with any certainty that the advice was the sole reason
for the A, the coincidence was not lost on either the class or myself.)

Writing about nationalist processes of assimilation, Gellner argues
that, "Far from reveling in the defiant individual will, nationalists delight
in feelings of submission or incorporation in a continuous entity greater,
more persistent, and more legitimate than the isolated self" (133). In
other words, nationalism subsumes the "I" within the "we" of "we the
people." I know that no serious teacher of writing would relish the suggestion that they spend their countless hours reading student papers
because they want to educate students in the ways of anonymity or to

crush their students' individual voices, to disrespect their cultures, or to assimilate them as drones in the service of elite culture. At the same time, I cannot deny that in the view of this important historian, Ernest Gellner, the efforts of teachers to do the best jobs that they can may be no match for an educational system that has been set up to achieve nationalist ends. Or, at the very least, if teachers are not vigilant, they will find themselves serving elements of a fundamentalist, nationalist ideology that they would otherwise eschew if these elements were not hiding behind the democratic rationales of the curricula they teach.

In their 1929 landmark ethnography, *Middletown*, Robert S. and Helen Merrell Lynd report on the state of education in Middletown, America (a.k.a. Muncie, Indiana). Anyone who has read the book will remember the oft-quoted beginning of the chapter, "The Things Children Learn": "The school, like the factory, is a thoroughly regimented world. Immovable seats in orderly rows fix the sphere of activity of each child" (1929, 188). From that grim beginning, the Lynds paint a gray picture of "lesson-textbook-recitation" days of enforced behavior, seat work, and skills training, including those deemed necessary for good citizenship, earning a living, and taking up one's place in society— in the factories and stores, as workers and consumers. Significantly, the Lynds' study ends up coming back, again and again, to the forces pressing the people of Middletown into alignment with the national identity of the day, an array of influences that stretches far beyond the Pledge of Allegiance recited by every student at the start of every school day: "Civic loyalty and patriotism are but two of the pressures tending to mold Middletown into common habits of thought and action. Every aspect of Middletown's life has felt something of this same tendency: standardized processes in industry; nationally advertised products used, eaten, worn in Middletown homes; standardized curriculum, text-books, teachers in the schools; the very play-time of the people running into certain molds, with national movie films, nationally edited magazines, and standardized music contests" (490–491). All of these phenomena shape the citizens of Middletown so that they will fulfill predictable and patriotic life patterns, thus ensuring the continued health of the national character.

The Lynds returned to Middletown eight years later, in 1937, to see what changes had occurred in their absence, and they reported their research in a follow-up book, *Middletown in Transition*. And things had indeed changed in the years between the two studies. The Lynds found a growing number of students in school and a Middletown focused on the expansion of its colleges where "[e]ducation was becoming 'scientific' with a vengeance; 'measurement' was in the saddle in all departments, from teaching to administration; and administration ceased to be the business of veteran teachers and became a series of specialties, its offices filled by specially trained persons" (1937, 205). The Lynds were witnessing "academic capitalism" in Middletown, America (Slaughter and Leslie 1999; Slaughter and Rhoades 2009).

The Lynds found conflict between the rich and poor of Middletown and between loyalty to timeworn traditions and commitment to the modern innovations of 1937. The local government responded to these tensions "simply as it must using the old words," such as proclaiming their commitment to following "The American Way" when trying to reconcile civic tensions (510). The Lynds also found conflicts in the schools. Competing interests struggled over the content of the curriculum and instruction—literally over what function the schools were to serve:

> There is conflict over the question of whose purposes the schools are supposedly fulfilling: Are these purposes those of the parent who wants education for *his* child in order that, through the acquisition of certain skills and knowledge or, more important, certain symbolic labels of an "educated person," he may achieve a larger measure of success than the parent himself has known? Or are they those of the citizen who wants, on the one hand, to have the fundamentals of community life, including its politico-economic mores, transmitted unchanged, and, on the other, to use the schools as an instrument of change sufficiently to bring any alien or backward children in the community up to these familiar standards. Or those of the teacher, with ideas derived from outside Middletown, loyal to a code of his own and obeying its philosophy? Or those of the taxpayers, businessmen, and the school board members, whose chief emphasis is on the "successful" and "progressive" schools, to be sure, but within the limits of a practical, sound, unextravagant budget? Or are they the purposes of anyone of the pressure groups who want to teach the children patriotism, health, thrift, character building, religion—or any to the other values more or less accepted by the community as a whole but become an emotionally weighted "cause" with one special group? (232)

I quote the Lynds at length here because they so clearly delineate the constituencies holding stakes in the content and shape of the education being provided in Middletown's schools and colleges. Reading the Lynds is an important lesson in how to see, and we compositionists can learn from their vision and unflinching honesty.

But if we follow the Lynds, what will we see? Specifically, we find that we compositionists have some serious questions to ask ourselves about what our mission actually is—not what we say or think it is, but what it actually is. For instance, what professional standards do we follow? Are we sure what they are or from where they originate? Do we teach, despite our stated and valued democratic purposes, students to aspire to elite culture when we teach them the sanctioned written and oral forms of society's elite? While there is certainly nothing wrong with wanting our students to achieve discursive fluency and improve their writing, and while it is noble to hope that all our students will better their lots in life in some way, isn't there a problem with how many of us—perhaps all of us—sanction certain discursive forms and styles, choose some over others for practice—and for the A's?

Gellner warns us that "nationalism is opportunistically selective in the respect it accords to tradition" (133). Nationalist ideology renders some cultural traditions more respectable than others, grants more academic currency to some than to others. This evaluation, Anthony Smith also tells us, is a result of how a nationalist ideology determines what a population values, and how the standards are "defined in terms of individual perceptions—usually those of a tiny minority of the given unit of population" (1971, 173). If this is so, if, the discursive forms we compositionists teach, the academic styles we call acceptable academic writing, are selected by a "tiny minority," shouldn't we compositionists be asking who this minority is and whose interests are being served in both the selection and the teaching? Are we the minority? If so, is it only some of us, or is it all of us? Is it the professors in the other disciplines that our courses are supposed to serve? Is it the deans, the provosts, the trustees? Is it the state legislators? Is it the national legislators? Whose nationalism is being served? Or, in a different vein, if we are serving nationalist ends by promoting what amounts to a hypothetical version of elite culture, to the exclusion of the styles of other American cultures, are we doing the right thing?

We have much to consider. Yes, we want students to learn the forms, values, and benefits of doing serious, scholarly writing because we see that serious, scholarly work can expand one's knowledge, vision, or horizons. But, is it also possible that our curricula are so traditionally, habitually, and unconditionally set in the service of a "tiny minority" that we are unable to see how we limit learning about options in writing even as we relegate the cultures of some students to second or third-class standing? Is it possible that because we have not sufficiently expanded our own knowledge, vision, and horizons we limit our students' opportunities for learning all they can about writing from us, even as we denigrate certain cultures through implicit and malignant neglect of the traditions that sanction them?

Despite how conspiratorial this all sounds, I believe that the answer is yes to both questions. The theories of one historian and sociologist after another bears this conclusion out. We teach in the service of nationalist objectives and the implications of our actions extend farther than we writing teachers have yet acknowledged or understood. Yes, a number of compositionists—for instance, Elaine Richardson (2003)—have explained how racism has affected their lives, both in and out of the academy and how teaching writing can address racism. And perhaps the teaching of writing has changed, to an extent, as a result of such work. But I hope that literacy educators will also follow Richardson's lead and study how our pedagogies promote, where they do, a nationalism that is specifically detrimental to students. If we do, maybe then, after much hard work, we will come to see how we teach against the international communication that could lead to cooperation and the solving of pressing problems that the entire world faces.

A DECENT NATION

As I reported in Part 1, "Cage: The Provincial Composition," in *The Decent Society,* political theorist Avashai Margalit (1996) argues that when a nation's agencies humiliate its citizens, these agencies denote an indecent society. I want to extend this definition here. When it has the power to do so, an indecent society will initiate economic policies that exploit and humiliate the citizens of developing nations as well. An indecent society will exercise what it claims to be its military options in the name of spreading a favorite "-ism," whether it be democracy or religion or any ideology. When it does so, it will be in the name of principles that have become empty slogans that pit "us" against "them." When it does so, it is granting free reign to run amok patriotic fervor and nationalist hubris and, potentially—or probably—greed. This, too, is indecent.

My country's government, on many occasions, has exploited without conscience, or even, in some cases, awareness, and waged war without cause. My country has acted, in light of Margalit's theory, indecently. It needs, now, to recover decency. It will have to face the facts of what it has done in Iraq and Afghanistan and elsewhere and it will need to heal, not in the same way that the countries of Iraq and Afghanistan will need to heal, but in the full light of its actions.

It need not have been this way. There are, after all, proud nations whose governments treat their citizens and the citizens of the world with respect. These nations establish social programs to promote the well-being of all of their citizens. These nations do not entertain profiteering desires and designs on either its own citizens or the citizens or resources of other nations. They do not declare their right to invade other nations. Many even cooperate with the governments of other countries to address world problems such as global climate change. But my country, the United States, has sometimes been an example of a state that does not contribute to world health even when the majority of its citizens would. We need to understand how this can be so. As citizens, we need to understand the state and how nationalism incorporates us and sometimes commits us to courses of action we would not otherwise entertain if we were thinking clearly.

But seeing will not be easy. In *Banal Nationalism,* Michael Billig analyzes how we are continually "flagged" (his term) as we go about our daily lives. According to Billig, we are so completely indoctrinated to the national character of the country in which we live that nationalism may rightfully be called common sense (1995, 4). Our news services are textured by an us/them rhetoric; our advertising promotes a citizenship of possession; our national sports teams encourage international competition; our living spaces contain icons of nationhood; national flags fly over our buildings; they are pinned to the lapels of our politicians; they wave on our postage stamps; and they hang at the front of many of our classrooms. In other words, nationality is all around us. "Nationalism," Billig tells us, "far from being an intermittent mood in established nations, is the endemic condition" (6). And that is the danger: nationalism is everywhere, always active, always ready, running deeply within us, blinding us to other ways of thinking and seeing. It keeps us alert and in a state of preparedness so that when the government calls, when a "crisis occurs, and the moral aura of nationalism is invoked: heads will be nodded, flags waved and tanks will roll" (4).

Clearly, it is time to bring out the flags, but this time to tag our ethnocentrism for display in the public square. Maybe if we can learn to see the content of our centrisms, we can learn to see ourselves, the standards we raise high, salute, and follow. Maybe, too, if we can analyze the beliefs we espouse, we will learn to see and understand the ways in which we all hang together. If so, we might better be able to see and even feel the deeper complexities of our nation, the connections among what once appeared to be separate problems: such as our dependence on fossil fuels and our willingness to go to war with oil-rich nations. As teachers, maybe then we might better be able to see our teaching in terms of its relation to the economic and political realities it supports, even as so many of us speak in contradiction to current economic and political realities.

According to the Iraqi-born historian, Ellie Kedourie, the conservative and controversial (as evidenced in his more vitriolic contributions to *The New York Review of Books*) founder of the *Middle East Quarterly,* nationalism is an illness. He wrote that nationalism is "a passionate assertion of the will, but at the core of this passion is a void, and all its activity is the frenzy of despair; it is a search for the unattainable which, once attained, destroys and annihilates" (1960, 89). We used to see this level of nationalism in the actions of George W. Bush's administration, which behaved precisely as if the unattainable, the perfect union of US national identity *was* attainable, but in particularly dangerous, neoliberal terms, and on a global scale.

Indeed, Kedourie believed that nationalism, an ideology invented in the nation-states of the West, is a disease of the mind and spirit which leads, among other things, to the trampling of individual rights, to the wholesale oppression of people, to the privileging of initiatives for the establishment of cultural and ethnic purity, and to the rise of dangerous forms of fundamentalist politics.

Dangerous indeed. According to Anthony D. Smith: "It is the fatal combination of ethnicity and nationalism, as 'ethno-nationalism,' that, in the tradition of Elie Kedourie, provokes the greatest fear and condemnation. But . . . it is precisely this combination that, whether it is tacit or 'unflagged,' as in parts of the West, or explicit and explosive, as in Eastern Europe and parts of Africa and Asia, most requires to be addressed. The fact that it is so deeply ingrained and routinised ('enhabited,' in Michael Billig's term) in the West, also requires explanation" (1998, 219).

Ok, then, let's try to explain it. When it is unleashed in its most rabid forms, the "ethno" at the heart of nationalism fuels intolerance, fundamentalism, and even ethnic cleansing campaigns. Witness it in the sectarian and fringe groups whose nationalism drives them to acts of terrorism. See it in the building of walls and fences designed to keep people out, while keeping hate in. See it in the colonial exploitation of The World Bank Group and the International Monetary Fund. See it, too, in the freewheeling use of economic and military power by nations that go it alone, reveling in their rogue status. It is we against them; it is the integrity of hate.

Perhaps Kedourie was right. Perhaps nationalism *is* a disease. Perhaps it is an infection that takes up residence in each of us, where it controls our actions so that we call for allegiance beyond reason. We dismiss the humanity of those we deem different and dangerous and call on everyone like us to join with us, to become even more like us or become different and dangerous, too. From here it is a short series of dehumanizing steps to seeing war as a solution for international grievances, as a relief from the disturbances of difference, and the disruptions of dangerous dissent. In unsettled times, nationalism blinds us to the suffering of others and prevents us from seeing how our choices can sometimes contribute to that suffering. In unsettled times, nationalism festers in our minds until we no longer see the consequences of occupation before we invade. In unsettled times, nationalism supports our home-grown insecurities and homeland racism. No, nationalism is not an illness. It is what we believe in and align ourselves with, even when we are not aware that we are doing so. The fact is that clinical metaphors seldom seem accurate and too often serve to absolve people from responsibility. No, the truth of the pain and suffering our blind allegiances cause should be motive enough for contrition.

A NATION'S CULTURAL CENTRISM

"Banal nationalism"—again, in Michael Billig's terms—encourages us to prop up a single-minded version of elite culture in our composition classes. Banal nationalism calls on us to continue to inculcate a simplified version of a national culture in our students. Banal nationalism tells us that we are correct when we assume that Eurocentric culture is the source or foundation of pedagogy for college composition. Banal nationalism blinds us to the search for possibilities for answering today's needs for broader and deeper cultural understandings. How many of us ever ask ourselves what Eurocentrism means beyond its status, depending on our politics, as a shibboleth for what is right or wrong with culture, us or them? Indeed, even a cursory look at Sharon Crowley and Debra Hawhee's *Ancient Rhetorics for Modern Students* (2008) demonstrates, within the contents of this textbook, at least, that even if there were many ancient rhetoricians working in various cultural settings, there is only one ancient tradition that modern students need.

In his book, *Eurocentrism,* economist, political theorist, and development planner, Samir Amin (1989) explains that while Eurocentric thought is particularly persuasive in privileging its own truth claims, the fact is that other cultural perspectives are equally productive. Eurocentrism, like any centrism, is limited by the specificity of its own historicity, even as it repudiates other cultural perspectives, making them available in only limited ways (which accounts for the general failure of liberal, multicultural theory in the academy). But it is unreasonable to think that Eurocentrism can or could obscure its own temporality forever. The fact is that we need the wisdom of multiple cultural traditions if we wish to understand concepts as complex as the march of history and issues that complicate and stress the current world situation.

Compositionists have found Eurocentric rhetoric's impressive prescriptive power to be foundational for understanding the production and reception of discourse; indeed, the normalizing power of Eurocentrism persuades us that its rhetoric is the natural tradition for properly guiding the composing of all discourse. Some might say that this state of affairs is curious given that so many of our profession's leaders have been telling us to expand our vision. In just one recent collection, Bruce Horner, Min-Zhan Lu and Paul Kei Matsuda's *Cross-Language Relations in Composition*, several compositionists and linguists argue, not just the importance, but the necessity of embracing the ethnic and cultural differences our students represent. Kate Mangelsdorf reminds us that our students do not leave their various literacies at the door when they enter our classrooms (Horner, Lu, and Matsuda 2010, 113–126). Gail Hawisher, Cynthia Selfe, Yi-Huey Guo and Lu Liu argue that "The ecology of literacy is seldom monocultural" (70). Paul Kei Matsuda reminds us that linguistic homogeneity is a myth anyway (81–96). Suresh Canagarajah argues that resonance among languages in writing is not a problem but a gift for writers (158–179). These facts have important implications for our pedagogies; namely, as Min-Zhan Lu correctly tells us, that we compositionists need to develop an international perspective on our work (42–56).

So why don't we? Herein lies the obvious though nonetheless mystifying problem for compositionists: because it is a centrism, Eurocentrism's claim to authority rests on the power of its pretense to being the only legitimate, as Amin calls it, "cultural tributary" in the world. Even though other tributaries flow and fill their branches with meaning and beliefs as rich and deep as the Eurocentric, we American teachers of writing cannot and do not fully utilize—even if we recognize—their value because they lie beyond the familiarity and safety of our horizons. Or, as Ella Shohat and Robert Stam (1994, 4) explain, Eurocentrism is a "form of vestigial thinking which permeates and structures contemporary practices and representations even after the formal end of colonialism." It is a "buried epistemology" that "embeds, takes for granted, and 'normalizes' the hierarchical power relations generated by colonialism and imperialism" (2). The result for composition teachers is tangible: we go on teaching writing, as John Mayher (1990) told us thirty years ago, by a common sense buried so deeply within us that we are sometimes hardly able to question it, let alone change it by deed. Amin explains it this way: "Eurocentrism is a paradigm which, like all paradigms, functions spontaneously, often in the gray areas of seemingly obvious facts and common sense. For this reason, it manifests itself in a variety of ways, as much in the expression of received ideas, popularized by the media, as in the erudite formulations of specialists in different areas of social science" (1989, vii).

Western rhetoric's long and deep tradition has spread, in one form or another, across the planet and into every writing classroom in the

West (and through conquests of one sort or another, many if not most in the East as well). We use Western rhetoric, in some form, to govern, negotiate, and disseminate information and order. We use it to establish decorum—a decorum that reflects "us." We employ its power to assert our rights and our justifications, to bring all the groups of our territory together—to reinforce the nation and its reach. We invoke it and promote it and every day administer it in composition classrooms. And the price of this cultural centrism is high. As Robert Stam (1995, 98) explains it: "Eurocentrism, like Renaissance perspective in painting, envisions the world from a single privileged point. It maps the world in a cartography that centralizes and augments Europe while literally 'belittling' Africa, and organizes everyday language in binaristic cultural hierarchies implicitly flattering to Europe (our nations/their tribes; our religions/their superstitions; our culture/their folklore)." An imperialism of epistemology as much as economy, Eurocentrism is dominance presented in the name of reason, stability, democracy, and national tradition, resting in the negation of the other. And the self-justifying arguments it calls forth in the academy are long-lived in traditional arguments for standards, conservative forms of assessment, and excellence in education. At the root of many calls for more stringent forms of gate-keeping, of course, is fear of the great unwashed hordes of students, the ones best served by some other college, especially ones in the students' own communities, the ones we can underfund while looking the other way. Calls for purity of language-use often, in this sense, fulfill one characteristic of racist thinking. As Étienne Balibar (2000, 55) writes in "Racism and Nationalism": "Most racist philosophies present themselves as inversions of the theme of progress in terms of decadence, degeneracy, and the degradation of the national culture, identity and integrity." Degradation. Otherness as an attack on integrity. In order to counter Eurocentrism, we will have to relearn its history and analyze its rhetoric as well as its epistemology. We will need to develop a counter-understanding that conserves what is best in the tradition while countering its universalist claims and drawing on the wisdom of other traditions.

Colonialism gave Western rhetoric to the world. The British took rhetoric and the teaching of literature to India and China and Australia. The United States took it to the Pacific, and, with the French, Spanish, Dutch, and Portuguese, who brought their own versions of rhetoric, to the Caribbean. And the colonial powers spread their literatures through their education systems. Teacher-centered, authoritarian, and hierarchical, colonial pedagogy is a form of teaching and an orientation toward meaning that matched up well with the patriarchy and authoritarianism of the imperial West. And the fit provided imperialist states with a powerful avenue for inculcating colonial ideology and consolidating colonial power. Many of us have seen the pedagogy in one form or another in our lifetimes: the teacher standing at the front of the room telling us what the poem means, what our reading means, what our writing means, even what our experience means.

The political and social mechanisms of colonialism are at work in the modern state and in our schools and universities. We can find them in the enforcement of Eurocentric discourse standards, the arbitrary and systematic privileging of Eurocentric forms and styles of discourse over others. We can witness the vestiges of colonialism in the rhetorical manners our evaluation processes sanction, and in those we prohibit, in the discriminatory language policies our writing programs sanction, and in exclusionary responses to public forums for the communication of cultural and alternative thinking and identity. If we look for them, we will find them, sadly, in our own habitual patterns of action and thought.

Even when we acknowledge or laud the existence of other rhetorical traditions, many of us who work with graduate students still lead them to the realization that there is only one tradition on which to base their teaching. We may introduce a variation on Western rhetoric in our classes, say, perhaps, Western feminist rhetoric, but too often, even today, it is presented as a supplemental rhetoric. And we do so even though it is past time we stopped supplementing and started supplying. As Ronald and Ritchie (2006, 5) say in *Teaching Rhetorica*: "We're not simply interested in how we *add* . . . women rhetors to our courses, how we stir them into the canon we already teach or use them or texts for classes. We believe instead that they provide a catalyst for examining how their presence might affect the kind of classroom structures, projects, and goals we might consider." The contributors to Eileen Schell and K. J. Rawson's *Rhetorica in Motion* (2010) would agree, I imagine, with Ronald and Ritchie. Feminist rhetorical studies are and have been enacted in a multitude of places and in a variety of directions. They have produced sophisticated research methodologies and agendas. Feminist rhetoricians are—and have been—pursuing answers to some of the most challenging questions facing researchers and teachers alike. To put it simply, they are changing our thinking about who we are and what we imagine could be our future.

Indeed, by now we should have had enough of the reductive sorts of multiculturalism (and, indeed, that we have not is testament to Eurocentric liberalism's power to limit our thinking). Adding "other" rhetorics to the multi-mix does nothing to change the fact that we still mostly teach our graduate students that they will really need to learn only one, white, male rhetorical tradition. They will learn it in our graduate classes, and they will learn it when they get their first teaching job. They will understand that the selection of composition textbooks, even though they contain shrunken versions of professional grade thinking about rhetoric, is good enough for their students and fine enough for them to adopt. Sadly, even as our graduate students follow multicultural commitments by adopting multicultural readers, they will actually be teaching the thinking, styles and manners sanctioned by textbook companies, even as they convince themselves that they are critical thinkers. Even as they laud the National Council of Teachers of English's efforts to convince the citizens of the United States of the necessity and beauty of language diversity, they will take up their exhausting roles as defenders of the national language and elite style when they pick up their red—or any other color—pens and start marking errors in form, logic, or grammar; which is not to say that students—and professors—never make such errors. It *is* to say that gatekeeping is a genuine, restrictive and default identity we writing teachers too easily take up when we read student writing. A textbook, some peer response group work, some computer instruction, and a commitment to working hard and reading papers late into the night while doing committee work on weekends and vacations, all the while attending conferences and writing blogs, articles and books—we have condemned graduate students to crushing workloads and little time for questioning a culturalism whose continuing history of imperialism, conquest and colonialism would otherwise make us all shrink in horror. Yes, we will ask our graduate students to be intellectually curious and critical and to enact imaginative teaching, and we will mean it. But, we, and they, may well be serving other masters even as we do so.

Our graduate students will mean well. They will be trying to do their jobs by trying to teach students how to write. And all the while, they will work hard in their service, with the well-being of their students in the forefront of their thinking. And all the while, they will support the reigning regime of neoliberal economic policy by putting their classrooms at the service of textbook companies and their international corporate owners. And, maybe, I should be saying "we"—well, I should definitely be saying "we."

So why does Western, Classical, Eurocentric rhetoric hold such sway? Why are some compositionists even eager to be called rhetoricians rather than writing teachers, claiming that when they teach writing they are actually teaching rhetoric?

One answer lies in the oft-discussed desire on the part of some writing professionals to legitimize the discipline of composition in the eyes of our colleagues in literature and the rest of the academy, even in the minds of administrators. It's a desire based on a misgiving that leads us to construct a service role for ourselves where we teach students to write for success in other classes and prepare students for productivity in the workplace, thus ensuring the value of our institutions' degrees. Of course, some will say that it is our aim to turn out students who will contribute to the common good of the community and country. And some will say that these are noble goals because, well, they are. But make no mistake: ideology is at work in claims to intellectual heritage, as it is in all knowledge claims. Classical rhetoric is a source of legitimatization precisely because it is recognized as an inheritance of the national cultural elite.

Theater critic Kiki Gounaridou explains the nature of the hold that the past has on scholars, teachers, students and artists this way:

> When a nation seeks to be reconnected with a sense of national identity, its cultural celebrations often express nostalgia for a past that defines a cultural high point in its history. This was the premise on which the seminar on "Composing National Identity Through the Reconstruction of National Culture" was based, during the 2002 American Society for Theatre Research (ASTR) Conference in Philadelphia. The seminar essays mainly addressed the use of theatre in the construction of national cultural identity. The participants discussed the relationship between political power and the construction or subversion of cultural identity, and explored the ways in which nations create a "neo-classical" culture in order to construct a new version of their national cultural identity. (2005, 1)

As many historians point out, nationalism needs reference to a heroic past in order to define or redefine a nation's people. And perhaps it does not always matter that the references and relations are largely fictive, or, at best, strained. Performance theorists Julie Holledge and Joanne Tompkins (2000, 443) state that "ancient Greece is the culture

that most Europeans and Easterners feel they 'own': it plays a wise ancestor role in the exalted heritage of western culture, when in reality most
cultures retain only a distant aesthetic appreciation of Greek theatre."
All that is required is the legitimacy and security that comes with the
inheritance of a sanctified past and the right to claim the authority it
bestows (something that men have traditionally accessed with greater
ease than women). With the glories of the past in hand, elitist nationalists and their minions can articulate who belongs not only to the "we" in
a "we the people," but in what capacity and to what degree. In this way,
nationalism acts as a "force for uniformity and rationalization" even as
"it also nurtures the fetishes of a national identity which derives from the
origins of the nation and has, allegedly, to be preserved from any form
of dispersal" (Balibar 2000, 54).

In other words, we compositionists teach select rhetorical forms,
transmit them, and do our parts to serve and preserve the nation's interests and inequalities as we do so. As conservators and transmitters of a
version of the Classical past, we stabilize, to some extent, cultural values
and serve the national identity.

But do we really conserve what we think we conserve? As Kiki
Gounaridou further reports on the 2002 American Society for Theatre
Research Conference, "the description of the seminar topic suggested,
'While this cultural 'neo-classicism' seeks to create an overall feeling
of . . . national identity, rarely is the classical culture presented in all its
complexities'" (1). This is certainly true of composition's use of Classical
rhetoric. Unless composition professors devote the entirety of their class
to the study of Classical rhetoric, they will cover only a small portion
of its complexity and speak in generalities about it as they do so. (Not
that one semester will necessarily yield deep study of the complexities
of Classical rhetoric, either.) But, there is another problem. Classical
rhetoric is about the composing, construction, memorizing, and delivery of speeches to, largely, fairly homogeneous audiences. As such, it can
hardly serve, in total, the class we call "composition," which is about the
composing and delivery of texts that can be written in and for a multitude of contexts and a multitude of audiences. Anyone can see that it's
not a match.

Still, some rhetorical theorists such as Janine Rider (1995), Kathleen
Blake Yancey (2006), Morris Young (2004) and Kathleen Welch
(1999), to name a very few, make convincing cases for why writing
teachers should endow the ancient offices of Classical rhetoric with

contemporary insights. Revisionist projects such as these reinvest the tradition with vitality, rendering it relevant to the work of writing teachers. Besides, there is wisdom in Julia Kristeva's admonition, that "The time has perhaps come for pursuing a critique of the national tradition without selling off its assets" (1993c, 46). As I hope to make explicitly clear throughout this book, I do not wish to auction off Classical rhetoric. The Classical rhetoricians posed central questions about the relation of discourse making to living that can help guide us, in certain uses and senses, on our own ways through life. I also, of course, appreciate the efficacy of Classical rhetoric in political situations. I applaud savvy writing program administrators and writing instructors who invoke the authority of Classical rhetoric to maintain the integrity of composition courses from meddling by people who look to balance university budgets by cutting writing course hours and tenure-track teaching positions. It can be useful indeed to have the academic, cultural capital of Aristotle in the bank when defending programmatic terrain and assets from pressures to turn composition classes into literature classes, or biology or sociology, or any number of other classes.

WHEN YOU DO THE RESEARCH

The prejudices of the nation have become big business. Sedimented in our cultural values, American nationalism mingles as both motive and product—both economy and ideology. It circulates in what we make, acquire, sell, export, put on, ingest, and absorb, in our ideas about how "we" do business, in who "we" are, not to mention who every other right-thinking person in the world should want to be. And all through this process of cultural creation and sedimentation, nationalism infects even the higher motives of our lives. Through the conduit of culture, American nationalism is incorporated into our universities as lifestyle-product, defining academic style and chic. And we compositionists have been distracted by our mistaken and under-theorized desire to serve our students, institutions, and nation, our commitments to our discipline and our desire to make names for ourselves in our own profession even as we have emulated the literary discipline. We compositionists have had our heads turned; consequently, we have not made the necessary turn to the study of the nation, nationalism, and internationalism. We have not needed to do so. The rhetoric of "our" cultural inheritance and its cultural and multicultural studies is all we have needed and needed to teach—or so we have seemed to think.

After all, cultures are logical—or so we are told by cultural theorist Greg Urban. But here we are not talking about logical thinking but about cultural circulation. According to Urban, cultures circulate by a "meta-cultural logic," a foundation of conscious and unconscious judgments that inspire, organize, and promote cultural activities, including the production of cultural objects. Indeed, as Urban points out, cultures usually follow more than one metacultural logic at a time. For instance, as cultures circulate, they distribute their preserved histories, which members reproduce so that others might adhere to tradition and maintain cultural coherence. When they do this, members are enacting a metacultural logic of "replication." But even as cultures replicate when members dedicate themselves to conserving traditional values, other members can still follow a metacultural logic of "newness" that inspires them to innovate and produce novelty for future development. And when cultures follow a metacultural logic of "dissemination," they circulate beyond their constituencies. Many move, as some nations aggressively do, outward, beyond their boundaries; they spread and sometimes accelerate in their development as they reach toward the future. (The nature of this movement will be affected by which logic—say, replication or newness—is more operative at a given time.) Finally, when cultures fail to develop by reaching outward or to the future, they run the risk of becoming subject to the forces of stagnation, entropy, and even dissolution.

In the United States, one of the dominant culture's leading lateral or replicant accelerants is, of course, the media, including, of particular interest for teachers of composition, the textbook publishing and teaching industry. Following logics of replication and newness, textbooks contain material that disseminates traditionally sanctioned forms of culture and national citizenship, but in slightly new ways. (Teachers will recognize the "slightly new" in the steady appearance of revised additions, or the reconfiguration of familiar subject matter under the rubric of the latest academic breakthrough.) Consequently, textbooks contain instructions for replicating the traditional, the comfortably known, even as each edition of the same text is packaged as the newest advancement in education.

Effectively taught to teacher and student alike, a textbook's pattern of maximum production and consumption inspires writing teachers to assign quickly written and evaluated texts (especially the ones that answer those questions for further discussion found at the end of selections in composition readers), and student texts serve both as conservation medium and useful propellant as the national culture progresses along its noisy pathways. In Urban's terms, student essays are easily discernable as rational (2001, 33), because they fulfill the metacultural logic of replication (they replicate—or attempt to—familiar, traditional form). We can grade them with relative ease (discounting the long and tedious hours we spend on them), and we can see ourselves comfortably in our traditional authority as we do so. And as we finish reading a set of papers, textbooks—or a teacher's assignment—quickly lead to another set, and the national culture is conserved, preserved, prolonged, and extended, all at the same time.

What fires the engines of this merchandising of composition? Money is the obvious answer, but there are two other factors driving the textbook industry's influence on composition. The first is faith and the other is habit.

I believe that the majority of composition teachers adopt textbooks for their classes because they believe that it is the right thing to do, that by doing so they give their students access to culture, and to, at least, potential success in the academy, their next class, be it a science or a social science, and in the workplace, as in "I am teaching my students what they need to secure a job." This line of reasoning, which follows a logic of dissemination, is more a leap of faith than it is a theory built on research. Urban explains: "The metaculture of dissemination that took shape in Europe—perhaps in the fifteenth and sixteenth centuries, but undoubtedly with older roots—is based upon this implicit faith. If people take up objects that are the embodiment of cultural learning and the result of cultural replication, one can have faith that some culture will pass to those people, even without regard to specific evidence of replication" (65). Clearly, one of the characteristics of modernity is a time-honored, habitual, if critically unexamined, faith in form—form itself being a manifestation of habit. It is a faith that people hold onto as they work, and it contributes to the replication and dissemination of culture. At the same time, one of modernism's other characteristics is a commitment to the breaking of form, as seen in the work of Ezra Pound. Modernity accommodates both impulses (which can become hardened into something like faiths). We will be drawn to one pole or the other of this dichotomy according to our inclination or, as Pierre Bourdieu (1977) told us, our habit. Habit inspires us to accept or adopt objects according to the degree to which they correspond with our already established inclinations and tastes, which are scripted by "class condition" and the "class conditioning it entails" (Bourdieu 1984, 101). Habit is, then, as with faith, a result of a metaculture of replication, and it is easily discernable in composition textbooks that provide and ask for the known. In other words, they present just enough of past forms to make us comfortable with our students' present writing, or uncomfortable when we deem that the writing just does not "measure up"—measuring up itself being both a tool and effect of class and racial conditioning.

Composition teachers adopt textbooks because that is what composition teachers from all across the country have traditionally done. Nothing is harder to change in a human being's mind than their habitual patterns of thought. So, composition teachers adopt textbooks because they have inherited the habit of mind that says adopting textbooks is precisely what good professors do, and they have faith that if they do so they are indeed good professors. They adopt them because textbooks promise to be the latest technology that respects tradition. They are, then, manifestations of the largest of corporate imperatives: they are products and they are everything for everyone. Corporations know that they must produce and sell the new in order to accelerate gains. They can only do this if what they produce appeals to those who: (1) want the familiar, (2) want the new, (3) want both at once or do not yet know that they want both at once. Textbooks are the perfect product. They were born in the still-persuasive Enlightenment, metacultural logic of dissemination, and they now reside in contradiction, endlessly reproducible, yet always new. They tell us that we are always the same and always ground-breaking and that everyone should have one if they wish to become like us. They are composition's embodiment of capitalism's motives and drive to create "we, the people." They are illogical, ubiquitous, expensive, critical within comfortable limits, and, largely, banal. They are the chief conduits through which we attempt to inculcate writing students with our voices. As Greg Urban tells us, "basic education still relies largely on tests of replication—how well students have internalized the culture of their teachers. The metaculture of modernity competes with metacultures of tradition, this being a key theme of our time" (66–67).

Anyone who has been watching the ties of Eurocentric education to capitalist ideology has seen the metaculture of dissemination working in high gear. We have witnessed the colonialist globalization of the Western tradition of rhetoric, and we are witnessing the globalization of English and World Bank literacy (Watkins 2003). We have witnessed the spread of English around the world in the name of international business development. Some of us have argued that composition is being turned into a business-serving preparation course textured by the failed development policies of Washington and the World Bank Group (Hurlbert and Hector-Mason 2006). Despite the warning cries published by African educators in *A Thousand Flowers: Social Struggles Against Structural Adjustments in African Universities* (Federici, Caffentzis and Alidou 2000), too many of us do not object to the attacks on teachers' unions and the closing of state schools and colleges; in fact, we indirectly or inadvertently support them.

Would we care if we knew that we ask students to buy textbooks, the profits from which, go to companies who produce textbooks that are adopted and exported by the World Bank to the detriment—and sometimes near or real extinction—of indigenous presses in economically developing nations? Graham Furniss (2006), a professor of African Language Literature at the School of Oriental and African Studies at the University of London, reports that the sharp decline in the Nigerian economy in the 1980s, which was caused, largely, by World Bank structural adjustment policies, brought about a sharp decline in an otherwise flourishing local, literary publishing market. And educator Jean-Clotaire Hymbound (cited in Mazrui 2000, 56) has argued that the decline in publishing also affected African textbook production: "[A] World Bank loan to the Central African Republic (CAR), supposedly intended to improve quality and accessibility of elementary education, came with a package of conditions requiring the nation to import its textbooks (and even French language charts) directly from France and Canada. This draconian move was justified on the grounds that printing in these western countries is cheaper than in the CAR, making their publication more affordable to the average African child."

In other words, the World Bank has both authorized control of the intellectual destiny of African children and weakened Africa's infrastructure, including its publishing houses, which produce and distribute local knowledge (Mazrui 2000, 56–57). In fact, in 2005 the Africa News Service reported that Longman was the largest publisher in Nigeria and that, indeed, their textbooks were being "widely adopted by various governments" for use in the implementation of universal education initiatives. Would we care if we knew that Longman was owned by Pearson, the largest producer of standardized tests in the world? Would we complain about the effects of standardized testing, including racial and class bias in standardized tests, as we adopt or produce Longman textbooks?

Would we teachers of writing care if we knew the managerial connections between the parent company of a major publisher of composition textbooks and the board of directors of a large German steel manufacturer, the major supplier of steel for the Germans in World War II, and the German and US militaries of today? Would we care if we knew that another of our major textbook companies is owned by a conglomerate which is a major supplier of educational publications for the US military? Would we care if we knew that we ask students to buy textbooks from companies, in other words, whose corporate conglomerates create profits from the arms industry?

Or, to be more specific, would we care if we knew that we ask students to buy texts from St. Martin's, a company whose parent ownership, according to *Vanity Fair*, has unexplained and unapologized-for origins in a Nazi past? Founded by the now deceased Georg von Holtzbrinck, the Holtzbrinck Publishing Group is run by his children (who have, admittedly, treated the Jewish publishers and authors they have acquired fairly and made impressive monetary grants to Israel, as well). Still, should we compostionists care that during the war Holtzbrinck, a member of the National Socialist party in Germany, published Nazi propaganda (even as a competitor of his used Jewish slave labor in printing plants)? Should we care that after that war, Holtzbrinck "subsequently filled his sales force with former Nazis who, because they were ostensibly barred from the book industry, could be had cheap" (Margolick 1998, 142)? And should we care "that the man in charge of one of Georg von Holtzbrinck's postwar magazines was a notorious former SS storm trooper who had once worked for Joseph Goebbels"? Should we care that "Georg von Holtzbrinck's wartime activities remain murky" (Landler 2002)?

What are we doing? Seriously, what are we doing? Yes, we teachers can miss information that is relevant to our teaching and adopt a textbook of which the profits go to corporations that operate in direct opposition to the intellectual values and morals for which we stand and teach. Still, it's not like we haven't been told. We've been told and told and warned again. Maybe it is time to look to different sources for guidance. Buddhist monk Thich Nhat Hanh writes:

> Millions of people make a living off the arms industry, manufacturing "conventional" and nuclear weapons. These so-called conventional weapons are sold to Third World countries, most of them underdeveloped. People in these countries need food, not guns, tanks, or bombs. The United States, Russia, and the United Kingdom are the primary suppliers of these weapons. Manufacturing and selling weapons is certainly not a Right Livelihood, but the responsibility for this situation does not lie solely with the workers in the arms industry. All of us—politicians, economists, and consumers—share the responsibility for the death and destruction caused by these weapons. We do not see clearly enough, we do not speak out, and we do not organize enough national debates on this huge problem. If we could discuss these issues globally, solutions could be found. New jobs must be created so that we do not have to live on the profits of weapons manufacturing. (1998, 46)

We teachers of writing who adopt textbooks without checking the actions and investments of the company or conglomerate producing them, all the while claiming to teach students to think critically—not to mention if we claim to be critical pedagogues or cultural studies or postcolonial specialists—ought to ask ourselves some important questions. And, of course, I think that the writers and editors of first-year composition textbooks ought to do the same and with, perhaps, a sharper edge. As Pound wrote: "The shortcomings of education and of the professor are best tackled by each man for himself; his first act must be an examination of his consciousness, and his second, the direction of his will toward the light. The first symptom he finds will, in all probability, be mental LAZINESS, lack of curiosity, desire to be undisturbed" (n.d.b, 59).

After years of studying this subject, I have come to some painful conclusions. As a profession, we sometimes don't much know or, as I sometimes fear, care about what we are doing. We adopt textbooks published by St. Martin's or Longman or whatever other press, but do we do our homework about the historical and international economic implications of these choices? Worse, we write or edit textbooks for these companies. Truly, what are we doing?

Kenneth Burke spent much of his career warning us about naturalized rhetorical habits. He cautioned us again and again about the rhetorical processes through which ideology authorizes or excludes critical lines of thinking and innovative discursive structures. No wonder that the use of composition textbooks is so prevalent; no wonder nationalists and other fundamentalists make such rabid formalists. As Burke wrote in *A Rhetoric of Motives:*

> We consider it a sign of flimsy thinking, indeed, to let anti-Communist hysteria bulldoze one into neglect of Marx. (We say "bulldoze," but we are aware that the typical pedagogue today is not "bulldozed" into such speculative crudity; he welcomes it, and even feels positively edified by it. If he cannot grace his country with any bright thoughts of his own, he can at least persuade himself that he is being a patriot in closing his mind to the bright thoughts of his opponents. No wonder the tendency is so widespread. It is a negative kind of accomplishment for which many can qualify.) (1969, 105)

I immediately want to defend my fellow compositionists from Burke's critique. But how does one counter-state the number of composition textbooks sold each year to first year students across this country? And how does one ignore the shockingly low sales of scholarship in composition, especially when there are so many people teaching writing (and I am not pointing a finger at adjunct faculty who are hardly supported in their attempts to learn their discipline)?

No, in fact, I do not want to point a finger at anyone; instead, I want to encourage my colleagues in composition to critique textbook companies and their corporate connections and textbook pedagogies and their content in order to ensure that they do not relegate us to the role of what Burke called "ideologists." Burke explained that ideologists are "specialists in words (or ideas)." They are "priests, philosophers, theoreticians, jurists"—and, I would add, teachers of writing—"who miss the bigger material picture because they see things too exclusively in terms of their specialty." Because they do not see their roles, for instance, in historical context, ideologists end up in the default position of being apologists for elite and ruling class ideology, and "in keeping with the nature of their specialty, perfect and systemize the ideas of the ruling class. And since the ruling class controls the main channels of expression, the ideas of the ruling class become the 'ruling ideas'" (105). And as historian after historian and sociologist after sociologist tell us, our classrooms are channel number one. It is past time we compositionists asked important questions about who and what controls the programming—and who serves them.

Now I am not saying here that there is never a reason to write, say, a book on argumentation that might be adopted for a relevant, perhaps upper-division, class. Such classes can be meaningful parts of any writing curriculum. I am also not saying that a writing teacher might not want to teach a unit on Western rhetoric, including argumentation, in their composition class—all of that depends on how the class is grounded in a larger literacy vision. What I am saying, or asking, is whether, as a profession, we are so blind or lazy that we act as classroom field reps or stable writers for the textbook companies, especially when the product we are selling does not represent state-of-the-art theory or pedagogy and actually contributes to what is, essentially, harmful in the world? Is it that we are so driven to achieve tenure and promotion and so afraid that we won't that we make such deals? If so, what makes us feel qualified to grade the quality of our students' critical thinking when our own is so feeble, or when we refuse to even own it? How do we turn off what we know—or don't we know it to begin with?

I don't know the answers to some of my questions, and maybe I don't want to know. The one conclusion I can come to regarding my profession is equally as painful, though: in its current state, with its textbooks, conventions and ideology, composition is a white, nationalist enterprise. As it is conceived and taught, it is about white identity, about adopting white identity, and being a conservative or a moderately liberal student. As Bonnie Lisle and Sandra Mano (1997, 12) put it: "Diversity is a hot topic in composition . . . But we detect a gap between professional talk and professional practice. A glance at current textbooks, which offer a rough measure of what goes on in most composition classrooms, suggests that, while the profession celebrates heteroglossia and difference, most rhetoric instruction remains monologic and ethnocentric." I don't mean to split hairs here, but this gap is more of a chasm. On the face of it, I know that most composition teachers would say that they are for multiculturalism, and I believe that they would be speaking honestly when they do. But good intentions do not, as they say, pay the bulldog. It is past time for change. Applied linguist Rico Lie's (2003) challenge to language educators is relevant here: we need to do serious study on how the media—textbooks—work through and on cultural identity and diversity. As Ezra Pound pointedly wrote, "An education that is not focused on the life of today and tomorrow is treason to the pupil" (n.d.b, 634).

THE GLOBAL NOTHING

Powerful national cultures have the impulse to disseminate themselves. So, what do we compositionists produce, under the logic of commercial production and consumption, for dissemination—for global export? I say, "Nothing." "Nothing?" you ask. "Even in our global economy? Really? Nothing?" "Yes," I reply, "really and literally, nothing."

In *The Globalization of Nothing*, George Ritzer argues that the West has raised the dissemination of global consumerism to new levels of efficiency by developing the art of exporting nothing. By nothing, Ritzer means that we export "*generally centrally conceived and controlled social forms that are comparatively devoid of distinctive content* [author's emphasis]" (2004, xi). Two examples of the social forms that Ritzer has in mind are shopping malls and credit cards. A mall is an exportable form that contains nothing in and of itself. It is administered from without by a management company, which decides, among other things, what will go into it, what its contents will be. A credit card works the same way. It is not itself money. Instead, a credit card is a form that represents the processes by which credit will be assigned, as administered by a central location, a bank or credit firm. (Actually money is nothing either—it is value legislated by law. It seems that in our time nothing, too, is sometimes a form that we fill with nothing.)

Ritzer further explains that globalizing nothing is less challenging than globalizing something: "[I]t is far easier to globalize largely empty forms than those that are loaded with content (although these days virtually everything is globalized, at least to some degree). The main reason is that that which has much content also offers much that has the potential not to fit into, even to conflict with, aspects of other cultures around the world; the more the content, the greater the chance that some phenomenon will not fit or be accepted" (xii).

I believe that we see the same globalization of nothing in the metacultural logic underwriting our composition textbooks. Writing textbooks provide empty forms that are controlled and sold by a handful of textbook companies. The forms, whether they be the modes of discourse or the argument or the even the essays called for by the "questions for discussion" in composition readers, are, indeed, empty. They contain no content other than the content conjured by student writers with which to fill them. Because the forms are empty, they do not, largely, conflict with the content of any classroom in almost any college or university. The forms are transient, fleeting, of momentary value; that is, the modes themselves, according to Robert Connors (1981), "rise and fall." As Ritzer explains, "empty forms have problems of their own in gaining and maintaining acceptance" (xii). And so thesis and purpose-driven texts and forms have all had their heydays as they, too, rise and fall.

The importance of this analysis is, I hope, clear. Composition textbooks provide little direction to the necessary things that writers need to do in the twenty-first century, such as explore composing processes among different peoples and enact alternatives in their writing, alternatives that would also stand against those forces that obstruct the possibility of international composition. Textbooks are nothing. They are the absence of cultural creativity. They do not, largely, call for it, and they do not, largely, promote it. The problem with nothing, of course, is that it is not something, and worse, in a pedagogy, it is a nothing that takes the place of something. Just as the mall takes the place of a farmer's market, the composition textbook takes the place of meaningful vision and writing. The globalization of nothing is, in this perspective, a displacement of the local, perhaps the unique and distinctive, perhaps even the sacred. It is the displacement of affiliation from the traditional to the transient, from the organic to the chemical, from the macrobiotic to the imported, from interpersonal to intrapersonal, even from the multicultural to the monocultural. In the composition class it is the displacement of relevance, significance, and meaning, to irrelevance, insignificance, and meaninglessness. It is a replication of standardization, and it is, I suspect, in student eyes, largely a waste of time. Of course, individual teachers and students find ways to insert themselves, their cultures and their meanings into the teaching and writing that they do—the most creative or resistant elements of human nature always will. Emptiness does not, after all, nullify the human imagination. In fact, it can, in rare instances, even inspire it (as in "power loves a vacuum").

I have met many teachers over the years who are completely dissatisfied with the textbooks they are using in their writing classes but push themselves to "use" them in some way, anyway, and so hide the emptiness they feel and too often see from their students—after all, students are not easily fooled. How much better it is when we offer students the opportunity to write something rather than fill the empty forms of nothing. Ritzer does not miss this insight:

> By the way, it is worth remembering that for us, unlike others, nothingness is *in the form* and *not in the person* who is associated with it, at least not necessarily. That is, as is made abundantly clear, many people do *not* find their relationships with empty forms substantively empty; they often see them as quite full of substance. The emptiness is not in them, but in the form. No matter how empty the form, it can be defined as full and, as has been pointed out previously, in a curious way an empty form lends itself to being defined as full since it can be defined in so many ways. Yet, most generally, it is undoubtedly a great struggle for a person to find substance in an empty form; it would be far easier in a form that is loaded with substance, that is something! (197)

Textbook descriptions are not, finally, even about writing. They are about giving students things to read and talk about so that class time is filled and writing is generated for assessment. They are about the textbook author's general thinking about writing or their idea of what constitutes college level and necessary readings. Or they contain grammar and MLA and APA information, and maybe some suggestions for researching. None of these things are in and of themselves bad things. Certainly, writing may lead to a need to know the APA or MLA format, to understand how to use a comma or to a desire to read what others may have said about our search, but that need comes in its time. Supplemental texts are always useful in that regard. And so we have libraries and the internet, and, yes, bookstores. But these are not the deeper rationale for encouraging students to write in the first place.

Textbooks are not immersion in the search for meaning and relevance through writing. Relevance is, with the help of a professional facilitator, attempting the articulation of an interpretation, for instance, of an episode in one's life, finding words to explain something that has perplexed us, an understanding of a moment the meaning of which has, until writing, eluded us. And writing is about striving to do these things with as much clarity, force, and beauty—and sometimes difference—as possible. That's what writing is about. As Ritzer says, it may be that sometimes people recognize the "advantages of nothing" (xv). Nothing writing pedagogies require little thought on the part of instructors and administrators. They tell the teacher what to do as they perpetuate old formalisms under new configurations of nothing. They promote stasis while preparing us to consume and to change nothing in the world of discourse that we inhabit.

We in composition have been hearing warnings about the failure of content in composition textbooks for years. Back in 1978, Charles Cooper, Lee Odell and Cynthia Courts complained about the Warriner's *English Grammar and Composition,* a text whose adoption was so ubiquitous it may fairly have once been called a national textbook:

> According to Warriner's *English Grammar and Composition*—a typical practical stylist handbook, perhaps the most widely used in public schools—the chief problem in writing well is choosing language, syntax, and organizational patterns that are consistent with the practice of "educated people," those whose speech and writing define "good English." This practice, supposedly distinguished by such characteristics as correctness, conciseness, and clarity, is appropriate for every situation in which one is "writing carefully." In all these situations—"serious articles, 'literary essays,' essay-type answers on examinations, research papers, and formal speeches"—a writer adopts a polite, earnest persona that is eager not to confuse or offend an audience that has assimilated the principles of standard English. By and large, the writer's chief purpose is to present information and ideas in a clear, orderly fashion to an audience that, so far as we can determine, has no emotional investment in either the writer or the piece or in the subject being discussed. In judging writing, Warriner makes an assumption that the qualities of "good" writing remain essentially the same, no matter what the mode or purpose of the writing.
>
> It seems pointless to attack the point of view epitomized in Warriner's text; we can just let I. A. Richards (1936) dismiss it with his phrase "the ususal postcard's worth of crude common sense." (1978, 1)

Cooper, Odell and Court's dismissal of the vacuous, classist attitude embodied in the Warriner textbook was justified, of course. But where are we today?

The contributors to Gale and Gale's *(Re)Visioning Composition Textbooks: Conflicts of Culture, Ideology and Pedagogy* have brought the critique closer to date and closer to the mark: the national culture and nationalist ideology which the textbooks are designed to perpetuate. In his essay, "In Case of Fire, Throw In," David Bleich argues that "the patronizing language of textbooks helps to perpetuate the hierarchical structures of society. These structures render coercive speech by an authoritative class of people to a less authoritative. . . . My discomfort with textbooks is connected to their promoting of social values that few, including nonacademics, question. They are part of a structure of commerce and pedagogy that many are not willing to change" (1999, 35). I know Bleich's discomfort well. As does Joseph Janangelo. In the same volume he argues against the moralizing tone and content (142) found in the largely fictitious, reductive narratives told by textbooks about students and writing. It is a narrative of industry being rewarded by merit and advancement (94). It is a narrative with which "the writing program controls students by having the text show the discernible progress that a good student makes by obediently following the rules of a handbook-and teacher-dictated drafting process. The good student text thus serves as an exemplary narrative and a shaming device that both models and moralizes the kind of writing, and writing behavior that a program demands from its students" (95). But as a writing program adopts textbooks for its teachers, it serves more than its own ends. As Janangelo explains, the composition textbook's narrative of industry and success "contains" weak (i.e., different) writing and in so doing "initiates" students into a society supported by composition's call for conformity. To put this all another way, composition textbooks reinscribe the contradictory ideology of industrious individualism and social conformity in the United States (99–112). It is no wonder that James Thomas Zebroski, in his article "Textbook Advertisements" in the foregoing compilation, so ably connects composition's textbooks to class struggle, a conflict where the textbook's patrician content denies the rights, language, and discourse of the working class students that the textbook is purported to serve.

Such power! In the same collection, LizBeth Bryant, in "A Textbook's Theory," demonstrates that a composition textbook does not even need to reflect what we compositionists know about writing from our own research for us to adopt it. What, then, does the composition textbook need to do? Simply claim the status of "rhetoric." As Michael Kleine explains in "Teaching from a Single Textbook 'Rhetoric': The Potential Heaviness of the Book": "What is troubling about a written rhetoric is not that it is arbitrary and persuasive, but that too often it postures, as does The Law, as a kind of transcendent discourse, free of values and persuasive force—really not as a discourse at all, but a foundational truth" (137). And what can one say in the presence of the transcendental and the face of a foundational truth? Very little—or a lot if one chooses to deal with the reality of the subsidence cracks.

Of course, some teachers will continue to say that the textbook companies offer "tradition." But what is this tradition? On the whole, it is a pale tradition that valorizes the production of school writings and pro-motes the completion of exercises and assignments to certify the mas-tery of the conventions of something called "academic discourse," that impressionistic term applied to a kind of writing—though there is dis-agreement about what kind of writing it is—produced in the academy. However we describe this tradition, one thing remains the same: even a cursory glance at textbooks of the last fifty years demonstrates that noth-ing much changes in them even as our students continue to change. What was once argument is now multiculturalism; what was once multi-culturalism is now cultural studies; what was once cultural studies is now argument again—circulation without progress.

What do we expect? Most English academics do not ask composi-tionists to teach students to compose the unique, the, in some way, local, sacred, and perhaps abnormal text (in Richard Rorty's sense as explained by Xin Liu Gale [1996] in *Postmodern Authority*). Instead, we compositionists are charged to train our composition students for instrumental production. As poet Juliana Spahr puts it: "Clarity as a purely rhetorical attribute serves the purpose of a classical feature in lan-guage, namely, its instrumentality. To write is to communicate, express, witness, impose, instruct, redeem, or save—at any rate to *mean* and to send out *an unambiguous message*. Writing thus reduced to a mere vehicle of thought may be *used* to orient toward a goal or to sustain an act, but it does not constitute an act in itself" (2001, 119). So, as we teach writ-ing, writing, too, can become nothing. It is an instrument or vehicle; the content is added value that is measured out in grades. Compositionists have claimed the Western tradition of rhetoric as its foundation, even as its *raison d'etre*. We argue for the role of argument, the role of audience, even for the political purpose of writing a text. We have given up the idea that we should encourage students to explore the role of writing as "an act in itself," as something.

Instead, composition textbooks encourage a posturing and mimick-ing of the nation's elite. Sandra Jamieson (1997) has argued that the readers the textbook companies are selling, even the glossy, multicul-tural readers, perpetuate racism by requiring students to adopt, in their writing—again, for those end-of-the-essay questions for further thought and writing—white, male, liberal identities. The reader literally autho-rizes and promotes, in other words, whiteness and patriarchy. In this perspective, the process of "adopting" a textbook takes on new and trou-bling, to say the least, ramifications.

And in an article, "A Place in Which To Stand," that I published in *Relations, Locations, Positions* (Hurlbert 2006), I argue that because textbooks promise to be relevant wherever they are adopted, they must present material in a decontextualized fashion. The result is that they encourage students to see composing as a trans-situational process that they must follow to fulfill the ecological demands of the illusory null-geography that the textbooks themselves maintain—a geography where problems such as global heating are alleviated by more exemplary effort on the part of students, the poor and working class.

So, what is the answer to textbooks? *(Re)Visioning Composition Textbooks* contains two (besides David Bleich's "In Case of Fire, Throw In"). Peter Mortensen writes:

> . . . it would do good simply to have students ask some basic questions about the materiality of their textbooks. Thumb through to the copyright page. Notice who is credited for doing what. Who authored the rhetoric or edited the reader? Where does this person teach? What is his or her scholarly expertise? Who was the commissioning editor? Who published the book? Who printed it? And where? A union shop in the United States? Somewhere else in the world? Then close the book and ask how it got into the classroom. Who ordered it—and why? What wasn't chosen—and why? Who is teaching the class—and why? (Gale and Gale 1999, 227)

Mortenson is right. This would be a good beginning indeed.

Xin Liu Gale offers another strategy, that, as compositionists, "We need to resist the increasing control of the corporate culture of textbook publishing companies over the content textbooks and make textbooks truly part of the 'disciplinary matrix' of composition and rhetoric" (206). Truly, that the textbook companies do not create books that represent the best insights of composition researchers is a problem. But I do not think that we will be able to change this by negotiating from a position of weakness, which is surely the position we inhabit as long as the textbooks continue to make huge profits for their corporate publishers and fill our classrooms with nothing.

Consequently, I propose, here, a third option (the reasons for which I discuss more fully in the next section), in collaboration, I hope, with Gale, though my thinking here may perhaps be more radical than hers. I propose that we break the textbook companies' stranglehold on composition studies; that we get them out of the exhibition halls of our national conferences (and then learn to celebrate the new kind of conferences we would have in place of the annual, national, industry celebrations we currently have); that we more openly and strongly encourage all writing teachers to eschew the use of a composition textbook of any kind, and that, as a profession, we join to help writing program administrators fight for funding to hire qualified compositionists and to support writing teachers who are trying to learn to teach writing rather than the content of required textbooks (and we will need to do both at once as our universities are unlikely to halt the practice of adjuncting the teaching of composition any time soon).

Until then, what I suggest will no doubt take a long time to happen—if it does at all—let us agree to at least one, basic, student-centered principle: that to teach writing we will have students experience composing and conceptualize that experience, including what they learn from, and want to inspire in, others. There is hope in this one single proposal because there is hope in the aesthetic realm of composition. There is hope in reaching for local writing that gestures toward or participates in the global realm, in striving for the formally creative, linguistically innovative work—something unique that draws people together for the common good. This redefining will draw on various cultural traditions, blends them and reorients them toward the future and toward the conservation and reinvention of life.

Our reliance on textbooks, with their commitment to replication and tradition, puts us at risk of appearing more and more antiquated, out of touch with the world, and, in worst case scenarios, even expendable. As we hold to traditional forms that have been reduced to nothing, our fate may be harsh. As modernity and global heating accelerate, any commitment to conserving empty forms that are disconnected from the pressing meanings of everyday life may seem more and more irrelevant and unsustainable.

AND SO?

In order to construct pedagogies that resist racism, we need to understand our responses to others. The quest for this knowledge will take us to the origins of who we are. It is a journey through dark places where we confront truths about ourselves we might otherwise like to avoid. Julia Kristeva (1993a) maps the path in her collection, *Nations Without Nationalism*. Specifically, she explains how the origins of our racism can be found in the psychosexual processes of individuation where the unconscious processes that lead us to become ourselves also lead us to construct and maintain social commitments. Unfortunately, some of these commitments follow nationalist and racist impulses.

> In the beginning was hatred, Freud said basically (contrary to the well-known biblical and evangelical statement), as he discovered that the human child differentiates itself from its mother through rejection affect, through the scream of anger and hatred that accompanies it, and through the "no" sign as prototype of language and of all symbolism. To recognize the impetus of that hatred aroused by the other, within our own psychic dramas of psychosexual individuation—that is what psychoanalysis leads us to. It thus links its own adventure with the meditations each one of us is called upon to engage in when confronted with the fascination and horror that a different being produces in us, such meditations being prerequisite to any legal and political settlement of the immigration problem. (1993c, 29–30)

Racism's roots can be traced to our origins, to the processes of subjectivity through which we become who we are. Of course, this does not mean that we must necessarily be racist or even entertain racism. Nor does it mean that individuals are synonymous with the nation in which they live. It does mean, though, that we have some hard and unsettling work ahead of us if we want to resist racism. As Kristeva writes, "The complex relationships between cause and effect that govern social groups obviously do not coincide with the laws of the unconscious regarding a subject, but these unconscious determinations remain a constituent part, an essential one, of social and therefore national dynamics" (1993b, 50). If this is true, and I believe that it is, then we must learn ourselves, if we are to understand our affiliations—and our hatreds.

We compositionists must learn what we ignore when we commit to the extension of one cultural tributary to the exclusion of all others. We must learn the racism at the heart of our curriculum. We must learn the pain we both endure and perpetuate if we hope to animate our personal agency and possibility of a different way of teaching and being in the world—our agency. And I say this because I believe that education is still our best avenue for freeing ourselves from the cult of origins that informs the teaching of writing in our schools, colleges and universities: "Indeed, I am convinced that, in the long run, only a thorough investigation of our remarkable relationship with both the *other* and *strangeness within ourselves* can lead people to give up hunting for the scapegoat outside their group, a search that allows them to withdraw into their own 'sanctum' thus purified: is not the worship of one's 'very own'; of which the 'national' is the collective configuration, the *common denominator* that we imagine we have as 'our own,' precisely, along with other 'own and proper' people like us?" (1993b, 50–51).

We must learn ourselves as we learn about others because we must know ourselves if we are to know how and what we make of others. It is precisely in these processes that nationalism resides, and with hard and honest work we can find it there. We may seek anonymity in our national affiliation, in our relationship to others whom we deem to be like us. But, finally, this sort of affiliating will not, in and of itself, bring us peace. As Kristeva explains it, "devotees of origins anxiously seek shelter among their own, hoping to suppress the conflicts they have with them by projecting them on others—the strangers" (1993c, 3–4). We need to liberate ourselves of our conflict with our own kind by relegating responsibility onto others whom we deem to be different. After all, someone has to be responsible. We need to learn, in other words, how to free ourselves from the "cult of origins" that binds us to our hatreds and separates us from others and limits the possibilities for joining in cooperative action. We must learn, ultimately, that we are the strangers, that when we look at others, we look at ourselves.

"National pride" Kristeva writes, "is comparable, from a psychological standpoint, to the *good narcissistic image* that the child gets from its mother and proceeds, through the intersecting play of identification demands emanating from both parents, to elaborate into an ego ideal" (1993b, 52). When a child witnesses violence, or when a child's ego is damaged by humiliation, censure, loss, or the withholding of love, a child can develop a narcissistic syndrome. The symptoms of narcissism, contrary to the popular meaning of the word, can also include be self-loathing and fear, manifesting themselves in unsanctioned and unfocused hubris, in depression, withdrawal, or aggression, or some combination from the list (Hurlbert 2002). In other words, out of humiliation comes shame and the responses to shame, including:

> *Hatred of oneself,* for when exposed to violence, individuals despair of their own qualities, undervalue their own achievements and yearnings, run down their own freedoms whose preservation leaves so much to chance; and so they withdraw into a sullen, warm private world, unnamable and biological, the impregnable "aloofness" of a weird primal paradise—family, ethnicity, nation, race.
>
> A defensive hatred, the cult of origins easily backslides to a persecuting hatred. (Kristeva 1993c, 3)

Shame works against us. Instead of restoring the possibility of agency, it debilitates us. It locks us away in our own self-recriminations and retributions. We are damaged as we witness terrorism at home and abroad. We are damaged as we witness the violence of war and poverty and killing on the streets every day. We bear witness to that which tears at the hearts and minds of who we are, and we compensate for our fears and misgivings by retreating to the mystical realm of imagined origins and national affiliation. We stand with those whom we perceive to be like us; we stand against those whom we imagine would hurt us. But when it is our country at war, it is our "kind" perpetrating the violence. It is "we the people" who war with others. And as we applaud our nation's victories and give thanks for our good fortune, deep inside we know that we are the ones responsible, directly or indirectly, for the violence and the humiliation of others. We are the ones doing the damage, doing the killing, and we, too, are humiliated. Our shame leads to racism as we seek to reject this terrible strangeness within ourselves, as we endure depression's self-loathing, as embodied in the shame of our developed narcissism. We are the ones who hate, but it is so much easier to hate others than it is to uncover our hatred of ourselves and face the shame we endure.

In *Schemes of Shame: Psychoanalysis, Shame, and Writing,* Joseph Adamson, Hilary Clark and their contributors also explain writing's role in the process of restoring the self from the ravages of shame. As they articulate it, shame paralyzes the self by locking it in a struggle between the need for self-preservation and the fury of guilt, between commitment to the self and a humiliating voice from the past (1999, 11). Shame is a destructive emotion, one where the self continues to tear at the fabric and health of itself even as it seeks the peace of release and self-acceptance. Indeed, it is not hard to imagine the tremendous expenditure of energy that such a state of mind requires, nor is it hard to imagine the sense of powerlessness and even despair in the face of life's problems that might result. In this state, the subject's ability to act on behalf of their health, let alone the health of others, is undermined. Yet some seek health despite all. Some seek a necessary access to another that will allow them to reveal something of what troubles them, something about which they seek knowledge. Through artistic expression, some find a necessary revelation that reduces shame. Through writing, some explore the complications and contradictions of their lives—meaning making that marks the return of agency. Writing's artistic nature fosters this exploration. In and through the gifts of immediacy and distance through persona, writing enables self-discovery and, perhaps, recovery. But for a process to work in this way, writers "must be able to trust in an audience, in the willingness of others to see her as she is without undue fear of overexposure or invasion or rejection. This is why so many writers are so sensitive to the criticism of their work, seeing it as a rejection of themselves" (28–29). It is, obviously, hard to trust when one feels exposed, when one's hatreds, resentments, fears, and pain are intimated by the words on the page. It is hard and it is courageous, and writers do it much of the time. They trust and they explore their creativity. They trust and they write, and when they do, the desire to heal and contribute is stronger than the pull of isolation and the damaging power of shame. They write in love and, as Adamson and Clark tell us, this, too is a necessary ingredient for the restoration of the self (28–29). We compositionists have important keys already in our hands—if we would just use them.

In "Reflecting on Self-Relevant Experiences: Adult Age Differences," Cora Rice and Monisha Pasupathi (2010, 488) write that "telling a story serves the purpose of lowering the person's engagement with that story—rendering the story part of the personal past and less a part of the present and future." Their argument is that through the process of disclosing the past, a storyteller's engagement with the emotional content of the narrative is reduced. Using writing to explore a negative experience that would limit a person's subjectivity offers, then, positive emotional effects. Telling the narrative of a negative experience and examining and even critiquing its content is part of a human being's processes for maintaining and developing the self. It is one of the chief mechanisms a person has for restoring the possibility for taking action in the face of societal, as well as personal, ills.

Of course, healing from a cage of shame can take a lifetime and many retellings. It is obviously not a matter of writing the right thing, of healing the self one semester and then healing one's culture the next. Rather, it is a matter of working toward health. It is a matter of writing to unlock the cage of racism which keeps us from seeing ourselves as well as others, and then of figuring out how to unlatch and open a door, and finally, stepping through, of finding and accepting ourselves *in* the ways we need to work for peace.

A composition class begins with writers learning to look inward, to articulate and interpret experience, including one's gifts and challenges, loves and fears—as well as the "-isms" that haunt us. A composition class teaches writers how to form experience in print so that it can be interpreted and critiqued, to make a work that opens vision and understanding. As a teacher of writing, I want students to know what it feels like to write life—to know how good that feels—how it sends one, for instance, to bed at the end of the day hopeful and resolute that they can make something worth the making and the reading. And in this I propose that writing is a liberating activity, or at least that it creates opportunities for healing, for health, and for further actions. My point here is that we can help our students to claim writing in its importance, and that by doing so we help them heal from the effects of the textbook corporations' commodifications, the goal of which always is, again, to have teachers adopt their textbooks, the vehicles through which writing is turned into nothing for students. As George Ritzer points out, one can work to overcome the sense of loss that the corporate, nothing-product induces. We have the power of agency on our side. We can make pedagogical choices, in other words, that can help our students, and ourselves, to heal from the effects of the corporate production of nothing (2007, 203–216). We can help students experience writing as a craft, as the relevant and socially important subjective expression that it is, rather than as a corporate-sponsored production of nothing. The healing and the craft-pride that follows would restore and further develop agency and possibility, a hunger for something. Craft-pride would arise in the production of writing—not from a nationalist pride in a state-sponsored culture, which is, finally, a response to national fear and shame—but pride in the composing of something that crosses into the realm of health and relevancy, far more important commodities for a threatened world.

Internationalism inspires understanding and peace by standing as an antidote to Eurocentrism's universalist tendencies. One of the best ways to understand, work with, and live with others is to learn as much as we can about how they make meaning. Learning about others' cultural inheritances demonstrates respect. The better we communicate with others, the more we get to know about them and ourselves. The more we cooperate and collaborate with others, the more we construct structures and opportunities for tackling the difficult world problems we face.

As compositionists, we know these things. We all know that the best, most successful pedagogies honor all the cultural and national inheritances of the students in the room. There are, of course, many ways to enact this honoring, but student-centeredness has its bottom-line qualities. Specifically, it requires that we encourage each student to draw upon all their gifts, including the best, most humane endowments of race, gender, sexual preference—and nationality—in their attempts to learn about writing.

IN OTHER WORDS, IT CARRIES OVER

Greg Urban describes the effects of reading this way: "If you read a book you yourself have not written, culture carries over to you" (2001, 73). As we have seen, the concept of culture is hardly an inert, fixed entity or category, and neither is the ideology it serves—nationalism. The manifest of its contents and the itinerary of its course will depend on the theorist keeping track. For my analysis, the cultural content—the meaning, manner, style, thinking, emotions, and ideology—that is exchanged in the reading process affects the manner in which we compose.

This exchange is a material process and so can be traced (as Bruce Horner [2000] importantly taught us about material practices in *Terms of Work in Composition: A Materialist Critique*). How I think about my subject, how I go about the preparation to write—what I read, what research I do, what materials I gather—is textured by the books I read. Even how I sit at the computer is oriented by the manner in which the books I am writing about address me or how the subject matter that they deal with make me feel. At times I begin to write by attending to the text of another, not necessarily in the sense of having a book open next to me in order to type a quote from it into my text—though sometimes I do— but in the sense of having some energy of text or line of thinking from a text in my head. I attend to it as I compose so that my text is, in some way, a response. As a writer, I try to compose the energy of the other text into my own. I compose in relation, then, to a text that is literally in my head, and figuratively part of me, texturing, to a degree, my identity.

I seek out the writing of the other, then, because I am trying to work against the limitations on my abilities, to complete myself by listening to the other. This is the project of being human, but I will never fully engage in it if I do not continue to try and escape the baser strains contained in national and racial inheritances.

PART THREE

Key
The Composition Classroom

EXHIBIT A

In his *ABC of Reading*, Ezra Pound attempted a theory and method for the study of literature, though the book also contains a handful of "composition exercises" (1934, 64–65). The first half of the *ABC of Reading* is a compilation of criticism and writing assignments, a kind of guide for educators, whatever the types of literature or writing that they might teach. The composition exercises are mostly pedestrian, including such activities as having students exchange papers to identify and cut extraneous words in their writing. There are a few more interesting ideas, though, including having students exchange papers to look for words that are out of place and decide "whether this alteration makes the statement in any way more interesting or more energetic" (64).

The second half of the *ABC of Reading* contains a series of literary readings or "exhibits" for students. These "exhibits"—including Chaucer, John Donne, Robert Browning, and Walt Whitman—are Western to the point that they may be said to be as much an exhibition of Eurocentrism in literary studies as anything else. Despite Pound's claims about the necessity of intercultural exchange, he did not make the connection to the classroom. A mistake too often seen in the history of United States education; a mistake too often followed.

WHAT ARE YOU BURNING TO TELL THE WORLD?

My composition class begins with writers learning to look inward in order to articulate and interpret the many experiences of their lives and world, including one's gender, loves, fears, and prejudices. The goal is to have students write a lot so as to become better artists of and activists in their own lives. And in this process they learn to address their worlds.

On the surface of it, my pedagogy looks simple. In fact, my first-year composition class consists of the following few assignments (all of which I explain below in subsequent sections):

1. A book manuscript (which later becomes)

2. A desk-top published book

3. A foreword to a book written by another student in the class

4. The keeping of a response folder.

In *Letters for the Living: Teaching Writing in a Violent Age,* Michael Blitz and I (1998) described the pedagogy we developed for a first-year composition class in which we have students write semester-long projects, short books—some might call them chapbooks—on what they are burning to tell the world. Over the years that have passed since the publication of *Letters for the Living,* I have continued to develop our pedagogy. Specifically, I additionally ask students to interpret and write about the significance of their books from different rhetorical perspectives. I now also have each student write a foreword for a book written by one of their colleagues in the room. In these forewords, each student identifies and discusses the key issue in the book they are reading, and each student connects the book to larger cultural or historical issues or trends. (This work often requires some research, but as research writing is taught in a class subsequent from composition at my university, research is not a requirement in my class.)

The assigned length of my students' books varies from semester to semester, depending on the size of the class and the number of classes I am teaching, but usually the books run from fifteen to twenty, single-spaced, typed pages—though I can imagine teaching situations where I would set different, even shorter, page requirements. The goal is, as writing teachers know, to get students to write as much as possible because practice is the best way to facilitate the development of writing fluency. At the same time, it is important not to assign so much writing that students become frustrated with work they think they can never complete.

In addition, I now also have students write, at various times during the semester, about what they are learning about writing from someone else in the room, or what insights they can learn and apply from an excerpt about rhetoric from rhetorical traditions other than the Eurocentric (I occasionally, when there is a space in the class schedule, hand out an excerpt or explain a principle in class—more on this below). I do this so that students will learn how we develop awareness about how to write from others and not only from teachers. I do this so that students might begin to experience the international dimension of composing. I do this so that they develop the lifelong learning practices in which writers engage or could meaningfully engage.

Again, I start my class on the opening day by asking my first-year students to consider the question, "What are you burning to tell the world?" At this initial point, my students generally wonder what it is they could possibly write. At the beginning of what is usually the second or third class, I have the students sit in a whole class circle to discuss possible book topics, and I use occasional breakout groups when I sense that students need time to discuss these topics among themselves. By the end of two to three of these whole class and group discussions, my students generally know what it is they are going to write about, or, at least, have a pretty good idea about how to get to it (though some students, usually a handful in each class, require individual appointments with me before they find their book topics).

After this period of invention, the class schedule is simple. For the first half of the semester, students draft (sometimes in, but mostly out of, class) or have class writing workshops (see the next section). At midterm they hand in manuscripts of their books (these manuscripts are not entire drafts of the books. Usually I do not ask for the last quarter to a third of the books at midterm, as the students are still writing them). For the second half of the semester, the students finish and revise their books, write a foreword for one of their colleagues, continue the workshops, and desktop publish (after class presentations on desktop publishing) the final version of their book—something done electronically, in some cases, as well. The forms and styles of the books are established through class discussion, with all of the students offering ideas to each other, and through individual conferences.

THE CLASS WORKSHOP

I assign no outside readings in my composition classes beyond the students' writing and any forewords or other sources that the students choose to read for inspiration as they write their books or forewords. There are also no grammar lessons outside of the editing of the manuscripts that I do with students during individual conferences.

The class workshop takes the form of discussions about the students' writing. On assigned days, a student distributes to each member of the class a copy of one page from either the book or foreword they are writing. This is done during the class immediately preceding the one in which the writing will be discussed. (That way each student comes to class having already thought about the writing and with already prepared comments. That way, too, all the students have read the same page of writing and our class discussion can go deeply into both praise and suggestions for revision.) These workshops are student-centered, with the students sitting in one large circle and taking turns at offering response to a page from one student's book. Each student has a turn—and a responsibility—to offer something in response, whether it is praise or a suggestion for revision. Students need training, of course, in how to do this. I begin by telling my students that they must use the following comment forms in responding to their colleagues' papers:

How would it change your meaning if you added _____?

How would it change your meaning if you cut _____?

How would it change your meaning if you moved _____ to _____?

How would it change your meaning if you combined _____ and _____?

I like _____ because _____.

I'd like to know more about _____.

I constructed these comments after reading Ann Berthoff's essay on marginal commentary, "Learning the Uses of Chaos." This article demonstrates Berthoff's abiding interest in hermeneutics and deepens the meaning of expressivist thought in composition far beyond the typical academic reductions, even as it anticipates—lays the groundwork for—much of postprocess theory: "We should focus on the shifting character of meaning and the role of perspective and context, and we can do so by raising such questions as . . . : 'How does it change your meaning if you put it this way?'" (1979, 71). To Berthoff's focus on meaning, I have spliced common but useful revisions, the initial ideas for which I got while reading Quintilian's well-worn list of revisions for speech writers: "Addition, excision, and alteration" (X. iv. 1).

Berthoff suggests that when we respond to student writing, we should only ask questions that lead to a reconsideration of the meaning, and we should ask questions because they leave authority for texts squarely in the hands of students. And since student writers—indeed, most writers—can quickly take offense when their writing is criticized, I insist on students using questions when responding to each other's work. Questions are not commands for revision, and so, hopefully, they do not siphon agency. In addition to questions, I have the students offer statements that tell writers what they are doing well. Positive response is instructive when it is specific and detailed, rather than ambiguous, as in "Good writing"; consequently, I have the students explain why they think something is good when they do, as in "I like _____ because _____."

I ask students to make four of these comments per page of writing in the workshops (and they may use or reuse any of the comment questions or statements that I provide any number of times that they wish). As the semester progresses, the students internalize these questions and the transformation that I seek begins to happen: the students begin to apply the questions to their own writing—even, as they frequently report, when they are writing—and reading—for other classes. When this transition occurs, the students experience considerable growth as writers. They have an understanding of what their readers experience when they read, and they think about how to meet the needs of readers.

In addition to the four questions or positive statements, I also ask students to write short notes to the writers at the end of the workshop papers. These notes reflect connection to the content of the writing, the emotion the reader felt, or the continued thinking that writing leads them to do. They may even be personal words of praise or encouragement, which, surely, all writers also need.

As the final part of the workshop process, I ask students to photocopy the papers to which they respond. At the end of the semester, or during writing conferences, I have students analyze their responses to their colleagues' workshop papers. This gives them opportunity to articulate and examine the significance of the skills they develop over time as they respond to the writing of others.

BOOKS

The majority of the students who enroll in my writing classes at Indiana University of Pennsylvania are European American, but many of my students are also African, Asian, Latin, or Native Americans, who come from cities like Pittsburgh, Philadelphia, or elsewhere, or even the neighboring countryside. Other students in my undergraduate classes come from other states and cities, from around the world, from Asia or Africa or the Middle East. They are, in other words, of different races and nationalities.

Over the years that I have been asking them to write books on what they are burning to tell the world, I have seen students write about a wide range of subject matter. I have received books, no matter the country of origin, in which students have written about families in divorce, absent parents, present parents, themselves as parents, death of loved ones, neglect, abandonment, abuse, violence, illness, the failure of relationships, alcoholism, addiction, crime, racism, ecological issues, vegetarianism, occupations, the transition from high school to college, survival, love, respect for role models, home towns and trips to distant places, including coming to America, meeting people, growing and changing.

Some critics have complained that my pedagogy is an expressivist "anything goes" plan for a composition course, a class where students can write about anything that they want to write, even books about their pets or prom nights. That is a misreading of what I do. During class discussions I make clear to my students that books have to have a point, a tension, a critical question, a personal, and social significance—a reason for being that keeps students and their university audience (the class, including me) interested for the entire semester—and beyond. A book about how much a student likes his girlfriend, for instance, is unlikely to interest many students or teachers for very long—if at all—unless there is an underlying question or issue. Frankly, the other students are often ready to say this, as is this teacher. The goal is to offer careful, effective advice and help students learn how to hear it and make positive use of it.

In this regard, my pedagogy is a cultural and political project. It is a pedagogy that helps students learn how to use personal experience in order to access and identify, critique and respond to systemic and historical issues. My project is at the confluence of the psychological and sociological elements of composition studies (and thus meets the writing requirements of most colleges in one way or another). It is this point of confluence, it seems to me, that is unfortunately lost in many discussions of cultural and critical studies, where anthology pieces or a teacher's particular interests and ideological investments are too often, from what I have seen of pedagogies and materials from around the country, the center of class study. Many of my students' books are about the experience of living in the United States, but the life issues my students explore are certainly often applicable to other living circumstances. Who does not suffer pain, violence, disappointment, loneliness, and fear in life, or some combination of these? In other words, my students are addressing the world in their books. They are healing. They are restoring the psychological possibility for action.

Of course, some students write about international travel and the lessons learned. For instance, a few years ago, a student wrote his book about his deployment experience as a US Army Ranger in the former Yugoslavia:

> The Serbian had gone out the back of the house and had one of the Kosovar people tied and was dragging her with him. Just as I exited the back door, the soldier dropped his hostage and turned toward my Ranger teammate and me. As he turned and fired, I fired a warning shot in his direction. His round hit my teammate in the leg. I fired three rounds. I knew I hit him. The soldier quickly dropped to the ground and then rolled over onto his side. As I approached him to check to see if he were still alive, I noticed he was still breathing and showing his hand, as if to say, "I give up." After removing his weapon, I rolled him onto his stomach and saw that I struck him in his upper left shoulder. I then applied a pressure dressing to the wound to help stop the bleeding.
>
> I had actually just tried to kill a man.

This, too, is the truth of international experience and exchange: it is sometimes conflicted, confusing, and contradictory. The troubling fallout can follow a person home. Another of my students recently wrote about such a return. In her book, she wrote about how her decision to go back to college was part of a resolution to reconstruct her life after her husband came home a changed man after his fifteen-month deployment in the Gulf War:

Sometimes I look back on those fifteen months as the best part of our marriage. Matt would tell me about his feelings for me. Matt complimented me and told me how beautiful I was. He made me feel special. Now he doesn't even look at me.

Instead of coming home and renewing his marriage, Matt spent all his time in the garage behind the house, working on cars.

I tried and tried talking to Matt about how I felt, and he did not seem to understand. I did not deserve to be treated as a maid that cleans up after him all the time . . .

I am one who has never wanted to give up on anything. I have never believed in divorce and think that marriage should last a lifetime. Now I have to decide if I go against my beliefs and start a new chapter in my life. The decision to stay with Matt throughout the deployment was an easy one. But the decisions Matt made on his own after the deployment do not make it so easy to stay with him.

This writer had lived alone in the rural and unfinished farmhouse that she and her husband were working on before he was deployed. She faced fearful nights alone, waking up at every bump in the night, and every thought of the dangers her husband faced. When he came home, she expected things to be good again. Instead, Matt came home and shut her out. As a result, she had to begin to make decisions for herself, even though the roots of these judgments could be traced to the other side of the world and even the halls of government.

Students are telling us about their places—and ours on this planet. They are exploring the feelings they experience and the emotions they see in others. They are trying to understand life on earth—their own and their own in relation to others. And they are making connections.

A student from Malaysia recently took my composition class and wrote his book about his home. He wrote about the rural area in which he grew up, the beauty of the mornings, and the congestion and pollution of the neighboring city. He wrote of the house he grew up in through the imagery of youth—his "castle," which he both loved and hated. He loved his memories of the times he shared with his family there, but hated some of the history of the land—the civil war, the Malayan Emergency. It is a book of poetry and prose, visions and facts; it is a book about his sister, the "Princess playing in the garden," and it is a book about the residue of war, a vision in which the mountains my student played in as a child disappear: "The mountains are gone / Covered by the corpses and the soil." It is a book about how history is always with us—how at times it seems to obliterate the present.

Seeing a connection between rural destruction and urban decay, a student from the United States, from the Bronx, wrote the foreword for this Malaysian student's book: "While the Bronx is nowhere near a mountainous area, the buildings that occupy the borough are my mountains. They too are multi-colored and range in size. I have found myself climbing these mountains as well, but my paths to the top were elevators, stairwells, and fire escapes. Interestingly enough, I have found the mountains I climbed gone as well. In their place, I find empty lots, filled with rubble and earth." Our students write about home and the loss of home, about the beauty and the fall from grace, as well as possible returns. A student from Taiwan recently wrote her mixed-genre book about how she lives the tension of leaving home while carrying her home with her wherever she goes, even to the university where I teach:

> My town
> Green
> Mountains teach me
> In a silent way
> The Green teaches me
> To view the world with broad visions
>
> Leave my town
> Carry The Green in my heart
> Every night I fall asleep
> I dream a Green dream
> Whenever, wherever
> Green days
> My everything . . .
> I'm from a Green Dream.

Another student, from South Korea, who was studying in the United States, took my class and also wrote a mixed-genre book with, in parts, a decidedly poetic feel in which he portrayed the gritty aspects of the difficult lives of the men and women working in the old fish market in the seacoast city of Busan:

The *iljimae* (married women) who work in *Jagalchi* Fish Market are a tough breed.

Here and there, crying seagulls recall strong iljimae in early morning, though the sun doesn't show up yet. Kind-hearted iljimae feed them on a piece of their meat. However, they are pissed off. To make their hungers up, seagulls are begging like dogs. Aunt's handkerchief tied to her head tightly flutters roughly through salted wind.

Today fisher hasn't caught anything, just desperation. Looking at the bitter sky, hearing his wife's deploring sound, smoking toxic cigarette. His forehead has one more wrinkle. His hands and heart become hardened skin. Their baby is crying and crying continually.

"Let's go to *pochangmacha*!" Nice smell of boiling seafood come out of tent covered with red nylon cloths on the *Jagalchi* Street and attracting passengers wanting a drink.

"Let's drink until getting drunk. I will buy *soju* to all you guys! We have everything in our hand. We can do anything in the world. Enjoy your life! Toast damn world! I am rich man! I am rich guy! Rich . . . Rich . . . God damn money."

"An ancient said from once upon a time, man's life has to be short and thick. Just today we forget all things." Especially today's shot is really bitter like biting gallbladder. "Why does my tear come out of my eye? Why do I want to cry the whole night?" Deep sigh. Deep smoke.

WHY A BOOK?

Several educators have explored the value of having students write and publish books as part of informed grade school, high school, and college curricula. Nancie Atwell (1987) has described ways for publishing school writing, including the important role that publishing plays in classroom student writing groups. Anne Wescott Dodd, Ellen Jo Ljung, Brenda Szedeli, and Sheryl L. Guth (1993) have discussed the crucial ways that publishing inspires students to see the social significance of their work. Janet Irby (1993) has explained how encouraging student publication can help to inspire the development of active, rather than passive, forms of subjectivity. Maria Varelas, Christine C. Pappas, Sofia Kokkino, and Ibett Ortiz (2010) have even argued that having students create and publish illustrated science books encourages learning at the same time that it provides windows into student understanding of science and their world. Lastly, Tim Laquintano (2010) explains that one of the best ways to help students be ready for the world that awaits them upon graduation is to help them understand the digital nature of writing and publishing. As Lacquitano reports, the dawn of the ebook era continues to blur the distinction between writer and reader by placing each in ever-more collaborative relationships. We teach for and in a world of books whose interactive dimensions are yet to be fully explored and understood.

As for myself, years of reading, study, and teaching all lead me to the same conclusions: students who write for publication tend to invest a tremendous amount of effort in learning how to write. Moreover, students who write semester-long pieces remain in the recursive processes of reflecting, composing, revising, and editing. Indeed, by going over and over a single piece of writing as many times as possible, students learn more about writing than students who perform short, exercise writing. Students who write longer texts that emerge from organic needs, including their questions, concerns, and desires to explore the meaning of their lives and worlds, have greater opportunity for developing their understanding of the significance of meaning and meaning making, of critical thinking and coherence in form, and perhaps most importantly, of the consequences of meaning. They have greater chances to develop, in other words, a profound sense of craft. I am not alone in these observations. Patrick Finn (1999, 122) explains in *Literacy with an Attitude:* "It's commonplace for students who first begin to write lengthy papers to be surprised to find that what they wrote on page twelve is inconsistent with what they wrote on page two. With experience, writers are no longer surprised; they expect this to happen. Writing permits us to reflect on our knowledge and beliefs, notice inconsistencies, and work them out."

In "Longer, Deeper, Better," researchers Jay Simmons and Timothy McLaughlin report findings that support Finn's and my views. Their three-year study, "Producing Writers," for which they received a United States Department of Education's Fund for the Improvement of Postsecondary Education (FIPSE) grant, proceeded from the position that first-year developmental and ESL students need to be deprogrammed from the short, error-fixated, limited nature of five-paragraph, weekly theme writing. The participating teachers, who came from community and four-year colleges and universities, thus developed a writing course in which students wrote fewer but longer pieces along with accompanying texts in which the students reflected on their writing experiences.

Based on the portfolios the students produced, the researchers assessed the writing samples for such issues as length, ideas, organization, language and mechanics. But the results of the study go far beyond the quality of the writing:

> We find that in writing extended pieces (1,000 words or more), developmental and second-language writers, often cautious by nature and wary of error, stretch out as writers in ways not encouraged by shorter, more modest assignments. We find that students who are not prone to reflection gain much as writers by thinking about their pieces and by writing assignments that integrate reflective writing. We also find that assignments that bring reading and research into the mix enhance the process of exploration, reflection, and meaning making. We find that as students develop an enhanced sense of audience (through reading and responding to another's work), student writing becomes better shaped, better developed and more sharply focused. Above all, we find that challenging assignments, coupled with peer review and response, help *all* students to become better writers. (2003, 425)

The outside evaluators of the study agreed with the findings. As Simmons and McLaughlin report: "'Producing Writers' outside evaluators determined that our participants learned about their weaknesses, about editing, and about writers and what readers liked and disliked, thus confirming that increasing length and duration of work develops the 'habits, preferences, and judgments' of writers, what Gardner and Hatch would call 'abilities,' whatever the age. And length and duration increased with regular peer response to drafts of more challenging assignments" (421).

Craft is never only a matter of craft. Learning about our writing is learning about both what and how we think and know. It is learning about how we approach our work, how we see it through, and what is possible when we attend to our own words, how we take up our tools and media. Learning about our writing is a matter of learning about ourselves—everyone's life challenge. It should not be surprising for readers of Simmons and McLaughlin's article that when the students chose which of their semester writings to put in their portfolios for assessment, they chose the ones in which they felt the greatest sense of investment. Their personal writings on experience, with accompanying reflection, were most often the longest texts the students produced, and even the students themselves reported that they put more time and effort into them than they did their shorter cultural critique or persuasive pieces (424). The goal is, then, to encourage students to explore their experiences, and as they do so, to examine the critical implications—both for themselves and for an audience—a natural part of the reflective level of personal writing. And, simply stated, the best way to achieve these ends is to have students write longer pieces.

Only by writing long pieces can students learn these things. And, yet, they—we—still need others to give a full measure of meaning to our words.

FOREWORDS

At midterm each semester, when the students hand in manuscripts of their books, I distribute a copy of each student's manuscript to someone else in the class. I then ask each student to write a foreword for the manuscript that they received. I have several reasons for doing this, but I especially want my student writers to see one of their colleagues read and take their writing seriously, to treat it as worthy of study, as writing that presents issues over which students can connect, discuss, research, and establish some sort of affiliation—though these are not always so easy to do.

I remember one student who wrote about growing up African American in a largely white and, by his estimation, racist town in Pennsylvania. In that particular class, I had the students switch their books randomly for the writing of the forewords. As it turned out, the black student's book ended up in the hands of a white, male student who, earlier in the semester, had made a racially insensitive comment (though, to be honest, most of the time he was just quiet, speaking only when required in workshop sessions).

After the books were exchanged, I asked the students to sit in our whole class circle and discuss, one by one, the book they randomly received, especially what strategies they might use to write their forewords. When it came time for the white male to talk, he looked at the writer of the book, at me, and at the writer of the book again. He said, "I'm not sure I am the right person to write the foreword for your book. Maybe someone else should do it."

The writer looked him directly in the eyes from across the circle and said, "No, I think you are exactly the right person to write the foreword to my book." This writer could not have been more correct, of course (in fact, correct, brave, strong, and generous all at the same time). His classmate needed to come face to face with difference and address it if he were to change—to grow.

But sometimes learning emerges from a point of similarity. I remember one semester when a student raised his hand during a full class circle discussion and asked if he could write the foreword for a girl in the room whose book was about being hospitalized for the treatment of depression. He related to the class that he, too, was treated for depression, and so he thought he could bring some useful insight to the writing of the foreword. The girl looked at him with relief on her face. It was a look that seemed to say, "Thank God someone understands. I am not alone." Of course I could have been—and could still be—inscribing emotions onto her face that were not there, but I do not think so. But just as important as what that young woman was learning about compassion in that class moment, was the lesson being taught to me about bravery. I said that as I, too, had been treated for depression, I appreciated the honesty and strength of both of these writers. I suggested that indeed this young man could bring insight to the writing. And in that moment I felt I saw relief on the faces of both of these writers. And maybe I felt some myself.

UBUNTU: RHETORICAL PRINCIPLES AT WORK

As any writer knows, and as many others such as Marian Mohr (1984) and Morris Young (2004) have argued in various ways and from different perspectives, one of the challenges a compositionist must face is how to encourage students to revisit, re-see, and revise their work.

As I stated above, at points in the semester I ask students to consider their work in light of a principle from a rhetorical tradition other than the Eurocentric. One semester, in one of the first sessions of my composition class, when the students were just starting to write their books, I took a few minutes of class time to explain the concept of *ubuntu* (for a discussion of *ubuntu*, see Part 1, "Cage: The Provincial Composition"). As I explained to my students, *ubuntu*, or the spirit of harmony at the center of human being, requires that a speaker—or in the case of my classroom, a writer—use their words to reinforce unity and harmony among people, or restore it when it is damaged. I also discussed the fact that in this vision of the rhetorical moment, speaking or writing has unique and historical, as well as contemporary, significance. I explained that a writer whose composing is influenced by the concept of *ubuntu* might naturally seek the assent of his or her imagined readers. But *ubuntu's* historical component should lead a writer to seek, additionally, the blessing of those who have gone before, such as his or her ancestors, for the words he or she might write.

And so I asked each of my students to write an impromptu short letter to their ancestors and explain their book's topic and ask for their ancestors' approval for its writing. I told them that to gain their ancestors' approval, they would each need to articulate how they intended to use their books to establish or access unity and harmony with others.

One male student wrote to his ancestors about how he wanted his book to address the problem of the fat-rich diet of his family and how it was leading to ill-health: "Obviously we see that through the years our life style has been sedentary and synthetic. We live shorter, less meaningful lives, because through and since slavery we have lost our way of life . . . I want to break that mold and dream that I can do differently.

Well, at least what I eat and my physical health which I trust will lead me to spiritual and mental purity." Ahmad's quest for an organic approach to life, where he might connect his diet to his faith and contribute to the well-being of his family led him on a quest, as recorded in his book, for truth that might restore the harmony of balance to his family.

Another student explained to his ancestors the need he felt to tell the world about what he learned about fairness while doing service work in Mexico:

> I'm writing this story about my experiences in the country of Mexico while my friends and I built a house for a young couple who were newlyweds in one of the poorest cities in the country.
>
> I'm sharing this story because I believe that what I saw and what I witnessed should be shared with other people. Others should know the everyday struggles and hardships these people struggle through everyday. . . . I want people to know what it is like to know they won't live beyond the age of 65 just because of the hardships they endure.

Another student who had served in the Army in Iraq wrote a book in which she took up one of the hardest of roles in the face of nationalism, that of a truth-teller: "I'm writing a book about the untold stories of what really goes on in the military in Iraq. The topic is all the sex scandals, prostitution and soldiers overdosing while in Iraq. I feel I should write about this to let people back home worrying about their loved ones know. I think people . . . deserve to know the truth."

One student wrote to her ancestors to explain why she was writing a book about an experience where two convicted child pornographers tried to steal her sisters, ages five and seven, while they were in her care in a small town Wal-Mart:

> I care about my sisters. I never thought about how I would feel if they were to leave my life or anything would happen to them. I would never want anyone to feel the pain of seeing someone they love being taken away from them; I am most happy that I am able to tell them how much I care and love them.
>
> I want to write this book to show people to not always worry about the materialistic things in life and to care more about the people that matter—you never know the last time you can tell someone you love them.

That semester, several students wrote about the need to restore their families in some way. One student wrote to her ancestors about having a younger brother whom she did not know: "I think a lot about my brother each and every day. I think about how he is doing and how he is being raised. I decided to write my book about my brother to get my emotions out about him. I think maybe it will help me get through and possibly one day when he finds out the truth, I could show him my book."

And in writing to restore families, some recognized while writing to their ancestors, that they really wrote to restore themselves: "I'm writing this book because I have never really let out my true feelings about losing my grandma in our house fire. If other people can benefit from this book then I think that's wonderful . . . but really this book is to let out what I've been holding in so that I can sleep at night without worrying if my house will catch fire again."

And some wrote to explain to their ancestors that the need to heal superseded the need to keep family secrets. For instance, a gay student wrote to his ancestors to explain his need to write about his sexuality and how he had kept it hidden: "[I]t needs to be said. And not just for myself, but for others like me that may hear what I have to say some day." And in another and very different instance, a female student who cut herself wrote: "I need people to realize that this is okay to talk about, especially if they don't understand it. I want people to break free of the judgments and stereotypes. This part of my life shaped who I am, . . . and I want to explain why I felt that way." Or, as another female student wrote: "Dear Ancestors, I am writing a book in College Writing class about my eating disorder. I know you would be proud of me for even being in college and even more proud that I am writing. I know that you probably wouldn't understand anorexia and bulimia because you were used to never wasting food and eating and appreciating all of the food that you had. But I live in a very different generation where being very skinny is a good thing."

The ability to imagine past realities was—and is—a challenge. And perhaps the students sometimes get the past wrong or take a little longer to learn it. But in the telling—in explaining their purposes to their ancestors, my students also learned certain important lessons—not the least of which was gratitude. Indeed, some students explained the need to give thanks in the midst of hardships or the blessings of life. One student wrote to her ancestors about how her mother raised her, provided for her, and kept her safe in a difficult urban setting: "I am writing this book to honor my mother for all the work and sacrifice that was needed to raise three children by herself. Once my father died she had to assume the role of breadwinner and parent. Some people have difficulty with either of these roles, but my mom was a wonderful parent while keeping food on the table. My book is meant to inspire parents and children that have experienced loss in their lives."

And occasionally, a student picked a particular ancestor to whom they wished to write. One student I remember wrote her book about her broken family, difficult teenaged mistakes, and how getting a job in a small, Pennsylvania town offered her a chance to turn her life around. When asked to write to her ancestors to explain her book, she chose to write to the one closest to her:

> Ancestors, mainly Papa. I am writing a book for my English class. It's based on my transition while working at the pizza shop. I know you would approve because you told me how proud of me you were. . . . I know that all my other ancestors would also be proud to know what I've become and without working at the pizza shop who knows where I would have ended up. This book is my way of thanking Carl and Sharon [the owners of the shop] and also to congratulate myself and be proud of who I am.

And a rural student wrote:

> Dear Ancestors,
> You are the reason I am able to tell this story. It is about the lifestyle that you created for us, and I feel this story should be told. People need to know how a farmer lives and about the great people who do the farming.

To be honest, I cannot say with any certainty that all of these students needed to write to their ancestors to achieve these understandings of their purposes. Indeed, I do not believe that such a claim would be true. Yet I do think that any tool that a teacher can use to help students to rethink what they do in their writing is a valuable one. Besides, as students sometimes tell me, they take the activities of my class and apply them later in other writing circumstances. And, also to be honest, there are times when I can say with no uncertainty that the introduction of a rhetorical principle can have a profound effect on my students' thinking—and in the following section, I tell of such a semester.

MINDFUL TEACHING

One semester, I asked my first-year composition students to reconsider their books in light of the principles of communication that Thich Nhat Hanh (1998) discusses in *Interbeing*. Specifically, I asked my students to consider the ways in which their books inspired anger and suffering, or peace and healing; whether they facilitated or closed down communication between themselves and others.

Many of my students must have seen that facilitating or opening communication meant forgiving someone they were writing about, especially when the person caused them pain. It was not always easy for them. As one student wrote, "My baby cousin was killed by a drunk driver, and I want to get my point [about the effects of drinking and driving] across without being rude or hurtful. But it is difficult because I have anger towards people who drink and drive."

Another student wrote about forgiving his brother: "My book is about waking up and finding out that my brother tried to commit suicide and all the emotions I went through throughout the day. I believe my book will open communication because I am writing about how I felt and asking questions rather than judging. I'm looking for a reason, a cause; I'm not blaming anyone. I'm just searching." Such profound words: "I'm looking for a reason, a cause; I'm not blaming anyone. I'm just searching." How honest; how strong. So often our students, just like ourselves, are searching for the means and resources for forgiving someone. I have had so many students, over the years, who have written about the fathers who were not in their lives. And I have watched as they searched for healing. As one of my students recently wrote in her book, *The Dad I Never Had*, "I'm still healing from my dad not being in my life. I hope my book inspires others to forgive and forget, just like I am learning to do." And another wrote her book about her father who had spent most of her life in prison as a result of arrests related to his drug addiction. After talking about Hanh's position on using writing to open communication and inspire healing, she thought about her book in terms of her revising process: "This will be in the back of my head when I reread my pages. I want to be sure to be more understanding towards my biological father and his illness. I will try not to take my anger out on him in my writing." What an intelligent and mature response to her own writing, which easily could have turned into diatribe, into an infantile venting of rage. In another instance, a student discovered, through Hanh's teachings, an understanding of the living implications of rhetoric, a knowledge that has the power to enrich a student's life well beyond the end of any semester. When writing about her book in which she explores experiences with her alcoholic and physically abusive father: "I am telling the truth about everything my father has done to me and my family . . . at the end of the book I forgive my father. Knowing this makes me want to express everything I have experienced with my father and family as well. I hope my father will get to read this because of how truthful and meaningful it is to me." This student learned a sophisticated lesson, one that is rhetorical to be sure, but also so much more. Through knowing Hanh, she learned that by opening communication with another, a writer opens new, meaningful and productive communication with the self. And she may even have learned one of the most important life lessons of all if she can see its meaning: namely, that forgiveness is a path to truth.

Students also write about difference. One student recently wrote her book about a lesbian couple that opened a bakery in her small town. Her book is a story of prejudice, transcendence, and the love circulating in one kitchen in one small town in the world. It is the love of family. As the student wrote, "I would like to inspire people to be open to others that are different from themselves."

And sometimes our students simply write about feeling different. Responding to Hanh's teaching that communication that attempts to force people to one's viewpoint inspires anger and suffering, one student wrote about his book which portrays his difficult high school years in *Out*: "I am not trying to force my opinion onto anyone. I am simply writing about my experiences and how I felt after coming out with my homosexuality. I will not try to have angry undertones toward anyone, and I will end my book on a high note by explaining how I got through it and still felt good about who I am." Though he suffered at the hands of other students in his rural high school, this student chose a different path for himself.

And sometimes healing doesn't come easily. Indeed in one instance a student's writing about Hanh presented a problem. This student's book was about how a drunk driver crashed into her family's grocery store, the only one in her rural village and the only one for miles. The resulting fire razed the building and left the people, including the student's family, who depended on it, with a need that was not replaced: "I didn't know this man [the drunk driver], so I only have one view of him, a negative view that I carry with me all the time, that of a criminal. I would hope that I can show some sympathy toward him, but I don't know how much I will be able to. Reading Hanh, I want to portray him in the correct context, otherwise I will focus on how much I still despise that man." This student's words told me that her writing was both infused with anger but also with a desire to alter appearances. Hearing about Hanh taught her, I later found out, that if she wanted to produce "good writing" she had to sugarcoat her portrayal of the man who destroyed her family's store and her feelings about him. Hearing about Hanh led her to believe, I feared, that "good writing" was a whitewashing of events and thought. In this case, I used a writing conference to talk with the student about the value of reflection and honesty in writing.

Still some students were able to write tangibly and directly about healing. One student's book stands out in my memory for the strength of the writer. This particular student's book was a harrowing account of sexual assault in the stairwell of her high school. As she wrote about her book: "It tells the truth of my assault and makes others understand what it is like going through it and how it changed me. It will show the healing process I've gone though. It [knowing Hanh's principles of communication] will change my book from a more negative tone at the beginning to a more hopeful and uplifting tone towards the end."

How did hearing about Hanh help this student to achieve this ending? First, while she was planning to write of her recovery, which was certainly already underway, and while she was already coming to terms with the existence and nature of the young man who attacked her, hearing about Hanh's rhetorical principles helped her to control the trajectory of her book so that she portrayed her healing process without the need to rely on a clichéd narrative of forgiveness. Hanh's rhetorical principles helped her to tell the truth of her experience, but also the truth of who she is above and beyond the crime committed against her.

Another student wrote of the horrific child abuse she endured at the hands of her mother's boyfriend, an abuse that included being tied to a support brace in the basement of the family home and being beaten with a rope. Despite the shame that might haunt a young woman who has suffered such abuse, this student writes with a different purpose:

My book is going to inspire happiness, hope, resolution and healing. I think it will do that because I am giving a voice to those people who are afraid/not willing to talk about it [abuse]. I also think that because I am including lessons learned and how I gained hope, and how I deal with healing those open wounds, it will be able to somehow give hope to people to start a healing process. This book will also inspire outsiders because I am opening their eyes to issues that are ignored . . . it [knowing Hanh's principles of communication] will allow me to track what my real purpose is.

And for a student whose friend died in a crash that resulted from texting and driving, being able to track the purpose in a new way proved essential to the outcome of the book: "I plan on explaining the affects of texting and driving and state my opinion on the subject. I don't plan on telling readers not to do it, rather I will show them the consequences. I hadn't thought about opening and closing communication, but trying to open communication could lead to more ideas for me to put in my story. Instead of just saying texting and driving is bad, I can focus more on how upsetting the consequences can be." Not forcing one's opinion on another, in other words, can be another avenue for invention.

WHEN WE COMPOSE

When we compose we look to others: for words, but also for orientations to still other words that we get from conversations, from media, and from the books on our shelves and on the shelves of libraries. We look for rhetorical inspiration and strategies. We can help students learn this important lesson.

At a couple of points during the semester, I ask my students to write about a time when they learned something about writing by watching another student or hearing them talk about their writing, or by reading something that another student wrote in response to one of their drafts or for the class. I then ask the students to explain how what they learned changed their own writing process in some way.

The students report that by watching their colleagues use freewriting to produce first drafts, they learn to do the same. They claim that seeing one of their colleagues using dialogue encourages them to do the same as a way to make their writing come alive. Sometimes they report fresh or perhaps unexpected lessons. In one such instance, a student wrote: "I heard one student say how they had begun to write not only using their brain but their heart. However cheesy this sounds, it changed how I write. I began writing from inside my heart. When writing using your heart it really allows you to say things you wouldn't normally say." Another student wrote, "Chantel told me that she talked to her mom a lot [about her book while she was writing it]. I started to call my mom more often to ask her questions." And a third student recently wrote about learning from another student a lesson in opening herself to the demands of the honest portrayal of experience: "Aysia's book helped me. I struggled with opening up to write personal, raw, and real dialogue. Reading how open she was with all of this in her writing, and seeing how great it was, helped encourage me to do the same, which improved my writing." Lastly, a female student recently wrote, "Chuck explained how he wrote with his way of speaking. He did not care that he came from a certain place and slang was different. This situation encouraged me to write as I wanted to."

Countless theorists and writers, from Jacques Barzun (1992, 2002) to Édouard Glissant (1997) to Germaine W. Shames (1997), argue against provincial limits on our thinking. The fact is that the world begins in the next seat or at the next computer station. For educators, the international challenge is to encourage ever more tangible contacts among people and to make the less visible contacts discernible and available for interpretation. We can help our students learn these lessons, and perhaps when we do, we will be teaching writing better than we ever did before. Why? Because we will be teaching students what writers actually do, we will be teaching them to make their writing a reason and an occasion for interacting with others.

Why do writers look to others? We look to others for inspiration, for technique, and for bravery. We look to relearn honesty and to make use of our voices. We look to others to learn forgiveness and hope. And sometimes we look to others for physical orientation: the way someone sat at their laptop in a coffee shop, at a computer in a lab, or held their notebook on a bus, the way they frowned as they scribbled or typed their ideas in or on a tablet, the settling of their physical positioning in relation to their work. Or after writing: the intensity with which someone spoke of their writing, or the mere fact of their writing, the poet at the reading who arranges her manuscript pages on the lectern or tears her pages to shreds and throws them at the audience, the writer who leans forward, toward the audience to say something about their early work. Or your friends: the one who says they are writing again, has written a poem this morning, the one who is writing a book and has the tone of someone in it for the long haul, or the way a friend holds their recently self-published book, the grace with which they hand it to you, the shape of their signature that they have inscribed for you on the title page and the attention to the signing that it represents. The agency of others inspires our own. It is the values behind an action, but as we interpret it. It is others as we interpret their presence, their contribution to the world. It is about being open to the languages of others who have always already inscribed their cultural presences. It is about wanting to know more, to desire change in ourselves, our cultures, our nation. These things we learn; these things we teach.

NATIONAL RECALCITRANCE

Graduate students, like their professors, sometimes bring and give voice to the malignant side effects of nationalism in class. As I described in Part 1, "Cage: The Provincial Composition," I teach a class called Rhetorical Traditions. Mostly the class sessions are filled with exciting and insightful discussions with teachers from around the world, but there have been moments in my classes' study of various rhetorical perspectives where a student will say something that I wish I had not heard. I am thinking this moment of one class session where we were discussing Harriet Malinowitz's *Textual Orientations* (1995) and an Arab male from Saudi Arabia claimed that the book was not relevant to his experience as there are no gay people in his country. I still remember the uncomfortable quiet that followed his comment as the other students considered, I suppose, the veracity of this statement as well as how to respond to it. I know that so many things went through my head. I knew that I could not let the comment stand. "Do I tell him that he does not know his own country?" I thought. I immediately considered the implications of doing so. The risk of insulting the man to his face was probably higher than I could estimate. I thought back to an earlier semester when a European student in Rhetorical Traditions protested when she felt that our day's discussion of Eurocentric rhetoric was not respecting her national heritage. With a tone of exasperation, she said, "I object to all this talk about Eurocentrism. I am Italian, not Swedish." She was right to object, of course. Discussions of Eurocentrism are the kind of talk in which specifics are blurred in the sometimes necessary, broad, and essentializing strokes of language. She felt that the uniqueness of her nationality—and her identity—were coming under erasure in class discussions. As she spoke, I thought how white students might be more likely to speak their resistance to rhetorical pluralism if they felt that they had more to lose, that their specific heritage meant power they were loath to see questioned. And all of this reminded me of a black student in another class who had objected to the concept of Afrocentricity because she felt her identity connected to the United States and not Africa. At any rate, a lot was going through my mind as I considered the alternatives.

And in that moment—or, well, perhaps it was two—and maybe I am conflating moments together in my memory—another male, Saudi national spoke up, "Of course there are gay people in our country, but they remain invisible because they live in danger."

Resistance to multiculturalism can manifest in many ways. I remember a Christian graduate student from the United States who felt that reading Harriet Malinowitz's *Textual Orientations* was an immoral imposition. Or the one who complained, for religious reasons, that we were reading selections from The Holy Qur-An in our class's investigation into traditional thinking about language and rhetoric. Matters of religion are seldom far from the "us versus them" thinking at the heart of nationalism. At any rate, moments such as these can shake one's confidence in people and one's hope that things can indeed actually change, that educating teachers might make things better somehow for future writing students. Yes, it is important that students articulate their resistances, and certainly the questioning of the patriarchal and racialized power of Eurocentric rhetoric can touch deep and dark places of fear and resentment—can lead to moments of debilitating self-loathing (Kristeva 1993b, 3).

In *Minor Re/Visions,* Morris Young demonstrates how local, rhetorical choices, intentions, and agenda are affected by nationalism. In resistance to negative, traditional perceptions of writers of color other than white, and of local literatures and societies, he argues for processes of re/vision, the constructive work of rereading and reinterpreting our narratives for the possibilities they suggest for overcoming historical and structural power hierarchies—including racism. Young's sense of re/vision is markedly hopeful and affirmative, even as he is anything but blind to the obstacles. As he writes about *Minor Re/Visions*: "While I have argued throughout this book that re/vision is a central trope and practice that provides people of color and others in minor positions to narrate themselves into the American story, we have seen a change in the cultural imagination that has made re/vision a more difficult prospect. Anxiety and nostalgia have become more prevalent as American culture looks to resolve its fear and confusion in more comforting forms of nationalism" (2004, 195).

One way to cope with anxiety and resist nostalgia is to develop and expand our composing processes and teaching by studying rhetoric and composition theories from around the world. The idea is that by looking to others for inspiration as we compose, by learning from others about composing, we will be more open to the idea of fairness, justice, peace, and opportunities for health for all. The idea is to understand others by learning about their meanings, but also their meaning making methodologies, and the philosophies behind the methods. If we do so, we may expand our own processes, sometimes even making elements from the processes of others part of our own.

Still, even though as a teacher, I have felt impatience with some of the fears and recalcitrance that have surfaced in my twenty-some years of teaching Rhetorical Traditions, happily, I can say that there have been far more examples of students coming to healthy realizations about the realities of rhetoric and writing instruction. Many more have constructed powerful new takes on rhetorical fairness, and many more have, with each passing year, become inspired by the rhetorical and pedagogical possibilities that international perspectives make feasible.

I have directed or served on several dissertations by students who are citizens of other countries. In this work, I have been able to bear witness to stories, both painful and uplifting, that these students have told about their homelands and cultures. These homelands influence their citizens' composing, and this, too, needs to be studied and understood. I am thinking, as I write this, about a doctoral student who wanted to write her dissertation about how women in her conservative, Arab country publish their writing, often in exile, and so resist the traditional forms of patriarchal oppression they face each day in their homeland. This student was denied, not surprisingly, the permission she needed to write her dissertation by her government. Her project—and she and her project by necessity remain nameless here; indeed, even my description of it is careful—ended up dealing with how Arab women use literacy to meet their needs in various ways. My point is that this student's project became a lesson in writing one's way around censorship to achieve one's goals. And I am thinking about another student. She wrote two versions of her dissertation: one for consumption by her committee and one, a "sanitized" version, for government officials at home, the ones who would probably assign her a prison sentence when she returned home if they saw what she really wrote.

Students such as these teach about bravery, about strength in resisting oppression, about the human determination to make meaning in the face of authoritarian and fundamentalist governments, about the realities of composing in a dangerous world—about the human thirst for freedom and truthful expression.

THERE IS NO RHETORIC, BUT
THERE IS HOPE

In 2005, I taught an advanced doctoral seminar in literacy studies. The topic I chose for the class was "Rhetoric and Poetics." The fifteen students who took the class were educators from the United States and countries located across Asia and the Middle East.

We began each night's weekly session sitting in a circle, gathered around the teacher's desk, on which students arranged whatever food they brought to class to share during that night's session. Often the food reflected the students' home cultures so that the sharing had particular significance for all of us—as did the discussions. Anyone who has taught students from such countries as China, Japan, South Korea, and Taiwan will testify to the fact that speaking in class discussions is more of an unusual and potentially discomfiting experience for students from some countries than for others. Yet night after night, I noted to myself how each student, without my ever explicitly requesting that they do so, made contributions to the discussions. For some reason, in this class the students all talked and all respectfully listened. Maybe it was the food in the center of the circle that we shared. Maybe it was their desire to learn and their natural good will. Maybe it was the readings, such as Samir Amin's *The Liberal Virus: Permanent War and the Americanization of the World* (2004), Édouard Glissant's *Poetics of Relation* (1997), Aristotle's *Rhetoric* (1932), Pierre Joris's *A Nomad Poetics: Essays,* Tove Skutnabb-Kangas's *Linguistic Genocide in Education-Or Worldwide Diversity and Human Rights?* (2000) and writings by Rachel Blau DuPlessis (1985) and Julianna Spahr (2001). Maybe it was something I did. Maybe it was all of the above and more.

Not that all nights were totally comfortable. On one occasion, I thought I perceived some slight—some very slight—stiffening of the students from Taiwan when an idea about universal rights was articulated by a student from China. I remember being concerned and then stopping to think that of course international tensions would also be present in this classroom. We bring the world and our perspectives on it to class with us. It could not be otherwise.

At any rate, except for that incident, the class worked with genuine collegiality. This was one of those semesters where it all came together, where food combined with writing, where laughter combined with serious discussion, where no one in the class attempted in any overt way to dominate the conversation or position themselves for an A (though Lad Tobin might remind us that we do not always know what is going on behind the scenes).

In the course of the semester's reading, writing, and discussions, the students came to design the major project for the class: the writing of a rhetoric. The project, which the class published for a limited time on a webpage, "Toward an International Rhetoric," was made up of various, individual contributions from the students in the class, including descriptions of our working processes.

Some nights we discussed the readings, some nights we wrote in small groups gathered around a computer, sometimes each at their own computer (writing in which I participated). We constructed running outlines of our growing and accruing rhetoric, sometimes on the blackboard and sometimes through computer projection. We researched in and out of class, and during the weeks between classes we wrote and brought our draft work to class. We read each other's contributions to our text and revised.

As with many collaborative projects, this one changed over the course of the semester. For instance, the project went from being oriented toward the shape and tenor of an actual rhetoric, as in the style of Aristotle's *Rhetoric*, to a collection of writings on the idea of what an international rhetoric is (when it was decided that Aristotle's drive to categorize did not fit the students' contemporary needs to speak for change in rhetorical studies). The students' additions to the project were, by and large, theoretical and programmatic in the sense that, in them, the students articulated the principles for teaching and writing in an internationalist perspective to which they could, generally speaking, ascribe as they charted their pasts and planned their future careers in education.

For instance, a graduate student from Nepal, who had witnessed how both Western cultural imperialism and a Maoist-inspired, bloody civil war—with contributions by a disaffected and disengaged king— had ravaged parts of his country, wrote: "The international rhetoric should work toward liberating the people's minds from political, economic and cultural hegemony so that indigenous linguistic and cultural heritage, which is like an endangered species, could be protected." A student from South Korea felt that an international rhetoric must be a rhetoric that supports human rights. For her, an international rhetoric would teach literacy educators to "have ears, eyes and minds to listen, to read, to accept differences and enjoy them." She wrote that when a professor imposes a false identity on her students, as when a teacher refuses to accept and understand linguistic and rhetorical differences in writing, that the human rights of students are transgressed. So, for her, an international rhetoric would by necessity be a rhetoric of openness and patience.

A student from China said that since many cultures do not take persuasion as the primary goal of discourse, Western rhetoric is continually promoted in an exclusionary way. This student, who took her lead from Édouard Glissant's vision for a new world order of knowledge, wrote that an international rhetoric should promote "the space of difference . . . not exclusion" (Glissant 1997, 82). At the same time, a student from Taiwan wrote that an international rhetoric would have to "reduce hierarchy and bring equality." It would have to be "a journey from language diversity to discovery of all language speakers as acceptably different. Édouard Glissant captures the dynamics of this process, 'Accepting differences does, of course, upset the hierarchy of this scale . . . we need to bring an end to the very notion of a scale. Displace all reduction' (190)." In the course of her work, this student wrote about literacy education and her childhood in Taiwan: "The students used to write their compositions with only one conclusion—fight back to Mainland China and rescue our fellow brothers and sisters who are in suffering. The grade of our composition was better if we came to the conclusion of a consciousness to fight back to Mainland China. The literacy education— the reading content in the textbooks, the compositions we had to write, the internalization of the ideology—had made the students not possible to be creative and responsive to their given condition. We did not even understand that we were the oppressed." For this student, developing an international rhetoric might help students resist the coercion of education tied to nationalist agenda.

Tying the theme of nationalism and its power to aesthetics and education, a student from the United States wrote against the combined legacies of New Criticism and capitalism as they define higher education's ideological stance of detachment. In this, he followed the lead of Richard Ohmann, who wrote that "New Criticism insisted that 'the means to well-being and wholeness is through withdrawal from social action and the achievement of all-embracing states of mind'" (1996, 89). For this student, then, any international rhetoric would not only reverse the New Critical trajectory of withdrawal and detached objectivism, it would promote social action as a necessary form of well-being and wholeness.

In the conclusion to the project, the students articulated the sense of personal obligation, responsibility and agency upon which they felt an international rhetoric would have to rest. Their work suggested new motives for the study of rhetoric—motives beyond, or, at least, in addition to persuasion. Their work was a rough blueprint for articulating rhetorics of peace, choice, and health. As the students wrote, "Rhetoric, if used unselfishly, will move us toward mutual acceptance and understanding, toward reconciliation, toward peace. With each and every word we write, speak, sign, think, we choose. And those choices take on, cling to, and define the shape of our collective future."

This short summary does not do justice to the historical research the project contains, to the depth of the theory, and to the commitment that teaching students to write can and should contribute to the making of a better world. Certainly the project shows the imposed time limit that the students faced: they had one semester to read material that was new to them, to think about and research ideas that were new to them, and to write a project for which they had no model. But the project is worthy for a number of reasons, and not the least of these is what it represents: a group of educators from around the world studying literacy together and then deciding, with little more than the prompting of the texts that I selected for them to read, to write essays toward the creation of an international rhetoric founded on principles of respect, dignity, and diversity. Think about this for a moment: this group of international educators decided to write a theoretical plan as Thich Nhat Hanh suggested—and certainly many of the students cited him—for the "alleviation of suffering." The world might indeed begin to look and sound different if more educators were left to their professional devices and were free to give reign to their critical imaginations.

THE INTERNATIONAL SUSTAINABLE LITERACY PROJECT

In fall 2009, I taught another doctoral seminar in literacy. The topic of the class was "Writing and the Sustainability Crisis." I asked my students to study global climate change and to imagine together possibilities for teaching literacy in the face of it. My thinking was that as biospheric degradation continues and populations come under greater and greater stress, the impacts on human being and human relations will escalate. In this challenging future, I argue, the processes of meaning making available to we humans will become more and more critical to our existence as we search for meaning amidst crisis. In this regard, I think of literacy as a lifeboat for consciousness. And I firmly believe that the significance of our mental lifeboats will become clear to us as the climate crisis worsens.

So I asked my graduate students, many of them teachers and professors from around the world, to research current and predicted effects of global heating on their home countries and to articulate the ways in which they might teach literacy, whether it be composition or English as a second or foreign language, to address the situations in which they live. The project took on a life of its own.

We took our work to the 2011 Conference on College Composition and Communication as a roundtable entitled, "Global Educators for Hope: The International Sustainable-Literacy Project." The students presented research on how climate change is affecting their countries and how each is teaching students to use literacy to support themselves in the face of it. Hayat Messekher from Algeria talked about teaching students to research and participate in her country's political discourse on the subject. Tomoko Odo from Japan presented the Japanese tea ceremony and explained how she teaches students to write about traditional Japanese ceremonies and their ability to sustain social cohesion in the face of national stress. John L. Reilly from the United States talked about the satirical, political action and performance group, The Yes Men, and how their interventionist performances can inspire ecological action. Ibrahim Ashour from Syria wrote of passages in The

Holy Qur-An that speak to the responsibility people have to be stewards of the environment. Laura M. Oliver spoke of her students in West Virginia who research the effects of coal mining on their state's ecology. Kyung-Min Kim from South Korea spoke of teaching for transcultural understanding in order to encourage cooperation among otherwise competing interests in Korea. Wan-Ning Yeh from Taiwan talked about teaching poetry writing that addresses ecological degradation. And Pisarn Chamcharatsri from Thailand spoke of teaching students to remember the power of love as they argue against the deforestation of their country, an ecological exploitation that led to the subsequent devastating floods of 2011. This was an impressive roundtable, an example of international cooperation to address a global issue, a hopeful, even moving, event.

As it turns out, that conference roundtable was only the beginning; it was what we are now calling "Phase I." The members of the International Sustainable Literacy Project hope to encourage other educators to address our world ecological crisis and help students learn to use literacy to construct their own lifeboats for consciousness. Together, with the insights that come from the combination of various local perspectives from around the world, we can all teach against global climate change. And by doing it together, we support each other in the dark times that come from facing the ever-more-likely catastrophic effects of global heating. By doing it together, we learn to stand with all of the grace and strength our international composing and sharing affords us. So, the work of the International Sustainable Literacy Project continues. We now consider the conference roundtable the end of Phase I of the project. Phase II will consist, with the editorial leadership of John Reilly, Pisarn Chamcharatsri and myself, of the submission of our work for publication. To complete this work, the project will be joined by other educators from around the world. (I will not name the new participants here, yet, as they are just beginning to write their contributions.) These currently include an educator from Saudi Arabia who will explore how global heating is affecting drought conditions in the mountainous regions of the south; a Kenyan educator who will explain how drought is increasing Africa's refugee problems, a population she teaches; a Bermudan educator who will discuss the possible effects of sea level rise on her island home; a Russian educator will discuss how global heating is negatively impacting agriculture in a village near the Volga River; and a Libyan educator who will discuss the ruinous effects of Moamar Khaddafi's years of careless and exploitative environmental policies. And all of these college and university professors will discuss the ways in which their teaching will help their students to see the connection of their local conditions to the global environmental situation, and to find personally and socially significant ways of responding. Finally, we are bringing Derek Owens to Pennsylvania for a consultation session with the members of the project in spring 2012, a meeting at which the participants plan to ask him to write a foreword for the journal issue of our work.

In addition, we are beginning to make early plans for Phase III of the International Sustainable Literacy Project. In this phase we plan to begin spreading word of our project to our various home countries with the goal of inviting educators from around the world to continue the project in local, interconnected sites. The ultimate goal of the International Sustainable Literacy Project, then, is to encourage educators from all corners of the world to join together to do no less than teach to save the planet.

PART FOUR

Uncaged
The International Future of Composition

MISTAKES AND BEYOND

Ezra Pound's *Cantos* constitutes a large collection of poems—some seemingly in bits and pieces—that do not quite come together. Pound knew it. He believed that he had failed, that *The Cantos* did not deliver a center, a frame, a realized form. One sees intimations of such dark realizations in the earlier *Pisan Cantos*: Pound's recognition of his shortcomings, his inabilities, his illness, as if he were writing of his own failure when he wrote of "a man on whom the sun has gone the down" (1970, 430).

Allen Ginsberg met Pound late in the elder poet's life. As Ginsberg tells it, Pound hardly spoke. But when he did, he really did.

> Pound told me that the Cantos were "stupidity and ignorance all the way through," and were a failure and a "mess," and that his "greatest stupidity was stupid suburban anti-Semitic prejudice," he thought—as of 1967, when I talked to him. So I told him I thought that since the Cantos were for the first time a single person registering over the course of a lifetime all of his major obsessions and thoughts and the entire rainbow arc of his images and clingings and attachments and discoveries and perceptions, that they were an accurate representation of his mind and so couldn't be thought of in terms of success or failure, but only in terms of the actuality of their representation, and that since for the first time a human being had taken the whole spiritual world of thought through fifty years and followed the thoughts out to the end—so that he built a model of his consciousness over a fifty-year span—that they were a great human achievement. Mistakes and all—naturally. (Ginsberg 1974, 181)

Ginsberg was right, of course. Although *The Cantos* do not deliver organic wholeness, they are still a successful—at times brilliantly so—rendering of a human life, flaws and all.

The Cantos are also an early record of how a writer composes in international terms. They are a transcript of how contributions from many times and places come together in one person's consciousness. They are a demonstration of how influences are integrated into a person's subjectivity and recorded to produce new writing, thinking, and tradition. They are a tapestry of sounds woven from various cultures in an attempt to articulate the new person, a new nation, and a new age.

But what new person, nation, or age? There is no evading suspicion of Pound's political commitments. There is no overlooking the excesses of nationalism and imperialism. There is no excusing fascism's hatred and murders. And there is no knowing if the problem originated in the hate of a twisted heart, a self-inflicted stupidity, madness, nationalist social controls, or the evil of the age. The story of Ezra Pound is a cautionary tale of the need for developing and maintaining an informed critical consciousness through which one continues to question one's cherished ideas.

If we can, perhaps we should just say that *The Cantos* are as limited as their time, place, and composer. *The Cantos* are impenetrable arrogance and literary inspiration. They are political malignancy and cultural critique. They are a foundation for a poetics of cultural superiority and multicultural inclusiveness glimpsed but never realized. And just as the content of a book of poems might speak of the achievements and shortcomings of its writer, the content of a discipline might do the same for its practitioners. It is past time for composition studies to fulfill its international potential. It is to our credit that we have begun. And we begin because history will not let us rest. History will not let us accept racism. We have the responsibility to turn from Pound. But, and this is key, that turn will not alone answer. We may condemn and dismiss Pound, but he will continue to stand at the center of the modern aesthetic—with its postmodern correctives—informing so much of writing, and teaching, in our time. We have his legacy. Every day, every moment, every class, we teachers stand in history, and our pedagogies endorse or resist that history. Our poetics and our rhetorics present us with intricate historical problems that we must continue to address. We must face the complexities if we are to free ourselves of the horrors of history. We must accept the historical demand that we learn our pasts so that we may know who we are. At the end, I despise, as we all do, the hateful portions of Pound's legacy. I fear and loathe fascism, even as I worry about the remnants of its ideology reincarnated in unfettered forms of nationalism. At the same time, I recognize that even a damaged person can create knowledge and beauty, though accepting that fact is difficult. We teachers of writing must rededicate ourselves to facing the challenges of history if we are to embrace our promise. And so I look within myself, and for the best in my students, for ways of healing.

INTERNATIONAL COMPOSITION #3

I admire all teachers of writing, but especially those who commit themselves to studying the traditions of rhetoric and poetics from cultures
and countries other than their own. I admire teachers who learn about
philosophies and religions and create visions of life without ethnic and
racial prejudice. I admire teachers who open themselves to others with
intelligence and humility and generosity and a willingness of spirit to
learn and change as they explore the international nature of composing. We have barely begun to ask the most challenging research questions. If we continue to work for it, we can articulate new insights into
the nature and necessity of composing, into the ways in which we are all
united on our life-journeys for meaning, health, happiness, and fulfill-
ment. We will be enlarged by this work; we will be strengthened in our
spirits, in our being.

Imagine a graduate program in International Composition Studies.
Such a program might take any number of focuses and contain a variety
of courses. As I think about its construction, I try to envision what a program would need to include to encourage the teaching of writing in an
international key—perhaps such courses as these:

Theories of International Composition

Teaching International Composition

International Rhetorical Studies

Composing: Rhetorics, Cultures, and Nations

Theories of Self and Other

Rhetoric and Imperialism

Post-Imperial Poetics and Rhetoric

Nationalism, Internationalism, and Transnationalism

Multiculturalism, Interculturalism, and Transculturalism

Globalization, Cosmopolitanism, and Composition

International Creative Writing and Composition

Sustainable Literacy Studies

Whole International Language Teaching

Globalized Language and Writing Studies

Globalized Economics and Literacy Studies

Literacy and Language for International Cooperation

Composition and National and International Activism

Internationalism in Applied Linguistics

Post-Imperial TESOL Studies

World Englishes and World Compositions

The International Writing Program

The International Writing Center

Service-Learning Around the World

Research Methodologies in International Contexts

Hermeneutics and International Meanings

Assessment in National and International Perspectives

Theories of Professional Writing in Global Perspective

Professional Writing for International Exchange

International Computerized Composing

Readers will no doubt have ideas about what courses to add, combine or cut from my list. But, for now, the courses I propose move from theoretical and historical concerns to the study of international composition in various instances and applications. They include courses in poetics and linguistics because both are intimately linked to composition and because as exchange and migration across cultural and national boundaries accelerate, as they surely will, we compositionists will continue to draw ever more deeply on the insights of poetics and applied linguistics to develop our understanding of how composing and writing work, what the possibilities are, who our students are, and even who we are and how we should teach. Composition has always been an interdisciplinary discipline. As we orient ourselves for greater responsiveness to global perspectives, we will more than ever need to marshal the collective wisdom of the other disciplines, including, of course, world politics, but also world philosophies and science.

Am I hopeful that I will see such a graduate program in my lifetime? Yes.

First, many existing graduate programs in international studies emerged in the nineties, and they continue to explore a wide variety of subjects. These international studies programs have focused on such disciplines as administration, development, diplomacy, economics, education policy, international affairs, law, politics, marketing, security, and sociology, and some have focused on geographic areas such as European or Middle Eastern Studies. Now, international studies programs have additionally begun to focus on such subject areas as environmental and sustainability studies, international media and technical communications, non-profit organizations and missions, peace and human rights, psychology, nursing, social justice, and service-learning management (though the names of themes such as "social justice," are also employed in some schools as new designations for traditional subject areas). Imagine how a writing program with an international perspective might create composition courses at all levels to contribute to international studies in its various manifestations. The future for the significance of composition could not be more promising.

Second, there are tenure track positions for the graduates of such a program; indeed, jobs that point to our international future are already available in composition. Here I will just mention two from the many I have seen. The graduate program in composition and TESOL in which I teach has, in the past several years, advertised for compositionists whose chief teaching and research interest is multicultural rhetorical studies. In a recent semester, Colorado State University–Pueblo also offered an assistant professor position in English, a specialist in rhetoric and composition with preferred secondary research interests in "constructions of culture, race, ethnicity, gender, or class in relation to literary or rhetorical studies." In addition, anyone who has kept on eye on the job market for the past several years knows that the demand for ESL writing studies experts continues to grow. It is reasonable to expect that as the field of composition develops in the coming years, the need for compositionists with international vision will continue to increase with it.

ON THE ROAD WITH INTERNATIONAL COMPOSITION

The many journals and books I have cited throughout the course of *National Healing* prove that there are ample opportunities for doing and sharing internationalist work in composition. Indeed, we need to continue to disseminate information on how we do our work, what our philosophical, theoretical, and political sources are, and what our pedagogies are—in short, how we write and teach writing, wherever that may be.

Here, I would just like to point to a couple of important, related sources. Certainly *The Journal of Second Language Writing* is widely known to compositionists, but there are other relevant journals, as well. For instance, there is *The International Journal of Innovation in English Language Teaching and Research* (Widodo et al. 2004–2012). Its inaugural issue, "Critical Perspectives on English Language Teaching and Research: Implications for Globalization and Multiculturalism," was published in September of 2011. As the journal's website states, the challenges of globalization call for greater scholarly dialogue on how educators from various parts of the world teach multilingual students.

And there are journals such as Michael Pemberton's *Across the Disciplines: Interdisciplinary Perspectives on Language, Learning, and Academic Writing* (1997–2012). It has published or reprinted articles and talks such as John Harbord's "Writing in Central and Eastern Europe: Stakeholders and Directions in Initiating Change" (2010). In it, Harbord, who is the Director of the Center for Writing at the Central European University in Budapest, reports on the relative lack of status that writing instruction holds in Eastern Europe. Rather than giving up in the face of this reality, Harbord begins to plot a course for future development of the discipline in Europe by calling for the translation of writing across and in the disciplines in first-language teaching situations to second-language contexts, where practical and by appropriately trained teachers. In addition, *Across the Disciplines* will feature an upcoming issue entitled "Writing across the Curriculum and Second Language Writers" that will be edited by composition scholars Michelle Cox and Terry Myers Zawacki.

There are also recent books, such as *Reinventing Identities in Second Language Writing* (Cox et al. 2010), that stand as breakthrough publications in international composition studies. This collection contains such fine essays as Immaculée Harushimana's "Colonial Language Writing Identities" (2010) in which she investigates colonialist perceptions of and commitments to academic discourse in Africa. Harushimana explains how Western conceptions of academic discourse have taken root in Africa in such a way that academic discourse has become synonymous with education and privilege. Academic discourse writing serves the purposes of the cultural elite, and when success in writing is materially connected to the ability to feed one's family, as Harushimana points out, the result is heightened sensitivity in students to criticism of their writing. The result is, finally, the development of resistant attitudes in students that hinder writing development.

Lastly, there are book series, such as the Studies in Writing Series edited by Gert Rijlaarsdam (n.d.) of the Netherlands. This series is part of the International Series on the Research of Learning and Instruction of Writing and includes books such as *Teaching Writing in Chinese Speaking Areas*, edited by Mark Shui-Kee Shum and De-lu Zhang. As its webpage attests, this series is devoted to publishing international perspectives on writing because internationalist thinking "allows for the establishment of working networks of writing researchers from across the globe and from all disciplines involved in writing studies." The editorial objectives on the webpage for the series states: "Studies in Writing provides a forum for research from established researchers, as well as contributions from young researchers. Fields of research covered are cognitive, socio cognitive and developmental psychology, psycholinguistics, text linguistics, curriculum development and instructional science." The series editor expresses interest in issues such as writing and media, collaborative writing, writing in the workplace, document design, the teaching of writing, including responding to and assessing writing, as well as research on the composing process.

At the 2010 Conference in College Composition and Communication in Louisville, Kentucky, David Russell chaired a session designed to orient the audience to directions beyond composition's traditional borders. "What Should CCCC Do (And Not Do) To Support the Globalization of Writing Studies?" brought together writing researchers from Canada, Egypt, Switzerland, and the United States to call for international sharing of research about writing and its teaching. In addition, at the

2011 CCCC in Atlanta, Russell chaired another session, "Globalization and Publishing Writing Research: An Editors' Roundtable Sponsored by the CCCC Committee on Globalization of Postsecondary Writing Instruction and Research." On this panel, several publishers of journals and books spoke about how they are attempting to foster the publishing of writing research from around the world through special issues and welcoming editorial practices.

Composition is on the move. Even as the offering of composition as its own course of study comes under greater scrutiny and budget pressures in the United States, we may find that it is being taught with increasing frequency overseas. Certainly, the interest is there. For instance, a conference entitled "University Literacies: Knowledge, Writing, Disciplines" (2010), recently held at the Université Charles de Gaulle in Lille, France, brought together scholars from around the world to share research on writing practices, genres, discipline, epistemology, and culture. In the United Kingdom, the Writing Development in Higher Education Conference, the recent theme for which was "Sustainable Writing Development: Approaches and Challenges" (2010), created a forum for researchers to present their work on issues ranging from writing centers, writing groups, exam writing, and writing in the disciplines. The conference also covered pedagogical concerns, such as how to teach library research papers, writing problems, as well as formal and rhetorical concerns of academic writing, and all in the context of British settings, but in reference to American and French research and practice. And in the United States we have the annual International Conference on Writing Research, "Writing Research Across Borders" (2011). The fourth meeting of this conference was held February 17–20, 2011, at George Mason University in Washington, DC. As its website states, the focus of the conference is "on writing development across the lifespan, including the impact of new technologies on learning to write, early acquisition of writing, writing across grade levels (K–20), writing in the disciplines and professions, and writing in the workplace or other community and institutional settings." Why? Because "[a]s societies become more knowledge-intensive and communication technologies draw us more closely together, the importance of writing in economic, scientific, civic, personal, and social development becomes more apparent." Finally, in the United States there are also annual conferences such as the Conference on Intercultural Rhetoric and Discourse, the sixth meeting of which was held at Georgia State University in 2010. This conference brings together scholars to discuss theoretical as well as empirical, intercultural research into "language- and culture-specific studies," "practical applications," and "teaching and classroom practices . . . in school, college, and the professions."

These conferences are just four of the many important beginnings we have to build on. As writing research continues to be exchanged across borders, change will follow as more and more educators affect their local schools and central governments—and what dialogues such conferences could foster. What insights could be composed as scholars from around the world continue to develop international understanding of the teaching of writing. Perhaps, one day, this incredible gift of a course in writing, this most significant of curricular offerings, will come back to the United States, expanded and richer for its migration. (And while composition has not traditionally existed as an independent, stand-alone course around the world, we may reasonably expect things to change in the coming years as graduate students from other countries come to the United States to study composition and TESOL.) And perhaps we will no longer recognize our course once it comes home again. And perhaps some of us will feel a need to save it from scientific mechanization and constricting ties to disciplinary demands from across the curriculum. Whatever these future, international dialogues, the meaning of the discipline we call "composition" will no doubt deepen in the years to come.

WORLD ENGLISHES; WORLD COMPOSITIONS

As poet Gerrit Lansing writes in "La p(l)age poetique":

> Poetics will be planetary or not at all (*hommage* á Andre Breton):
>   its data and resource are unrestricted by any "tradition."
> The word of sin was always Restriction, and, in the bondage-scene of verse,
> was always, at its best, high play (game of Decorum, the keeping, the
> conventions apt to some local time-crystal).
>
> The dead hand, or confusion of times, was ever to take the living
> rules of one historical moment and try to fasten them down on another
> time. Pseudomorphosis. The restricted notion of "form" never furthers.
> (Lansing 2003, 134)

Not just poetics, of course, but rhetoric as well "will be planetary or not at all." Rhetoric has also been subject to the "dead hand, or confusion of times." Rhetoric has also been the terrain of control and the desire for certainty and security. The decisions we compositionists face in the coming years between a planetary perspective and the restrictions of the anti-life drive of cultural purity, between the search for sustainable composing in the face of ecological crisis (and its attendant economic and political crises) and the oppression of class-based rules of discursive decorum, will become more acute. Linguists and TESOL educators are already facing this juncture as they decide how best to serve the needs of the times in general and the world's students in particular. It is the search for equity and peace, sustainability and survival. It is nothing less.

In its global reach, English represents both imperialism and cultural exchange, both conquest and variety. The linguists who take a global approach to language study recognize that "there is indeed greater emphasis today than in the past on capturing the expanding fusions and hybridizations of linguistic forms and the unprecedented variations in global functions of world Englishes" (Kachru, Kachru and Nelson 2009, xvii). This recognition of and respect for variety in English usage has caused linguists to open their discipline to the study of creativity and language politics on an international scale, study from which we compositionists can learn and to which we should certainly contribute.

Applied linguistics is expanding at a rate too fast and with a scholarly production far too great to overview here. Instead, let me merely point to the fact that compositionists share respect, with the proponents of the world English, globalization and international language studies movements, for multicultural and progressive language use. In "World Englishes and Culture Wars," Braj B. Kachru explains, "The concept world Englishes . . . emphasizes the pluricentricity of the language and its cross-cultural reincarnations" (2009, 446). According to Kachru, the world English movement in linguistics is a canon-busting, theoretical orientation that resists those with power who would attempt to legislate for homogenized standards of linguistic purity. He suggests that "we need a perspective of 'variousness'" (465) in which English language educators teach from the vision that English is not one language but a variety of languages, each connected to local contexts and to each other, each offering unique opportunities for creative performance and understanding and each enriching the other with creativity. We need to act from this insight, Kachru argues, "if we do not want to continue walling up the world visions—including African and Asian—in this unique, cultural and linguistic resource of our times, world Englishes" (466). In "Literary Creativity in World Englishes," Edwin Thumboo explains how people from different geographical settings exchange and borrow from one another to create new literary forms. He argues that these forms are worthy of study in their own right and not by measurement to mother-tongue standards. He calls for a "comparative spirit" in literary, world English analysis that "is sensitively attentive and exploratory" and that will lead to an understanding of "whether we can ultimately attempt an overview of all literatures in English" (2009, 422). In *Cultural Globalization and Language Education,* B. Kumaravadivelu argues that to understand either the relation of the local to global articulations, or the tension between cultural impulses toward heterogeneity or homogenization in language development, applied linguists need "to develop global cultural consciousness" (2006, 7). Even from these few quotes it should be clear that applied linguistics is undergoing a major shift that bears obvious theoretical and political kinship with an international composition studies as I propose in this book.

But, there is a catch. Kachru claims that the world English movement may not support an international perspective per se: "I have avoided the term *international language* with English. The term 'international' used with 'English' is misleading in more than one sense: it signals an *international* English in terms of acceptance, proficiency, functions, norms, pragmatic unity and creativity. That is actually far from true—that is not the current international functional profile of the English language and never was" (2009, 449). This point would seem similar to one made by Alastair Pennycook. In his book, *Critical Applied Linguistics* (2001), which he developed from earlier work in his Longman text, *The Cultural Politics of English as an International Language* (1994), Pennycook argues that the linking of English to the concept of internationalism solidifies English as the single, default language for international communication, leaving local languages to serve contextual and indigenous uses exclusively. Internationalism will not serve, in Pennycook's opinion, because it denotes the systemic conservativism of language superiority at work in traditional manifestations of international thought and relations.

No one can deny the validity of Kachru and Pennycook's critiques. English language education has a long and sordid history as a vehicle for imperialist acculturation projects in lands occupied by colonialist powers (and indeed, the world Englishes movement may face a similar critique because the equality invoked by the act belies the reality that all Englishes simply are not equal). But composition studies deserves a different kind of attention. It is a relatively new discipline; its reach has been confined, largely, to the United States. Consequently, composition has not had the international presence that TESOL has had and has not, as a scholarly discipline, been historically associated with imperialist designs. The challenge that we compositionists face as we "go international" with our discipline is one of critical consciousness. We need to develop a new level of disciplinary critique. We will need to develop the international vision that allows us to delineate and eschew the colonialist ideology at work in the nationalism of exclusive rhetorical commitments. And we will need to watch for and root out imperialist ideologies when they creep into our work. We need to do this work so that we may resist the oppressive pedagogical practices that are founded in elitist discursive allegiances and so we may neutralize the oppressive economic practices and arrangements that are embodied in compositionists' relationships to the teaching materials we adopt. And these are but some of the challenges we face now and will face in the coming years. History will judge us by what we do, not what we say. If we make resources of the rhetorical and composition traditions of others as we pursue the impulses of academic capitalism, we will have missed our chance to contribute something that is new in both deed as well as thought. Diverse and far-flung educators have demonstrated that it is possible to connect students across class, state, and national borders. They have shown that this work can be done with authenticity and can accomplish student-centered objectives, achieve new understandings of language use and writing, and affect lives in genuine and specific ways (Barksdale, Watson, and Park 2007; Bell 1992; Bellanca and Stirling 2011; Benson et al. 2002; Blitz and Hurlbert 1998; Christian 1997; Gabor 2009; Gillis 1994; Hsu 2009; Kern 1995, 1996; Mabasa 2005; Sipe 2000; Snyder 2002; Stiver 1996; Ware and Kramsch 2005; Warner 1995; Warschauer 1996, 1999; Wright 1992). Perhaps no project exhibited these qualities more so than the international sharing of writings and conversation—not to mention meals—in the international project that connected writers from Syracuse University and the Federation of Worker Writers in England. The exchange inspired the publication of critical and heartfelt writings by working class students attempting to come to terms with the seemingly alien world of the academy. The volume produced by these writers, *Pro(se)letariats,* which is published by Steve Parks's New Community Press, is a call to teachers to recreate education in the name of equity, fairness, and care. The book ends with a manifesto of five tenants. One of these reads: "All educators must move from subconsciously teaching students to be Westernized versions of 'them' to teaching the essential equality among all individuals and cultures" (Burns et al. 2010, 117). I hope that *National Healing* responds to this principle; indeed, I would ask all educators to respond to it. To begin, we will need, especially in our uncertain, changing world, and in the words that end *Pro(se)letariats,* to "teach a global humanity (not the humanities) based on an alternative sense of history and where cooperative values and restorative justice are primary" (117). An international perspective is composition's contribution to this effort. Our international history begins now.

SECURING COMPOSITION; SAVING THE PLANET

Maybe we compositionists will be wise and lucky enough to save our writing classes from administrative mishandlings and the budgetary axes that will continue to swing as the boney fingers of the international economic crisis, those who caused it, and those who benefit from it, continue to tighten their grip on our colleges. But, of course, the future is anything but certain. With the erosion of the traditional justifications for the humanities, we compositionists have watched as literature has lost support for the offering of its various period and genre courses. The traditional rationale for composition, our service role, may not be far behind. If writing across the curriculum compositionists successfully convince administrators to transfer the teaching of writing to the other disciplines, and if the abolitionist-compositionists continue to wage war on the universal writing class, we may see the ground on which we stand slip away from us too. In some respects, writing program administrators are on the front line. It is well-known that these administrators often work against impossible odds, and since I have never been one, I am loath to offer advice to these hard-working individuals. But it seems to me that internationalism might prove a useful tool in any rationale a writing program administrator—or any compositionist—might make for funding. Tying the teaching of writing to changing global realities, changing demographics, overseas recruitment of students, and preparation for careers in various kinds of international work might be useful for convincing administrators to support composition scholarship, proper training for writing teachers as they develop their own visions for the teaching of writing, and, perhaps, even tenure track lines for international writing specialists. Indeed, many universities already have language institutes for helping students to achieve academic success in US classrooms. Perhaps in some contexts it might be possible to establish international writing institutes that combine the work of language institutes with the teaching of writing in general. These would present locations for the broad study of writing, from first year to graduate course work to writing center work to creative and professional writing, and language and literacy research in relation to composition.

Whatever we do, I believe that in order to secure the future of our most important of courses, we compositionists need to join together to articulate new rationales for composition, new reasons for the necessity of writing studies. We must remember the central role of composing in a person's life and world participation, design our classes to facilitate it, and create persuasive demonstrations of the need. And we will, again, need to stop calling for the abolishing of the universal composition class, the default argument of those without a vision for its relevance or the meaning of its global purpose. And we will need to stop calling for service versions of writing across the curriculum, ones where composition classes are filled with the content of other disciplines to help out those who do not know what to do with writing class time. In this day and age, we compositionists need, more than ever, a healthy dose of street smarts. And we need visions and rationale beyond textbook-driven and textbook-related nationalist and, ultimately, racist curricula. We need visions and rationale as deep and meaningful and life-affirming as the act of writing itself is. And we need to base our visions and rationale in the realities of our already international world and existence. After all, composition—indeed, the humanities in general—is not merely about enriching the individual. It is, or should be, about preparing individuals to live in a world of international cultural exchange—something for which the composition class is uniquely situated and for which writing across the disciplines could and should be instituted; that is, to serve composition's essential, internationalist goals.

Composition is the first academic discipline to be fully about composing in writing. This is our originality, our unique contribution. Combined with student-centered pedagogical theory, we are ready to study our students' various composing processes as cultural practices. We in composition stand, in other words, on the threshold of fascinating courses of lifelong study offering fresh orientations to composing and writing. We have it in our power to exchange information about local composing processes, to learn respect for differing composing processes, and, in doing so, to articulate new ways of communicating through writing and new ways for working together and bringing writers together to achieve productive social ends. And because we study the meaning that writers make for the world, maybe, as compositionists, we can help, finally, to the extent that we ever can, to lead the way to alternative, healthier forms of world citizenship.

The fact is that the blind nationalism that has plagued the United States can make one feel that they are facing a thousand demons on a thousand sides. As a citizen of a nation that has practiced imperialism in the name of national interest and security, I have firsthand knowledge of the way in which nationalism affects the international scene. As a citizen of the United States, I talk first and foremost about my own country's need to heal. I do so because my country needs to find peace and health if it is to contribute to world peace and health in decent, honest and fair ways. The United States is one of the world's major superpowers; consequently, the responsibility for healing policy and behavior lies doubly in this land. Even in the face of the devastating economic and emotional results of having blindly followed nationalist affiliation to the point that we started an unjust war in Iraq, and even as patriotism is written into law designed to control US citizens, we must act.

Present national and international realities and tensions make it possible, I believe, for teachers of composition such as myself to recognize, finally, the degree to which our teaching supports, despite how politically aware compositionists generally are, a cultural purity which, in turn, sustains nationalism in the United States. I honor the degree to which my fellow compositionists work hard to address racism in our classrooms. Ours is a dedicated profession, and my colleagues in it teach with, largely, admirable, humane, and progressive goals and motives. But the fact remains that even with the best efforts of compositionists who teach against crushing odds and workloads, the ideology of nationalism too often undermines their best efforts at combating racism because, in the United States, nationalism still endorses one cultural centrism. The healing of one man or woman does not, in and of itself, of course, heal a nation, but I believe that the healing about which I am speaking comes first from within, by each starting with his or her own thinking and actions.

When teaching fulfills a nationalist ideological mission, compositionists enact a pedagogy that is both antithetical to sound writing instruction and damaging to students, the state, and even the world. Nationalism leads compositionists to teach writing in such a way as to underwrite a monocultural version of the national identity. In so doing, we fulfill our roles in maintaining US nationalist ideology and policy. And so, I am arguing that we compositionists must once again reclaim our classrooms, as we did in the eighties when we followed the lead of scholarly pioneers such as Ann Berthoff. This time we must do it for student-centered teaching within an international vision of composing and writing instruction and in light of internationalist goals for ending racism and state-sponsored violence.

We do not have time to wait. We face environmental degradation on a global scale. We face the possibility of continuing wars as resources become more and more scarce. Perhaps by learning how to write in ways that at least make cooperation a genuine possibility we will be better equipped to communicate and work together to end conflict and face the dangers of impending, global, environmental change of monumental proportions. Perhaps we will be able to answer them as we learn to make new meaning of our world and how we live in it. We cannot afford to delay creating cooperative relations with people from around the world in order to address our global crisis. We compositionists of a political bent do not have time to waste dreaming of some future age in which to act. We must begin now to learn from and with each other and in the demographic and political configurations in which we actually live. We must make actual, not theoretical, change. Through action, we can claim our stakes in the local lives and political discourses of our cities and state governments. We must change, too. We must monitor racism and violence, and we must understand them. We must root them out of our subjectivities and out of our relations with others. Healing is possible and writing is one of the vehicles. I believe this because I have seen it: in sites, in people, a process, ongoing and surprising. Writing can help us to open the cages that would keep us locked away from the world and the better people we would become. We must learn new ways.

LEARNING NEW WAYS #2

It's another New Orleans morning. A man and a woman sit at a nearby table. A woman comes into the coffee shop and approaches them. The man stands up, gives her a hug and introduces her to the woman with whom he is sitting, "This is my daughter."

"Oh," the sitting woman says with a laugh as she shakes hands with the daughter, "No wonder there are tears in your eyes!"

All three laugh and the daughter responds, "No, I've earned these tears all by myself. They are my own."

They do not laugh this time.

The daughter sits down and the three begin to talk.

CODA

In his introduction to *The Pisan Cantos,* Richard Sieburth explains how, when Ezra Pound was arrested in 1945, in Rapalo, Italy, for making treasonous radio broadcasts during World War II, he was taken to the US Army's Disciplinary Training Center, which was located in a dusty field north of Pisa:

> Pound was the only civilian inmate in the camp and, in the temporary absence of its commander, Lieutenant Colonel John L. Steele, overzealous subordinates, no doubt awed by the Washington cable's warnings about escape or suicide, had decided to confine their dangerous war criminal in one of the camp's "death cells"—a six-by-six-foot steel cage, open to the elements, which had been specially reinforced the night before Pound's arrival with sections of heavy "airstrip" steel mesh normally used to lay down temporary runways.
>
> Washington had stipulated that the prisoner be accorded no preferential treatment. Orders were therefore given that he be held completely incommunicado: isolated in his cell under the constant observation of a special guard, with the Mediterranean sun beating down on him all day and floodlights trained on him all night, his eyes badly inflamed by all the dust and glare, he was allowed no exercise privileges, no bed, no belt, no shoelaces, and above all, no verbal contact with the world around him—except for daily conversations with the camp's Roman Catholic chaplain. . . . Pound initially held up fairly well under the circumstances. Witnesses at the DTC later remembered him as reading his Confucius for hours on end, contemplating the surrounding landscape, engaging in shadow boxing, fencing, and imaginary tennis matches in his cage, and ingeniously arranging the tiny pup tent which, out of sheer mercy, had eventually been issued to him to protect him from the wind and sun and rain of the Pisan plain.
>
> But after some two and a half weeks of this, the prisoner foundered. (Sieburth 2003, xii–xiii)

NATIONAL HEALING

Part 1. Cage

1.   Six steps east
        north, west, south
        a cage
        or a thought
        trapped
        in a fence
        a soul
        dragging
        emptiness
        circulation
        without progress
            a cage
            a self
            a river bends
            crescent blue light

        as daylight fails
        I stitch
        versions
        of my self
        from shadows
        and bits
        of a monument
        to forgetting
        words blow
        through papers
        about a square
        pinning me
        to shadows
        sliding across
        a compound

        in this
        floodlight
        I arrange
        pieces

of this life
into one
at least
intentional fallacy:
the writer did matter
even as words
measure
a jagged path
to uneven suns
blind
to the history
of falls
into
bottomless
selves

       mountains
       turning
       blue and silver
       moonlight
       cage mesh

and I dreamt
I flew up
out of this cage
and over this yard
over a land
all new
all free.

2.   A life
spent trying
to be yourself
where everyone
sees you
stupid-faced
figuring
on feet scraping
across a
concrete floor

like you are
expecting
someone
who never shows
it's like an ending
that it's not
it's like a beginning
knowing
you weren't
looked for
as if
this cage
were not you
it's like wanting
to be new
but you aren't
it's like living
two impulses
instead of neither
it's like looking
for an answer
in a square
that never existed
wishing for relief
from a sun
or a self
rummaging
through graceless relics
lying in
a square
released
from a dream
and flying
into a punishing
white
sky

it's your broken
presence

in a wrong time
and the wrong things
they gave you
the wrong self
you gave yourself
it's blowing
across a square
toward you
crying
a night-caged
wind
it's like
the mechanized
jerk of your hand
connected to no one
unlocking a cage
and finding
another
trick life
disappearing
clown act
and slow dissolve
to you saying
   "it's going to be another hot one"
to no one
and nothing
other than
the one night
you heard
a voice
from another cage
as you made figures
a geometry
of a limited self
one parallel line
one edge of a square
theorum:
the difference
between you

and everyone else
the difference
you search
the twisted
creases
of a heart
mesh fence for
some sign
that you aren't
hung on
a cage
drying in the sun
        a parade ground
        a sea of faces.

Part 2. Circulations

1.   A city
       a sky
       the mountains
       you drift
       from fear
       to shining idea
       and back
       making
       a monument
       of impulses
       and second
       thoughts
       wondering
       why it is
       so far
       to the river
       still farther
       to the mountains
       circling
       the cage
       spitting stick
       curses
       through

mesh holes the
size of fists

a cage
or a city
at war
with itself
a bombed out
enclave
without a clue
without a key
you would
turn a city
in a bottle
and
if you could
turn a cage
into a city
it would be
the city
you always
dreamt
the one
you always
believed
could be
new.

2.   At night
you make
the sounds
you hear
when no one
is listening
like saying
this is me
reaching
my hands
into the

night sky
higher
than
the hours
higher than
a cage
fantastic
face and words
thoughts and hands
not bleeding
still eyes
locked
on a mountain
that took
a life
but raised
a soul
      a light
      above
      the other
      fading
      mountains.

Part 3. Key

1.   The key is
    writing it
    so well
    that you
    cannot tell
    the thing
    from the
    thing made
    so when it
    takes you in
    surprise
    you know
    what was
    twisting
    and tying

your thoughts
to a loss
inside
another loss
squatting
in a cage
in a square
looking up
cutting eyes on
the sky
and the need
to look
into the faces
of the many
versions of a self
it's like expecting
to see
and not
it's like
the living
without end
that ends
when you least
expect it
it begins again
consuming your sin
      a serrated sun.

Part 4. Uncaged

1.   It comes
       finally
       to the need
       to heal
       and searching
       the skies
       to find
       words
       you don't remember
       and the way

to say them
so they will hold
the scalding
concrete mist
rising from
square
and field
obscuring
this lock
you fill
with shards
of broken
dreams until
you find
improvised
a key
a light.

2.   And in this light
open becomes door
and admission
becomes words
from other times and others' dreams
geometries of being and necessary visions on necessary ways
light moving across the surface of a mind as it moves across the
surface of a building. Trajectories. The process of being open.

it is this: if you listen when you write you know how the words of another
come to life in a room full of doors and windows and people in a garden and someone sings light from one country to another and you try
whether you know it or not to get back to the process of becoming new
in a new place and a new way out of pasts that have picked you clean or
that you dreamt you ditched craving to be new in the service of a cause
you put fingers to keys

in a quarter
in a square
at the end
of a street

in the dark
and fog
a cage door
a lock
a room full of doors
a room full of windows

and what is true now slips out of my shaking hands in a piazza where everyone knows these tricks if the devil is right outside your door or right inside your door or right inside your details so that you become no one other than who the guards say you are or worse closer inside who you say you are

unless
you
write yourself
out

it's like
walking
to the front
of a cage
and reaching
through the bars
and turning the
key that
was maybe
always
there
though you
did not know it

and if the key reappears on a ring of keys your sweating hands work them fever-burned in the hot sun and counting on shutting out the present and letting in the past and trying to grab a future and the keys you might have seen if you had been thinking this is all that matters and no turning back no coming back no natural disaster no wrong mountains migrating over the cage I see them filtering through their orange light telling me how the keys turn to sarcasm in a laugh across a square a wine

glass falls upon beating pigeon wings as they pick at stray monarchs in
all I survey in so much motion and meeting then maybe a new life is possible though where it is supposed to come from I think I see in the bot-
tom of a tin cup I kick in protest just to hear the clatter of hope across
the square in the respiration of a sun

                    it's like sitting
                    on concrete steps
                    of a church
                    in a square
                    staring
                    at nothing
                    smiling
                    at everything
                    coming true
                    joy, pain
                    sad beginnings
                    new endings
                    transfers
                    losses
                    the sky
                    when a door
                    opens
                    when
                    a window
                    falls
                    a promise
                    a man made
                    standing beside
                    his words
                    dense mesh
                    once holding
                    him down
                    now
                    holding
                    him up
                    the sun
                    turns
                    a life

unfinished
turns
a nation
letting go
the mountains
on wings
a promise
holding on
the stars
coming closer
a world
set free

it's like turning around toward the sun behind you turning around toward the flood plain behind you leading to a city on a crescent river where you realize even if you are still where you were when you started and sometimes that is enough to know that even if you are still you have taken a step out of some version of some sort of pain because you stood over the edge of a river at night even though you haven't gotten much past the door of the cage or down the road out of town

you've at least
seen
a way
and say it
to no one
so maybe
some day
the words
will mean something
or more
to someone
because you were
finally leaving
finally walking
into town
a white hot piazza
past quarters
of people packing
as city walls

fall before roads
you stop
surprised by words
coming up
from the river
across the plain
up from ashes
down from mountains
words
not about you
but about a world
where people meet
as locks
tick, grab
and let go
wing magic
of bright truth
where
a scream
in the night
is also
a moment
beyond pain
        people meet
you see it,
now, finally,
a city of people
a world
a sun
a river bends
a sky
we've learned
to live
with
a world
given freely
by everyone
each in
different words

a promise
a question
that never sounds
like one

together, then,

   a prayer, a promise,
   a city, a river
   becomes a crescent
of blue light
   a river and a process
   of being open
   and standing
   by our words
someone says,
"No, I've earned these tears
all by myself.
They are my own."
and someone says,
this is the way
out of here
and knowing this
   I am staying.
   There are the
   cages we open
   and the ones
   still closed—
   it is a time
   and it is the time it takes—
   it is learning a new way.
   Oh process of being open.
in the lowland
in the damaged land
by the river
coming down
to us
we learn
together
to rise

rebuilding

   a city

our homes

   rebuilding

ourselves

   together.

   Oh process of being open.

   We become ourselves.

How we heal.

REFERENCES

Adamson, Joseph, and Hilary Clark. 1999. "Introduction: Shame, Affect, Writing." In *Schemes of Shame: Psychoanalysis, Shame, and Writing*, ed. Joseph Adamson and Hilary Clark, 1–34. Albany: State University of New York Press.

Adamson, Joseph, and Hilary Clark, eds. 1999. *Schemes of Shame: Psychoanalysis, Shame, and Writing*. *SUNY Series in Psychoanalysis and Culture*. Albany: State University of New York Press.

Ahmad, Aijaz. 1992. *In Theory: Classes, Nations, Literatures*. New York: Verso.

Ahmad, Aijaz. 1995. "Postcolonialism: What's in a Name?" In *Late Imperial Culture*, ed. Román De La Campa, E. Ann Kaplan, and Michael Sprinker, 11–32. London: Verso.

'Ali, Hadrat. 1995. *Living and Dying with Grace: Counsels of Hadrat 'Ali*. Trans. Thomas Cleary. Boston: Shambala Books.

al-Jahiz, Abu 'Uthman 'Amr ibn Bahr. 1999. *Avarice and the Avaricious*. Trans. Jim Colville. The Kegan Paul Arabia Library Vol. V. New York: Kegan Paul International.

Althusser, Louis. 1971. *Lenin and Philosophy and Other Essays*. Trans. Ben Brewster. New York: Monthly Review Press.

Althusser, Louis, and Étienne Balibar. 2009. *Reading Capital*. New York: Verso.

Ames, Roger T., with Wimal Dissanayake and Thomas P. Kasulis, eds. 1994. *Self as Person in Asian Theory and Practice*. Albany: State University of New York Press.

Amin, Samir. 1989. *Eurocentrism*. Trans. Russel Moore. New York: Monthly Review Press.

Amin, Samir. 2004. *The Liberal Virus: Permanent War and the Americanization of the World*. New York: The Monthly Review Press.

Anderson, Benedict. 1998. *The Spectre of Comparisons: Nationalism, Southeast Asia, and the World*. London: Verso.

Anderson, Benedict. 1983. *Imagined Communities: Reflections on the Origin and Spread of Nationalism*. Rev. ed. London: Verso.

Anderson, Charles M., and Marian M. MacCurdy. 2000. "Introduction." In *Writing and Healing: Toward an Informed Practice*, ed. Charles M. Anderson and Marian M. MacCurdy, 1–24. Refiguring English Studies. Urbana, IL: National Council of Teachers of English.

Anyon, Jean. 1980. "Social Class and the Hidden Curriculum of Work." *Journal of Education* 162 (1): 67–92.

Anyon, Jean. 1981. "Social Class and School Knowledge." *Curriculum Inquiry* 11 (1): 3–42. http://dx.doi.org/10.2307/1179509.

Anyon, Jean. 1997. *Ghetto Schooling: A Political Economy of Urban Educational Reform*. New York: Teachers College Press.

Arebi, Saddeka. 1994. *Women and Words in Saudi Arabia: The Politics of Literary Discourse*. New York: Columbia University Press.

Aristotle. 1932. *The Rhetoric of Aristotle*. Trans. Lane Cooper. Englewood Cliffs, NJ: Prentice Hall.

Asante, Molefi Kete. 1998. *The Afrocentric Idea*. Rev. ed. Philadelphia: Temple University Press.

Ashcroft, Bill, Gareth Griffiths, and Helen Tiffin, eds. 1995. *The Post-Colonial Studies Reader*. New York: Routledge.

Atwell, Nancie. 1987. *In the Middle: Writing, Reading, and Learning with Adolescents*. Upper Montclair, NJ: Boynton/Cook.

Augustine of Hippo, St. 1961. *The Confessions*. New York: Penguin.

Augustine, St. 1986. *On Christian Doctrine*. New York: Macmillan.

Baca, Damián, and Victor Villaneuva, eds. 2010. *Rhetorics of the Americas 3114 BC to 2012 CE*. New York: Palmgrave.

Bain, Alexander. 1890. *English Composition and Rhetoric*. Enlarged edition. New York: D. Appleton and Company.

Balibar, Étienne. 2004. *We, The People of Europe?: Reflections on Transnational Citizenship*. Translation/Transnation, ed. Emily Apter. Princeton, NJ: Princeton University Press.

Balibar, Étienne. "Racism and Nationalism. 2000. In *Race, Nation, Class: Ambiguous Identities* by Étienne Balibar and Immanuel Wallerstein, 37–67. Translator of Étienne Balibar, Chris Turner. London: Verso.

Barber, Karin, ed. 2006. *Africa's Hidden Histories: Everyday Literacy and Making the Self*. African Expressive Cultures. Bloomington: Indiana University Press.

Barksdale, Mary Alice, Carol Watson, and Eun Soo Park. 2007. "Pen Pal Letter Exchanges: Taking First Steps Toward Developing Cultural Understandings." *Reading Teacher* 61 (1): 58–68. http://dx.doi.org/10.1598/RT.61.1.6.

Barnstone, Tony, and Chou Ping. 1996. *The Art of Writing: Teachings of the Chinese Masters*. Boston: Shambala Books.

Bartholomae, David, with Anthony R. Petrosky. 1986. *Facts, Artifacts and Counterfacts: Reading and Writing in Theory and Practice*. Upper Montclair, NJ: Boynton/Cook.

Barzun, Jacques. 1992. *Begin Here: The Forgotten Conditions of Teaching and Learning*. Chicago: University of Chicago Press.

Barzun, Jacques. 2002. "Curing Provincialism: Why We Educate the Way We Do; A Conversation with Jacques Barzun." *American Educator* 26.3: 6, 10–11. Accessed June 9, 2009. ERIC (EJ660279).

Bawarshi, Anis, and Mary Jo Reiff. 2010. *Genre: An Introduction to History, Theory, Research, and Pedagogy*. West Lafayette, IN: Parlor Press.

Bazerman, Charles, Robert Krut, Karen Lunsford, Susan McLeod, Suzie Null, Paul Rogers, and Amanda Stansell, eds. 2010. *Traditions of Writing Research*. New York: Routledge.

Beaufort, Anne. 2007. *College Writing and Beyond: A New Framework for University Writing Instruction*. Logan: Utah State University Press.

Bell, Debbie. 1992. "Public School and University Compañeros: Changing Lives." In *Social Issues in the English Classroom*, ed. C. Mark Hurlbert and Samuel Totten, 174–95. Urbana, IL: National Council of Teachers of English.

Bellanca, James A., and Terry Stirling. 2011. *Classrooms without Borders: Using Internet Projects to Teach Communication and Collaboration*. New York: Teachers College Press.

Benson, Chris, and Scott Christian, with Dixie Goswami, and Walter H. Gooch, eds. 2002. *Writing to Make a Difference: Classroom Practices for Community Change*. The Practitioner Inquiry Series, ed. Marilyn Cochran-Smith and Susan L. Lytle. New York: Teachers College Press.

Benson, Thomas W., and Michael H. Prosser, eds. 1988. *Readings in Classical Rhetoric*. Mahwah, NJ: Lawrence Erlbaum.

Berlin, James A. 1984. *Writing Instruction in Nineteenth-Century American Colleges*. Studies in Writing and Rhetoric. Carbondale: Southern Illinois University Press.

Berlin, James A. 1987. *Rhetoric and Reality: Writing Instruction in American Colleges, 1900–1985*. Studies in Writing and Rhetoric. Carbondale: Southern Illinois University Press.

Berlin, James A. 1991. "Rhetoric, Poetic, and Culture: Contested Boundaries in English Study." *The Politics of Writing Instruction: Postsecondary*, ed. Richard Bullock and John Trimbur, 23–38. General editor, Charles Schuster. Portsmouth, NH: Boynton/Cook Heinemann.

Berlin, James A. 1996. *Rhetorics, Poetics, and Cultures: Refiguring English Studies*, ed. Stephen M. North. Urbana: National Council of Teachers of English.

Bernstein, Basil. 1971. *Theoretical Studies toward a Sociology of Education.* London: Routledge and Kegan Paul.

Bernstein, Basil. 1973. *Applied Studies towards a Sociology of Education.* London: Routledge and Kegan Paul.

Bernstein, Basil. 1973. *Towards a Theory of Educational Transmission.* London: Routledge and Kegan Paul.

Bernstein, Basil. 1990. *The Structuring of Pedagogic Discourse.* London: Routledge and Kegan Paul. http://dx.doi.org/10.4324/9780203011263.

Bernstein, Charles. 1992. "Pounding Fascism." In *A Poetics*, 121–27. Cambridge, MA: Harvard University Press.

Berthoff, Ann E. 1981. "The Intelligent Eye and the Thinking Hand." In *The Making of Meaning: Metaphors, Models, and Maxims for Writing Teachers*, 61–67. Upper Montclair, NJ: Boynton/Cook.

Berthoff, Ann E. "Learning the Uses of Chaos." In *The Making of Meaning: Metaphors, Models, and Maxims for Writing Teachers*, 68–72. Upper Montclair, NJ: Boynton/Cook.

Berthoff, Ann E. 1981. *The Making of Meaning: Metaphors, Models, and Maxims for Writing Teachers.* Upper Montclair, NJ: Boynton/Cook.

Berthoff, Ann E. 1984. *Reclaiming the Imagination: Philosophical Perspectives for Writers and Teachers of Writing.* Upper Montclair, NJ: Boynton/Cook.

Billig, Michael. 1995. *Banal Nationalism.* Thousand Oaks, CA: Sage.

Bizzaro, Resa Crane. 2004. "Shooting Our Last Arrow: Developing a Rhetoric of Identity for Unenrolled American Indians." *College English* 67 (1): 61–74. http://dx.doi.org/10.2307/4140725.

Bizzaro, Resa Crane. 2005. "'Making this Country Great': Native American Educational Sovereignty in North Carolina." In *Calling Cards: Theory and Practice in Studies of Race, Gender, and Culture*, ed. Jacqueline Jones Royster and Anne Marie Simpkins, 187–200. Stony Brook: State University of New York Press.

Bizzaro, Resa Crane. 2007. "Modern Indian Rhetorics: Survivance and Identity in the Twenty-First Century." *Journal of Advanced Composition* 27 (1–2): 419–25.

Bizzell, Patricia. 2002. "The Intellectual Work of 'Mixed' Forms of Academic Discourse." In *Alt/Dis: Alternative Discourses and the Academy*, ed. Christopher Schroeder, Helen Fox, and Patricia Bizzell, 1–10. Portsmouth, NH: Boynton/Cook Heinemann.

Bizzell, Patricia, and Bruce Herzberg, eds. 2001. *The Rhetorical Tradition: Readings from Classical Times to the Present.* 2nd ed. Boston: Bedford.

Blanche, Jerry D., ed. 1990. *Native American Reader: Stories, Speeches, and Poems.* Juneau, AK: Denali Press.

Bleich, David. 1999. "In Case of Fire, Throw In: What to Do with Textbooks Once You Switch to Sourcebooks." In *(Re)Visioning Composition Textbooks: Conflicts of Culture, Ideology and Pedagogy*, ed. Xin Liu Gale and Frederic Gale, 15–42. Albany: State University of New York Press.

Blitz, Michael, and C. Mark Hurlbert. 1989. "To: You, From: Michael Blitz and C. Mark Hurlbert, Re: Literacy Demands and Institutional Autobiography." *Works and Days: Essays in the Socio-Historical Dimension of Literature and the Arts 13* 7.1: 7–33.

Blitz, Michael, and C. Mark Hurlbert. 1998. *Letters for the Living: Teaching Writing in a Violent Age.* Refiguring English Studies. Urbana, IL: National Council of Teachers of English.

Bourdieu, Pierre. 1977. *Outline of a Theory of Practice.* Trans. Richard Nice. Cambridge Studies in Social and Cultural Anthropology 16, ed. Ernest Gellner, Jack Goody, Stephen Gudeman, Michael Herzfeld, and Jonathan Parry. Cambridge: Cambridge University Press.

Bourdieu, Pierre. 1984. *Distinction: A Social Critique of the Judgement of Taste*, trans. Richard Nice. Cambridge, MA: Harvard University Press.

Bowles, Samuel, and Herbert Gintis. 1976. *Schooling in Capitalist America: Educational Reform and the Contradictions of Economic Life.* New York: Basic Books.

Brand, Alice G. 2000. "Healing and the Brain." In *Writing and Healing: Toward an Informed Practice,* ed. Charles M. Anderson and Marian M. MacCurdy, 201–21. Refiguring English Studies. Urbana, IL: National Council of Teachers of English.

Brand, Dionne. 1984. *Winter Epigrams to Ernesto Cardenal in Defense of Claudia.* N.p.: Wacaro Productions.

Bridwell-Bowles, Lillian. 1995. "Discourse and Diversity: Experimental Writing within the Academy." In *Feminine Principles and Women's Experience in American Composition and Rhetoric,* ed. Louise Wetherbee Phelps and Janet Emig, 43–66. Pittsburgh Series in Composition, Literacy and Culture, ed. David Bartholomae and Jean Ferguson Carr. Pittsburgh: University of Pittsburgh Press.

Brittain, Carmina. 2002. *Transnational Messages: Experiences of Chinese and Mexican Immigrants in American Schools.* The New Americans: Recent Immigration and American Society, ed. Carola Suárez-Orozco and Marcelo Suárez-Orozco. New York: LFB Scholarly Publishing.

Bryant, LizBeth. "A Textbook's Theory: Current Composition Theory in Argument Textbooks." In *(Re)Visioning Composition Textbooks: Conflicts of Culture, Ideology and Pedagogy,* ed. Xin Liu Gale and Frederic Gale, 113–33. Albany: State University of New York Press.

Burke, Kenneth. 1968. "Lexicon Rhetoricae." In *Counter-Statement,* 123–83. Berkeley: University of California Press.

Burke, Kenneth. 1969. *A Rhetoric of Motives.* Berkeley: University of California Press.

Burns, Audrey, Alicia Landsberg, Evan Smith, and Jesse Uruchima, eds. 2010. *Pro(se) letariets: The Writing of the Trans-Atlantic Worker Writer Federation.* Philadelphia: New City Community Press.

Buttjes, Dieter, and Michael Byram, eds. 1991. *Mediating Languages and Cultures: Towards an Intercultural Theory of Foreign Language Education.* Multilingual Matters 60. Philadelphia: Multilingual Matters LTD.

Byram, Michael. 1989. *Cultural Studies in Foreign Language Education.* Multilingual Matters 46, ed. Derrick Sharp. Philadelphia: Multilingual Matters LTD.

Byram, Michael, and Veronica Esarte-Sarries. 1991. *Investigating Cultural Studies in Foreign Language Teaching: A Book for Teachers.* Multilingual Matters 62, ed. Derrick Sharp. Philadelphia: Multilingual Matters LTD.

Byram, Michael, and Michael Fleming, eds. 1998. *Language Learning in Intercultural Perspective: Approaches through Drama and Ethnography.* Cambridge Language Teaching Library. New York: Cambridge University Press.

Cahalan, James, and David Downing, eds. 1991. *Practicing Theory in Introductory Literature Courses.* Urbana, IL: National Council of Teachers of English.

Calafell, Bernadette M. 2010. "Rhetorics of Possibility: Challenging Textual Bias through the Theory of the Flesh." In *Rhetorica in Motion: Feminist Rhetorical Methods and Methodologies,* ed. Eileen E. Schell and K. J. Rawson, 104–17. Pittsburgh Series in Composition, Literacy, and Culture, ed. David Bartholomae and Jean Ferguson Carr. Pittsburgh: University of Pittsburgh Press.

Calinescu, Matei. 1987. *Five Faces of Modernity: Modernism, Avante-Garde, Decadence, Kitsch, Postmodernism.* Durham, NC: Duke University Press.

Campbell, George. 1963. *The Philosophy of Rhetoric.* Edited by Lloyd Bitzer. Landmarks in Rhetoric and Public Address, ed. David Potter. Carbondale: Southern Illinois University Press.

Campbell, Kermit E. 2005. *Gettin' Our Groove On: Rhetoric, Language, and Literacy for the Hip Hop Generation.* African American Life Series, ed. Melba Joyce Boyd and Ronald Brown. Detroit: Wayne State University Press.

Canagarajah, A. Suresh. 2003. "Foreword." In *Language Diversity in the Classroom: From Intention to Practice*, ed. Geneva Smitherman and Victor Villaneuva, ix–xiv. Studies in Writing and Rhetoric. Carbandale: Southern Illinois University Press.

Canagarajah, A. Suresh. 2010. "A Rhetoric of Shuttling Between Languages." In *Cross-Language Relations in Composition*, ed. Bruce Horner, Min-Zhan Lu, and Paul Kei Matsuda, 158–79. Urbana: Southern Illinois University Press.

Cardenal, Ernesto. 1977. *Apocalypse and Other Poems*. Ed. Robert Pring-Mill and Donald D. Walsh; trans. Thomas Merton, Kenneth Rexroth, Mireya Jaimes-Freyre, Robert Pring-Mill, and Donald D. Walsh. New York: New Directions.

Cardenal, Ernesto. 1993. *Cosmic Canticle*. Trans. Jonathan Lyons. Williamtic, CT: Curbstone Press.

Cassirer, Ernst. 1944. *An Essay on Man: An Introduction to a Philosophy of Human Culture*. New Haven, CT: Yale University Press.

Cassirer, Ernst. 1946. *Language and Myth*. Trans. Susanne K. Langer. Dover Books on Western Philosophy. New York: Dover.

Cassirer, Ernst. 1955. *The Philosophy of Symbolic Forms*, Vol. 1: Language. Trans. Ralph Manheim. New Haven, CT: Yale University Press.

Cheah, Pheng, and Bruce Robbins, eds. 1998. *Cosmopolitics: Thinking and Feeling beyond the Nation*. Cultural Politics 14, edited by the Social Text Collective. Minneapolis: University of Minnesota Press.

Christian, Scott. 1997. *Exchanging Lives: Middle School Writers Online*. Urbana: National Council of Teacher of English.

Cicero. 1942. *De Oratore*. Trans. H. Rackham. Loeb Classical Library, ed. G. P. Goold. Cambridge, MA: Harvard University Press.

Cicero. 1949. *De Inventione*. Trans. H. M. Hubbell. Loeb Classical Library, ed. G. P. Goold. Cambridge, MA: Harvard University Press.

Collins, Daniel F. 2001. "Audience in Afrocentric Rhetoric: Promoting Human Agency and Social Change." In *Alternative Rhetorics: Challenges to the Rhetorical Tradition*, ed. Laura Gray-Rosendale and Sibylle Gruber, 185–200. Albany: State University of New York Press.

Combs, Steven C. 2005. *The Dao of Rhetoric*. Albany: State University of New York Press.

Condon, Frankie. 2012. *I Hope I Join the Band: Narrative, Affiliation, and Antiracist Rhetoric*. Logan: Utah State University Press.

Confucius. 1997. *The Analects of Confucius*, trans. Chichung Huang. New York: Oxford University Press.

Connors, Robert J. 1981. "The Rise and Fall of the Modes of Discourse." *College Composition and Communication* 32 (4): 444–55. http://dx.doi.org/10.2307/356607.

Cooper, Charles, Lee Odell, and Cynthia Courts. 1978. "Discourse Theory: Implications for Research in Composing." In *Research on Composing: Points of Departure*, ed. Charles Cooper and Lee Odell, 1–12. Urbana, IL: National Council of Teachers of English.

Cooper, Lane. 1932. *The Rhetoric of Aristotle: An Expanded Translation with Supplementary Examples for Students of Composition and Public Speaking*. Englewood Cliffs, NJ: Prentice-Hall.

Cook, Méira. 2005. *Writing Lovers: Reading Canadian Love Poetry by Women*. Montreal: McGill-Queen's University Press.

Corbett, Edward P.J. 1971. *Classical Rhetoric for the Modern Student*. 2nd ed. New York: Oxford University Press.

Cosgrove, Cornelius, and Nancy Barta-Smith. 2004. *Search of Eloquence: Cross-Disciplinary Conversations on the Role of Writing in Undergraduate Education*. Research and Teaching in Rhetoric and Composition, ed. Michael M. Williamson and David A. Jolliffe. Cresskill, NJ: Hampton Press.

Cox, Michelle, Jay Jordan, Chrisitina Ortmeier-Hooper, and Gwen Gray Schwartz, eds. 2010. *Reinventing Identities in Second Language Writing*. Urbana: National Council of Teachers of English.

Crowley, Sharon. 1998. *Composition in the University: Historical and Polemical Essays*. Pittsburgh Series in Composition, Literacy and Culture, ed. David Bartholomae and Jean Ferguson Carr. Pittsburgh: University of Pittsburgh Press.

Crowley, Sharon, and Deborah Hawhee. 2008. *Ancient Rhetorics for Contemporary Students*. 4th ed. New York: Longman.

Cullen, Robert. 1999. *Rhetoric for a Multicultural America*. 1st ed. New York: Longman.

Cushman, Ellen. 1998. *The Struggle and the Tools: Oral and Literate Strategies in an Inner City Community*. Albany: State University of New York Press.

Cushman, Ellen. 2005. "Face, Skins, and the Identity Politics of Rereading Race." *Rhetoric Review* 24: 378–82.

Cushman, Ellen. 2006. "Toward a Praxis of New Media: The Allotment Period in Cherokee History." *Reflections on Community-Based Writing Instruction* 4 (3): 124–43.

Cushman, Ellen. 2008. "Toward a Rhetoric of Self Representation: Identity Politics in Indian Country and Rhetoric and Composition." *College Composition and Communication* 60 (2): 321–65.

Davis, Robert L., and Mark F. Shadle. 2007. *Teaching Multiwriting: Researching and Composing with Multiple Genres, Media, Disciplines, and Cultures*. Carbondale: Southern Illinois University Press.

Dawes, Greg. 1993. "Poetry and 'Spiritual Materialism': Ernesto Cardenal." *Aesthetics and Revolution: Nicaraguan Poetry 1979–1990*, by Greg Dawes, 64–108. Minneapolis: University of Minnesota Press.

De La Campa, Román, E. Ann Kaplan, and Michael Sprinker, eds. 1995. *Late Imperial Culture*. London: Verso.

Delcambre, I., and Y. Reuter. 2010. "The French Didactics Approach to Writing, from Elementary School to University." In *Traditions of Writing Research*, ed. Charles Bazerman, Robert Krut, Karen Lunsford, Susan McLeod, Suzie Null, Paul Rogers, and Amanda Stansell, 17–43. New York: Routledge.

Derrida, Jacques. 1976. *Of Grammatology*. Trans. Gayatri Chakravorty Spivak. Baltimore: Johns Hopkins University Press.

Derrida, Jacques. 1983. *Dissemination*. Trans. Barbara Johnson. Chicago: University of Chicago Press.

Dessommes, Nancy Bishop. 2006. "Whiteness and Resistance: Investigating Student Concepts of White Privilege in the Writing Classroom." PhD diss., Indiana University of Pennsylvania, Indiana.

Devitt, Amy J. 2004. *Writing Genres*. Carbondale: Southern Illinois University Press.

Dewey, John. 1916. *Democracy and Education*. New York: The Free Press.

Dingo, Rebecca. 2007. "Making the Unfit, Fit: The Rhetoric of Mainstreaming in the World Bank's Commitment to Gender Equality and Disability Rights." *Wagadu: Journal of Transnational Women's and Gender Studies* 4 (Summer): 93–107.

Dingo, Rebecca. 2008. "Linking Transnational Logics: A Feminist Rhetorical Analysis of Public Policy Networks." *College English* 70 (5): 482–97.

Dingo, Rebecca. 2012. "Turning the Tables on the Megarhetoric of Women's Empowerment." In *The Megarhetorics of Global Development*, ed. Rebecca Dingo and J. Blake Scott, 174–98. Pittsburgh Series in Composition, Literacy, and Culture, ed. David Bartholomae and Jean Ferguson Carr. Pittsburgh: University of Pittsburgh Press.

Dingo, Rebecca, and J. Blake Scott. 2012. *The Megarhetorics of Global Development*. Pittsburgh Series in Composition, Literacy, and Culture, ed. David Bartholomae and Jean Ferguson Carr. Pittsburgh: University of Pittsburgh Press.

Dodd, Anne Wescott. 1986. "Publishing Opportunities for Student (and Teacher) Writers." *English Journal* 75 (3): 85–9. http://dx.doi.org/10.2307/818875.

Dodd, Anne Wescott, Ellen Jo Ljung, Brenda Szedeli, and Sheryl L. Guth. 1993. "A Symposium: Publishing Student Writing." *English Journal* 82 (2): 47–54. http://dx.doi.org/10.2307/819703.

Donahue, Christiane. 2009. "'Internationalization' and Composition Studies: Reorienting the Discourse." *College Composition and Communication* 61 (2): 212–43.

Downing, David, ed. 1994. *Changing Classroom Practices: Resources for Literary and Cultural Studies.* Urbana, IL: National Council of Teachers of English.

Downing, David B., Claude Mark Hurlbert, and Paula Mathieu, eds. 2002. *Beyond English Inc.: Curricular Reform in a Global Economy.* Portsmouth, NH: Boynton/Cook Heinemann.

DuPlessis, Rachel Blau. 1985. "For the Etruscans." In *The New Feminist Criticism: Essays on Women, Literature and Theory,* ed. Elaine Showalter, 271–91. New York: Pantheon.

Emig, Janet A. 1971. *The Composing Processes of Twelfth Graders.* Urbana, IL: National Council of Teachers of English.

Emig, Janet A. 1983. "Uses of the Unconscious in Composing." In *The Web of Meaning: Essays on Writing, Teaching, Learning, and Thinking,* by Janet Emig. Ed. Dixie Goswami and Maureen Butler, 46–53. Upper Montclair, NJ: Boynton/Cook.

Emig, Janet A. 1983. *The Web of Meaning: Essays on Writing, Teaching, Learning, and Thinking.* Ed. Dixie Goswami and Maureen Butler. Upper Montclair, NJ: Boynton/Cook.

Erasmus, Desiderius, of Rotterdam. 1963. *On Copia of Words and Ideas.* Trans. Donald B. King and H. David Rix. Mediaeval Philosophical Texts in Translation 12. Milwaukee: Marquette University Press.

Federici, Silvia, George Caffentzis, and Ousseina Alidou, eds. 2000. *A Thousand Flowers: Social Struggles against Structural Adjustments in African Universities.* Trenton, NJ: Africa World Press.

Fenollosa, Ernest. 1920. "The Chinese Written Character as a Medium for Poetry." In *Instigations of Ezra Pound,* by Ezra Pound, 357–88. Freeport, NY: Books for Libraries Press.

Fernheimer, Janice W., ed. 2010. *Composing Jewish Rhetorics.* Spec. Issue of *College English* 72.6.

Finn, Patrick. 1999. *Literacy with an Attitude: Educating Working-Class Children in Their Own Self-Interest.* Albany: State University of New York Press.

Flynn, Elizabeth. 1988. "Composing as a Woman." *College Composition and Communication* 39 (4): 423–35. http://dx.doi.org/10.2307/357697.

Flynn, Elizabeth. 2002. *Feminism beyond Modernism.* Carbondale: Southern Illinois University Press.

Foster, David, and David R. Russell. 2002. "Introduction: Rearticulating Articulation." In *Writing and Learning in Cross-National Perspective: Transitions from Secondary to Higher Education,* ed. David Foster and David R. Russell, 1–47. Urbana: National of Council of Teachers of English.

Foster, David, and David R. Russell eds. 2002. *Writing and Learning in Cross-National Perspective: Transitions from Secondary to Higher Education.* Urbana, IL: National of Council of Teachers of English.

Foster, John Bellamy. 2002. *Ecology against Capitalism.* N.p.: Monthly Review Press.

Foster, John Bellamy. 2009. *The Ecological Revolution: Making Peace with the Planet.* N.p.: Monthly Review Press.

Foster, John Bellamy, Brett Clark, and Richard York. 2010. *The Ecological Rift: Capitalism's War on the Earth.* N.p.: Monthly Review Press.

Foucault, Michel. 1970. *The Order of Things: An Archaeology of the Human Sciences.* New York: Pantheon.

Foucault, Michel. 1982. *The Archaeology of Knowledge and the Discourse on Language.* Trans. A.M. Sheridan Smith. New York: Vintage.

Fox, Helen. 1994. *Listening to the World: Cultural Issues in Academic Writing.* Urbana: National Council of Teachers of English.

Freire, Paulo. 1973. *Education for Critical Consciousness.* New York: Continuum.

Freire, Paulo. 2000. *Pedagogy of the Oppressed.* New York: Continuum.

Furniss, Graham. 2006. "Literary Circles, New Opportunities, and Continuing Debates in Hausa Literary Production." In *Africa's Hidden Histories: Everyday Literacy and Making the Self*, ed. Karin Barber, 416–34. African Expressive Cultures. Bloomington: Indiana University Press.

Gabor, Catherine. 2009. "Writing Partners: Service Learning as a Route to Authority for Basic Writers." *Journal of Basic Writing* 28 (1): 50–70.

Gale, Xin Liu. 1996. *Teachers, Discourses, and Authority in the Postmodern Composition Classroom.* Albany: State University of New York Press.

Gale, Xin Liu. 1999. "The 'Full Toolbox' and Critical Thinking: Conflicts and Contradictions in *The St. Martin's Guide to Writing*." In *(Re)Visioning Composition Textbooks: Conflicts of Culture, Ideology and Pedagogy*, ed. Xin Liu Gale and Frederic Gale, 185–213. Albany: State University of New York Press.

Gale, Xin Liu, and Frederic Gale, eds. 1999. *(Re)Visioning Composition Textbooks: Conflicts of Culture, Ideology and Pedagogy.* Albany: State University of New York Press.

Gallop, Jane, ed. 1995. *Pedagogy: The Question of Impersonation.* Bloomington: Indiana University Press.

Gannett, Cynthia. 1992. *Gender and the Journal: Diaries and Academic Discourse.* Albany: State University of New York Press.

Gardner, H., and T. Hatch. 1989. "Multiple Intelligences Go to School: Educational Implications of the Theory of Multiple Intelligences." *Educational Researcher* 18 (8): 4–10. http://dx.doi.org/10.2307/1176460.

Gates, Henry Louis, Jr. 1988. *The Signifying Monkey: A Theory of Afro-American Literary Criticism.* New York: Oxford University Press. Cited in Robert Cullen, *Rhetoric for a Multicultural America*, 1st ed. (New York: Longman, 1999).

Gellner, Ernest. 1983. *Nations and Nationalism.* Ithaca, NY: Cornell University Press.

Genung, John Franklin. 1891. *The Practical Elements of Rhetoric with Illustrative Examples.* Amherst, MA: Amherst Press of J. E. Williams.

Gillis, Candida. 1994. "Writing Partnerships: Expanding the Audiences for Student Writing." *English Journal* 83 (3): 64–7. http://dx.doi.org/10.2307/820930.

Gilyard, Keith, ed. 1999. *Race, Rhetoric and Composition.* Portsmouth, NH: Boynton/Cook Heinemann.

Gilyard, Keith, and Vorris Nunley, eds. 2004. *Rhetoric and Ethnicity.* Portsmouth, NH: Boynton/Cook Heinemann.

Ginsberg, Allen. 1974. "The Death of Ezra Pound." In *Allen Verbatim: Lectures on Poetry, Politics, Consciousness*, ed. Gordon Ball, 179–87. New York: McGraw-Hill.

Giroux, Henry A. 2000. *Impure Acts: The Practical Politics of Cultural Studies.* New York: Routledge.

Giroux, Henry A. 2001. *Theory and Resistance in Education.* Rev. ed. Critical Studies in Education and Culture Series. Santa Barbara, CA: Praeger.

Glissant, Édouard. 1997. *Poetics of Relation*, trans. Betsy Wing. Ann Arbor: University of Michigan Press.

"Global Educators for Peace: The International Sustainable-Literacy Project." 2011. Roundtable session at the annual meeting of the Conference on College Composition and Communication, Atlanta, Georgia, April 7–9.

"Globalization and Publishing Writing Research: An Editors' Roundtable Sponsored by the CCCC Committee on Globalization of Postsecondary Writing Instruction and Research." 2011. Panel at the annual meeting of the Conference on College Composition and Communication, Atlanta, Georgia, April 6–9.

Golden, James L., and Edward P.J. Corbett, eds. 1968. *The Rhetoric of Blair, Campbell, and Whately.* New York: Holt. Rinehart and Winston.

Goodburn, Amy. 1999. "Racing (Erasing) White Privilege in Teacher/Research Writing about Race." In *Race, Rhetoric and Composition,* ed. Keith Gilyard, 67–86. Portsmouth, NH: Boynton/Cook Heinemann.

Gounaridou, Kiki. 2005. "Theatre and Nationalism: Introductory Remarks and Acknowledgments." In *Staging Nationalism: Essays on Theatre and National Identity,* ed. Kiki Gounaridou, 1–10. Jefferson: McFarland & Company.

Graff, Gerald. 1992. *Beyond the Culture Wars: How Teaching the Conflicts Can Revitalize American Education.* New York: W. W. Norton.

Gray-Rosendale, Laura, and Sibylle Gruber. 2001. "Introduction: Moving beyond Traditions: Exploring the Need for 'Alternative Rhetorics.'" In *Alternative Rhetorics: Challenges to the Rhetorical Tradition,* ed. Laura Gray-Rosendale and Sibylle Gruber, 1–13. Albany: State University of New York Press.

Gray-Rosendale, Laura, and Sibylle Gruber, eds. 2001. *Alternative Rhetorics: Challenges to the Rhetorical Tradition.* Albany: State University of New York Press.

Grewal, Inderpal. 2006. *Transnational America: Feminisms, Diasporas, Neoliberalisms.* Next Wave: New Directions in Women's Studies, ed. Inderpal Grewal, Caren Kaplan, and Robin Eiegman. Durham, NH: Duke University Press.

Hall, David L. 1987. *Thinking through Confucius.* SUNY Series in Systematic Philosophy, ed. Robert Cummings Neville. Albany: State University of New York Press.

Hall, David L., and Roger T. Ames. 1995. *Anticipating China: Thinking through the Narratives of Chinese and Western Culture.* Albany: State University of New York Press.

Hall, David L., and Roger T. Ames. 1998. *Thinking from the Han: Self, Truth, and Transcendence in Chinese and Western Culture.* Albany: State University of New York Press.

Han Fei Tzu. 1964. *Basic Writings.* Ed. Wm. Theodore de Bary, trans. Burton Watson. New York: Columbia University Press.

Han Fei Tzu. 1964. "The Difficulties of Persuasion." In *Basic Writings by Han Fei Tzu,* ed. Wm. Theodore de Bary, trans. Burton Watson, 73–79. New York: Columbia University Press.

Han Fei Tzu. 1964. "Eminence in Learning." In *Basic Writings by Han Fei Tzu,* ed. Wm. Theodore de Bary, trans. Burton Watson, 118–29. New York: Columbia University Press.

Hanh, Thich Nhat. 1998. *Interbeing: Fourteen Guidelines for Engaged Buddhism.* Berkeley, CA: Parallax.

Hannerz, Ulf. 1996. *Transnational Connections: Culture, People, Places.* Comedia, ed. David Morely. New York: Routledge.

Harbord, John. 2010. "Writing in Central and Eastern Europe: Stakeholders and Directions in Initiating Change." *Across the Disciplines* 7.

Harushimana, Immaculée. 2010. "Colonial Language Writing Identities in Postcolonial Africa." In *Reinventing Identities in Second Language Writing,* ed. Michelle Cox, Jay Jordan, Christina Ortmeier-Hooper, and Gwen Gray Schwartz, 207–31. Urbana: National Council of Teachers of English.

Hashim, Abdah Najwa. 1994. "Fever in a Hot Night." In *Women and Words in Saudi Arabia: The Politics of Literary Discourse,* by Saddeka Arebi, 142–52. New York: Columbia University Press. Excerpt originally from *Assafar fi Lail Al-Ahzan (Travel in the Night of Sadness),* Jeddah: Tihama, 1981.

Hattori, Tomo, and Stuart Ching. 2008. "Reexamining the Between World-Trope in Cross-Cultural Composition Studies." In *Representations: Doing Asian American Rhetoric,* ed. LuMing Mao and Morris Young, 41–61. Logan: Utah State University Press.

Hawisher, Gail, Cynthia Selfe, Yi-Huey Guo, and Lu Liu. 2010. "Globalization, Guanxi, and Agency: Designing and Re-designing the Literacies of Cyberspace." In *Cross-Language Relations in Composition*, ed. Bruce Horner, Min-Zhan Lu, and Paul Kei Matsuda, Horner, Lu and Matsuda, 57–80. Urbana: Southern Illinois University Press.

Heath, Shirley Brice. 1983. *Ways with Words*. Cambridge: Cambridge University Press.

Hesford, Wendy S., and Eileen E. Schell, eds. 2008. *Configurations of Transnationality: Locating Feminist Rhetorics*. Special issue of *College English* 7.5.

Hesford, Wendy S., and Eileen E. Schell, eds. 2008. "Introduction: Configurations of Transnationality: Locating Feminist Rhetorics." In *Configurations of Transnationality: Locating Feminist Rhetorics*. Special issue of *College English* 7.5: 461–70.

Hitchcook, Peter. 2003. *Imaginary States: Studies in Cultural Transnationalism*. Transnational Cultural Series, ed. Ien Ang and Jon Stratton. Urbana: University of Illinois Press.

Holledge, Julie, and Joanne Tompkins. 2000. *Women's Intercultural Performance*. New York: Routledge.

Holling, Michelle A., and Bernadette M. Calafell, eds. 2011. *Latina/o Discourses in Vernacular Spaces: Somos de Una Voz?* New York: Lexington.

The Holy Qur-An. English Translation of the Meanings and Commentary. N.d. Revised and edited by The Presidency of Islamic Researches, IFTA, Call and Guidance. Saudi Arabia: The Custodian of the Two Holy Mosques of King Fahd Complex.

Horner, Bruce. 2000. *Terms of Work: A Materialist Critique*. Albany: State University of New York Press.

Horner, Bruce, Kelly Latchaw, Jospeh Lenz, Jody Swilky, and David Wolf. 2002. "Excavating the Ruins of Undergraduate English." In *Beyond English Inc.: Curricular Reform in a Global Economy*, ed. David B. Downing, Claude Mark Hurlbert, and Paula Mathieu, 75–92. Portsmouth, NH: Boynton/Cook Heinemann.

Horner, Bruce, Min-Zhan Lu, and Paul Kei Matsuda, eds. 2010. *Cross-Language Relations in Composition*. Urbana: Southern Illinois University Press.

Hsu, Cathy. 2009. "Writing Partnerships." *Reading Teacher* 63 (2): 153–8. http://dx.doi.org/10.1598/RT.63.2.6.

Huijen, Chen. 2010. "Modern "writingology:" in China." In *Traditions of Writing Research*, ed. Charles Bazerman, Robert Krut, Karen Lunsford, Susan McLeod, Suzie Null, Paul Rogers, and Amanda Stansell, 3–16. New York: Routledge.

Hurlbert, Claude. 2005. "The Corporate Conference" and "The Star System." In "Making 4Cs Matter More," by Claude Hurlbert, Derek Owens, and Robert Yagelski. *Writing on the Edge* 15.2: 67–91.

Hurlbert, Claude. 2006. "A Place in Which to Stand." In *Relations, Locations, Positions: Composition Theory for Writing Teachers*, ed. Peter Vandenberg, Sue Hum, and Jennifer Clary-Lemon, Vandenberg, 353–57. Urbana, IL: National Council of Teachers of English.

Hurlbert, Claude, and Anestine Hector-Mason. 2006. "Exporting the 'Violence of Literacy': Education According to UNESCO and The World Bank." *Composition Forum* 16 (Fall). Accessed May 10, 2010. http://compositionforum.com/issue/16/exporting-violence-literacy.php.

Hurlbert, C. Mark. 1988. "Rhetoric, Possessive Individualism and Beyond." *Writing Instructor* 8 (1): 8–14.

Hurlbert, C. Mark. 1989. "Toward Collectivist Composition: Transforming Social Relations through Classroom Practices." *The Writing Instructor* 8.4: 166–76.

Hurlbert, C. Mark. 1991. "The Walls We Don't See: Towards Collectivist Pedagogies as Political Struggle." In *Practicing Theory in Introductory Literature Courses*, ed. James Cahalan and David Downing, 131–48. Urbana: National Council of Teachers of English.

Hurlbert, C. Mark. 1995. "EN 731: Rhetorical Traditions." *Composition Studies* 23 (2): 38–44.

Hurlbert, C. Mark. 2002. "Review of *Smoke and Mirrors: The Hidden Context of Violence in Schools and Society.*" *Journal of Advanced Composition* 22 (1): 234–40.

Hurlbert, C. Mark, and Ann Marie Bodnar. 1994. "Collective Pain: Literature, War, and Small Change." In *Changing Classroom Practices: Resources for Literary and Cultural Studies,* ed. David Downing, 202–32. Urbana, IL: National Council of Teachers of English.

Hurlbert, C. Mark, and Samuel Totten, eds. 1992. *Social Issues in the English Classroom.* Urbana, IL: National Council of Teachers of English.

Hymbound, Jean-Clotaire. 1995. "La Logique de la Banque Mondiale." *Afrique Education* (September): 34. Cited in "The World Bank, the Language Question and the Future of African Education" by Alamin Mazrui, 43–59, in Silvia Federici, George Caffentzis, and Ousseina Alidou. *A Thousand Flowers: Social Struggles Against Structural Adjustments in African Universities,* (Trenton: Africa World Press, 2000).

"International Student Enrollment Increased by 5 Percent in 2010/11, Led by Strong Increase in Students From China." 2012. Institute of International Education, Inc. Accessed December 31, 2011. http://www.iie.org/Who-We-Are/News-and-Events/Press-Center/Press-Releases/2011/2011-11-14-Open-Doors-International-Students.

Irby, Janet. 1993. "Empowering the Disempowered: Publishing Student Voices." *English Journal* 82 (7): 50–4. http://dx.doi.org/10.2307/819794.

Iriye, Akira. 1997. *Cultural Internationalism and World Order.* Baltimore: Johns Hopkins University Press.

Iriye, Akira. 2002. *Global Community: The Role of International Organizations in the Making of the Contemporary World.* Berkeley: University of California Press.

Jamieson, Sandra. 1997. "Composition Readers and the Construction of Identity." In *Writing in Multicultural Settings,* ed. Carol Severino, Juan C. Guerra, and Johnnella E. Butler, 150–71. Research and Scholarship in Composition, ed. Lil Brannon et al. New York: Modern Language Association.

Janangelo, Joseph. 1999. "Appreciating Narratives of Containment and Contentment: Reading the Writing Handbook as Public Discourse." In *(Re)Visioning Composition Textbooks: Conflicts of Culture, Ideology and Pedagogy,* ed. Xin Liu Gale and Frederic Gale, 93–112. Albany: State University of New York Press.

Johnson, T. R. 2005. "Writing with the Ear." In *Refiguring Prose Style: Possibilities for Writing Pedagogy,* ed. T. R. Johnson and Tom Pace, 267–85. Logan: Utah State University Press.

Joris, Pierre. 2003. "The Millennium Will Be Nomadic or It Will Not: Notes Toward a Nomad Poetics (1996–2002)." In *A Nomad Poetics: Essays by Pierre Joris,* 25–55. Middletown, CT: Wesleyan University Press.

Jung, Julie. 2005. *Revisionary Rhetoric, Feminist Pedagogy, and Multigenre Texts.* Studies in Writing and Rhetoric. Carbondale: Southern Illinois University Press.

Kachru, Braj B. 2009. "World Englishes and Culture Wars." In *The Handbook of World Englishes,* ed. Braj B. Kachru, Yamuna Kachru, and Cecil L. Nelson, 446–71. Malden, MA: Wiley-Blackwell.

Kachru, Braj B., Yamuna Kachru, and Cecil L. Nelson, eds. 2009. *The Handbook of World Englishes.* Malden, MA: Wiley-Blackwell.

Kachru, Braj B., Yamuna Kachru, and Cecil L. Nelson. "Preface." In *The Handbook of World Englishes,* ed. Braj B. Kachru, Yamuna Kachru, and Cecil L. Nelson, xvii–xix. Malden, MA: Wiley-Blackwell.

Kalamaras, George. 1994. *Reclaiming the Tacit Tradition: Symbolic Form in the Rhetoric of Silence.* SUNY Series in Literacy, Culture, and Learning: Theory and Practice, ed. Alan C. Purves. Albany: State University of New York Press.

Kedourie, Elie. 1960. *Nationalism.* London: Verso.

Kells, Michelle Hall, Valerie Balester, and Victor Villaneuva, eds. 2004. *Latino/a Discourses: On Language, Identity, and Literacy Education.* CrossCurrents. Portsmouth, NH: Boynton/Cook Heinemann.

Kennedy, George A. 1998. *Comparative Rhetoric: An Historical and Cross-Cultural Introduction.* New York: Oxford University Press.

Kent, Thomas, ed. 1999. *Post-Process Theory: Beyond the Writing-Process Paradigm.* Carbondale: Southern Illinois University Press.

Kern, Richard. 1995. "Découvrir Berkeley: Students' Representations of Their World on the World Wide Web." In *Virtual Connections: Online Activities and Projects for Networking Language Learners,* ed. Mark Warschauer, 355–59. Second Language Teaching and Curriculum Center. Honolulu: University of Hawaii Press.

Kern, Richard. 1996. "Computer-Mediated Communication: Using E-Mail Exchanges to Explore Personal Histories in Two Cultures." In *Telecollaboration in Foreign Language Learning: Proceedings of the Hawai'i Symposium,* ed. Mark Warschauer, 105–20. Second Language Teaching & Curriculum Center. Technical Report #12. Honolulu: University of Hawaii at Manoa.

Kirklighter, Cristina. 2002. *Traversing the Democratic Borders of the Essay.* Albany: State University of New York Press.

Kittay, Jeffrey, and Wlad Godzich. 1987. *The Emergence of Prose: An Essay in Prosaics.* Minneapolis: University of Minnesota Press.

Kleine, Michael W. 1999. "Thinking from a Single Textbook 'Rhetoric': The Potential Heaviness of the Book." In *(Re)Visioning Composition Textbooks: Conflicts of Culture, Ideology and Pedagogy,* ed. Xin Liu Gale and Frederic Gale, 137–62. Albany: State University of New York Press.

Knoblauch, C. H., and Lil Brannon. 1984. *Rhetorical Traditions and the Teaching of Writing.* Upper Montclair, NJ: Boynton/Cook Heinemann.

Kornfield, Jack, with Gil Fronsdal, eds. 1993. *The Teachings of the Buddha.* Boston: Shambala Books.

Kristeva, Julia. 1993a. *Nations without Nationalism.* Trans. Leon S. Roudiez. European Perspectives: A Series in Social Thought and Cultural Criticism, ed. Lawrence D. Kritzman. New York: Columbia University Press.

Kristeva, Julia. 1993b. "Open Letter to Harlem Désir." In *Nations without Nationalism,* trans. Leon S. Roudiez, 49–64. European Perspectives: A Series in Social Thought and Cultural Criticism, ed. Lawrence D. Kritzman. New York: Columbia University Press.

Kristeva, Julia. 1993c. "What of Tomorrow's Nation?" In *Nations without Nationalism,* trans. Leon S. Roudiez, 1–47. European Perspectives: A Series in Social Thought and Cultural Criticism, ed. Lawrence D. Kritzman. New York: Columbia University Press.

Kumar, Amitava, ed. 2003. *World Bank Literature.* Minneapolis: University of Minnesota Press.

Kumaravadivelu, B. 2006. *Understanding Language Teaching: From Method to Postmethod.* ESL and Applied Linguistics Professional Series. Mahweh, NJ: Lawrence Erlbaum.

Kumaravadivelu, B. 2008. *Cultural Globalization and Language Education.* New Haven, CT: Yale University Press.

kynard, carmen. 2002. "'New Life in This Dormant Creature': Notes on Social Consciousness, Language, and Learning in a College Classroom." In *Alt/Dis: Alternative Discourses and the Academy,* ed. Christopher Schroeder, Helen Fox, and Patricia Bizzell, 31–39. Portsmouth, NH: Boynton/Cook Heinemann.

Laquintano, Tim. 2010. "Sustained Authorship: Digital Writing, Self-Publishing, and the Ebook." *Written Communication* 27 (4): 469–93. http://dx.doi.org/10.1177/0741088310377863.

Landler, Mark. 2002. "Another German Publisher Mulls Its Wartime Past." *The New York Times.* November 26, 2002. Accessed January 23, 2012. http://www.nytimes.com/2002/10/14/business/another-german-publisher-mulls-its-wartime-past.html?pagewanted=all&src=pm.

Lan, Haixia. 2002. "Contrastive Rhetoric: A Must in Cross-Cultural Inquiries." In *Alt/ Dis: Alternative Discourses and the Academy*, ed. Christopher Schroeder, Helen Fox, and Patricia Bizzell, 68–79. Portsmouth, NH: Boynton/Cook Heinemann.

Langer, Susanne K. 1942. *Philosophy in a New Key: A Study of Symbolism of Reason, Rite, and Art*. 3rd ed. Cambridge, MA: Harvard University Press.

Lansing, Gerrit. 2003. "La p(l)age poetique." *A February Sheaf*. Boston: Pressed Wafer.

Lao Tzu. 1988. *Tao Te Ching*, trans. Stephen Mitchell. New York: Harper Perennial.

Li, Xiao-Ming. 1996. "Good Writing." In *Cross-Cultural Context*. Albany: State University of New York Press.

Lie, Rico. 2003. *Spaces of Intercultural Communication: An Interdisciplinary Introduction to Communication, Culture, and Globalizing/ Localizing Identities*. International Association for Media and Communication Research. Cresskill, NJ: Hampton Press.

Lipson, Carol S. 2009. "Introduction." In *Ancient Non-Greek Rhetorics*, ed. Carole S. Lipson and Roberta A. Binkley, 3–35. Lauer Series in Rhetoric and Composition, ed. Catherine Hobbs, Patricia Sullivan, Thomas Rickert, and Jennifer Bay. West Lafayette, IN: Parlor.

Lisle, Bonnie, and Sandra Mano. 1997. "Embracing a Multicultural Rhetoric." In *Writing in Multicultural Settings*, ed. Carol Severino, Juan C. Guerra, and Johnnella E. Butler, 12–26. Research and Scholarship in Composition, ed. Lil Brannon et al. New York: Modern Language Association.

Livingstone, David W. 1987. "Upgrading and Opportunities." In *Critical Pedagogy and Cultural Power*, ed. David W. Livingstone and Contributors, 125–36. Critical Perspectives in Education Series. South Hadley, MA: Bergan and Garvey.

"Longman Focuses on Private, Public Schools Market." 2005. Africa News Service/ COMTEX. July 13. Accessed January 27, 2012. http://business.highbeam.com/3548/article-1G1-133983533/longman-focuses-private-public-schools-market.

Lu Ji. 1996. "Art of Writing." In *The Art of Writing: Teachings of the Chinese Masters*, ed. and trans. Tony Barnstone and Chou Ping, 1–20. Boston: Shambala Books.

Lu, Min-Zhan. 2010. "Living-English Work." In *Cross-Language Relations in Composition*, ed. Bruce Horner, Min-Zhan Lu, and Paul Kei Matsuda, 42–56. Urbana: Southern Illinois University Press.

Lu, Xing. 1998. *Rhetoric in Ancient China, Fifth to Third Century B.C.E.: A Comparison with Classical Greek Rhetoric*. Studies in Rhetoric/Communication, ed. Thomas W. Benson. Columbia: University of South Carolina Press.

Lu, Xing. 2004. *Rhetoric of the Chinese Cultural Revolution: The Impact on Chinese Thought, Culture and Communication*. Studies in Rhetoric/Communication, Ed. Thomas W. Benson. Columbia: University of South Carolina Press.

Lunsford, Andrea A. 1999a. *Foreword to Living Rhetoric and Composition: Stories of the Discipline*, ed. Duane Roen, Stuart C. Brown, and Theresa Enos, xi–xiii. Mahwah, NJ: Lawrence Erlbaum.

Lunsford, Andrea A. 1999b. "Toward a Mestiza Rhetoric: Gloria Anzaldúa on Composition and Postcoloniality." In *Race, Rhetoric, and the Postcolonial*, ed. Gary A. Olson and Lynn Worsham, 43–80. Albany: State University of New York Press.

Lunsford, Andrea A., and Karen J. Lunsford. 2008. "'Mistakes are a Fact of Life': A National Comparative Study." *College Composition and Communication* 59 (4): 781–806.

Lunsford, Andrea, and Lisa Ede. 2006. "Crimes of Writing and Reading." In *Teaching Rhetorica: Theory, Pedagogy, Practice*, ed. Kate Ronald and Joy Ritchie, 13–30. Portsmouth, NH: Boynton/Cook Heinemann.

Lynd, Robert S., and Helen Merrell Lynd. 1929. *Middletown: A Study in Contemporary American Culture*. New York: Harcourt, Brace, and Company.

Lynd, Robert S., and Helen Merrell Lynd. 1937. *Middletown in Transition: A Study in Cultural Conflicts*. New York: Harcourt Brace Jovanovich.

Lyons, Scott Richard. 2000. "Rhetorical Sovereignty: What Do American Indians Want from Writing?" *College Composition and Communication* 51 (3): 447–68. http://dx.doi.org/10.2307/358744.

Lyons, Scott Richard. 2009. "The Fine Art of Fencing: Nationalism, Hybridity, and the Search for a Native American Writing Pedagogy." *JAC: Journal of Advanced Composition* 29 (1–2): 77–105.

Lyotard, Jean-Francois. 1984. *The Postmodern Condition: A Report on Knowledge.* Trans. Geoff Bennington and Brian Massumi. Theory and History of Literature, Volume 10, ed. Wlad Godzich and Jochen Schulte-Sasse. Minneapolis: University of Minnesota Press.

Mabasa, Ignatius T. 2005. "Crossing Borders: Poetry and Young Writers in Zimbabwe." Poetry International. Zimbabwe-Poetry International. July 1, 2005. Accessed March 28, 2011. http://www.poetryinternational.org/piw_cms/cms/cms_module/index.php?obj_id=5729.

Mack, Nancy. 2002. "The Ins, Outs, and In-Betweens of Multigenre Writing." *English Journal* 92 (2): 91–8. http://dx.doi.org/10.2307/822231.

Malinowitz, Harriet. 1995. *Textual Orientations: Lesbian and Gay Students and the Making of Discourse Communities.* Portsmouth, NH: Boynton/Cook Heinemann.

Mall, Ram Adhar. 2004. "The Concept of an Intercultural Philosophy." Translated by Michael Kimmel. In *Intercultural Communication: A Global Reader*, ed. Fred E. Jandt, 315–27. Thousand Oaks, CA: Sage.

Mangelsdorf, Kate. 2010. "Spanglish as Alternative Discourse: Working against Language Demarcation." In *Cross-Language Relations in Composition*, ed. Bruce Horner, Min-Zhan Lu, and Paul Kei Matsuda, 113–26. Urbana: Southern Illinois University Press.

Mao, LuMing. 2004. "Uniqueness or Borderlands?: The Making of Asian American Rhetorics." In *Rhetoric and Ethnicity*, ed. Keith Gilyard and Vorris Nunley, 46–55. Portsmouth, NH: Boynton/Cook Heinemann.

Mao, LuMing. 2006. *Reading Chinese Fortune Cookie: The Making of Chinese American Rhetoric.* Logan: Utah State University Press.

Mao, LuMing. 2010. "Introduction: Searching for the Way: Between the Whats and Wheres of Chinese Rhetoric." In *Studying Chinese Rhetoric in the Twenty-First Century*, ed. LuMing Mao. Special Issue of *College English* 72.4: 329–49.

Mao, LuMing, and Morris Young, eds. 2008. *Representations: Doing Asian American Rhetoric.* Logan: Utah State University Press.

Margalit, Avishai. 1996. *The Decent Society.* Cambridge, MA: Harvard University Press.

Margolick, David. 1998. "The German Front." *Vanity Fair* (June): 120–45.

Marks, Joel, and Roger T. Ames. 1995. *Emotions in Asian Thought: A Dialogue in Comparative Philosophy.* Albany: State University of New York Press.

Matsuda, Paul Kei. 2002. "Alternative Discourses: A Synthesis." In *Alt/Dis: Alternative Discourses and the Academy*, ed. Christopher Schroeder, Helen Fox, and Patricia Bizzell, 191–96. Portsmouth, NH: Boynton/Cook Heinemann.

Matsuda, Paul Kei. 2010. "The Myth of Linguistic Homogeneity in U.S. College Composition." In *Cross-Language Relations in Composition*, ed. Bruce Horner, Min-Zhan Lu, and Paul Kei Matsuda, 81–96. Urbana: Southern Illinois University Press.

Mayher, John S. 1990. *Uncommon Sense: Theoretical Practice in Language Education.* Portsmouth, NH: Boynton/Cook Heinemann.

Mazrui, Alamin. 2000. "The World Bank, the Language Question and the Future of African Education." In *A Thousand Flowers: Social Struggles against Structural Adjustments in African Universities*, ed. Silvia Federici, George Caffentzis, and Ousseina Alidou, 43–59. Trenton, NJ: Africa World Press.

Mazumder, Bhashkar. N.d. "Upward Intergenerational Mobility in the United States." Economic Mobility Project. The Pew Charitable Trust. Accessed January 27, 2012.

http://www.pewtrusts.org/uploadedFiles/wwwpewtrustsorg/Reports/Economic_
Mobility/PEW_Upward%20EM%2014.pdf.

McCarthy, Lucille Parkinson. 1987. "A Stranger in Strange Lands: A College Student Writing across the Curriculum." *Research in the Teaching of English* 21 (3): 233–65.

McIntyre, Alice. 1997. *Making Meaning of Whiteness: Exploring Racial Identity with White Teachers.* Albany: State University of New York Press.

McPhail, Mark Lawrence. 1994. *The Rhetoric of Racism.* Lanham, MD: University Press of America.

Milner, Laura Alicia. 2005. "The Language of Loss: Transformation in the Telling, In and Beyond the Writing Classroom." PhD diss., Indiana University of Pennsylvania, Indiana.

Misson, Ray, and Wendy Morgan. 2006. *Critical Literacy and the Aesthetic: Transforming the English Classroom.* Refiguring English Studies. Urbana, IL: National Council of Teachers of English.

Mohr, Miriam. 1984. *Revision: The Rhythm of Meaning.* Upper Montclair, NJ: Boynton/Cook.

Mortensen, Peter. 1999. "Of Handbooks and Handbags: Composition Textbook Publishing after the Deal Decade." In *(Re)Visioning Composition Textbooks: Conflicts of Culture, Ideology and Pedagogy,* ed. Xin Liu Gale and Frederic Gale, 217–30. Albany: State University of New York Press.

Morton, Jelly Roll. 2005. Liner Notes. *Jelly Roll Morton: The Complete Library of Congress Recordings by Alan Lomax.* Rounder, CD.

Mudimbe, V. Y. 1988. *The Invention of Africa: Gnosis, Philosophy, and the Order of Knowledge. African Systems of Thought.* Ed. Charles S. Byrd and Ivan Karp. Bloomington: Indiana University Press.

Murphy, James J., Richard A. Katula, Forbes I. Hill, and Donovan J. Ochs, eds. 2003. *A Synoptic History of Classical Rhetoric.* 3rd ed. New York: Routledge.

Mutua, Kagendo, and Beth Blue Swadener, eds. 2004. *Decolonizing Research in Cross-Cultural Contexts.* Albany: State University of New York Press.

Myers, Carrie F. 1996. "Writing in the Dark: Composition and Motherhood." PhD diss., Indiana University of Pennsylvania.

National Council of Teachers of English. 1988, Updated 1992. Conference on College Composition and Communication. "CCCC Guideline on the National Language Policy." Accessed May 10, 2010. http://www.ncte.org/cccc/resources/positions/nationallang-policy.

Neel, Jasper. 1988. *Plato, Derrida, and Writing.* Carbondale: Southern Illinois University Press.

Nietzsche, Friedrich. 1949. *The Use and Abuse of History.* Trans. Adrian Collins. Indianapolis: Bobbs-Merrill.

Ohmann, Richard. 1996. *English in America.* Hanover, NH: Wesleyan University Press.

Oliver, Robert T. 1971. *Communication and Culture in Ancient India and China.* New York: Syracuse University Press.

O'Reilley, Mary Rose. 1993. *The Peaceable Classroom.* Portsmouth, NH: Boynton/Cook Heinemann.

Owens, Derek. 1990. "Beyond Eurocentric Discourse." In *Theory and Pedagogy,* ed. C. Mark Hurlbert. Special issue of *Works and Days: Essays in the Socio-Historical Dimensions of Literature and the Arts* 16.6: 87–101.

Owens, Derek. 1994. *Resisting Writings (and the Boundaries of Composition).* Dallas: Southern Methodist University Press.

Owens, Derek. 2001. *Composition and Sustainability: Teaching for a Threatened Generation.* Urbana: National Council of Teachers of English.

Pagnucci, Gian S. 2004. *Living the Narrative Life: Stories as a Tool for Meaning Making.* Portsmouth, NH: Boytnon/Cook Heinemann.

Peckham, Irvin. 2010. *Going North Thinking West: The Intersections of Social Class, Critical Thinking, and Politicized Writing Instruction.* Logan: Utah State University Press.

Pemberton, Michael. 1997–2012. *Across the Disciplines*. Accessed January 28, 2012. http://wac.colostate.edu/atd/.

Pennycook, Alastair. 1994. *The Cultural Politics of English as an International Language*. Language in Social Life Series, ed. Christopher N. Candlin. New York: Longman.

Pennycook, Alastair. 2001. *Critical Applied Linguistics*. New York: Routledge.

Pennycook, Alastair. 2007. *Global Englishes and Transcultural Flows*. New York: Routledge.

Pennycook, Alastair. 2010. *Language as a Local Practice*. New York: Routledge.

Perelman, C. H., and L. Olbrechts-Tyteca. 1969. *The New Rhetoric: A Treatise on Argumentation*, trans. John Wilkinson, and Purcell Weaver. Notre Dame, IN: University of Notre Dame Press.

Perl, Sondra. 2004. *Felt Sense: Writing with the Body*. Portsmouth, IN: Boynton/Cook Heinemann.

Perloff, Marjorie. 1985. "The Contemporary of Grandchildren: Pound's Influence." In *Ezra Pound among the Poets*, ed. George Bornstein, 195–229. Chicago: University of Chicago Press.

Petersen, Donald. 2001. *Early and Late: Selected Poems*. Chicago: Ivan R. Dee.

Phelps, Louise Wetherbee, and Janet Emig, eds. 1995. *Feminine Principles and Women's Experience in American Composition and Rhetoric*. Pittsburgh Series in Composition, Literacy and Culture. Pittsburgh: University of Pittsburgh Press.

Plato. 2005. *The Collected Dialogues of Plato: Including the Letters*. Bollingen Series LXXI, ed. Edith Hamilton and Huntington Cairns, trans. Lane Cooper. Princeton, NJ: Princeton University Press.

Pound, Ezra. N.d.a. "The Serious Artist." In *Literary Essays of Ezra Pound*, ed. T. S. Eliot, 41–57. New York: New Directions Press.

Pound, Ezra. N.d.b. "The Teacher's Mission." In *Literary Essays of Ezra Pound*. Ed. T. S. Eliot. New York: New Directions Press, 58–63. Originally published in *English Journal* 23 (October 8, 1934): 630–35.

Pound, Ezra. 1928. *TA HIO: The Great Learning*. University of Washington Chapbooks, 14, ed. Glenn Hughes. Seattle: University of Washington Book Store.

Pound, Ezra. 1934. *ABC of Reading*. New York: New Directions Press.

Pound, Ezra. 1970. *The Cantos of Ezra Pound*. New York: New Directions Press.

Pound, Ezra. 1973. "Mang Tsze: The Ethics of Mencius." In *Selected Prose: 1909–1965*, 81–97. New York: New Directions Press.

Powell, Malea. 1999. "Blood and Scholarship: One Mixed-Blood's Story." In *Race, Rhetoric and Composition*, ed. Keith Gilyard, 1–16. Portsmouth, NH: Boynton/Cook Heinemann.

Powell, Malea. 2004. "Extending the Hand of Empire: American Indians and the Indian Reform Movement, a Beginning." In *Rhetoric and Ethnicity*, ed. Keith Gilyard and Vorris Nunley, 37–45. Portsmouth, NH: Boynton/Cook Heinemann.

"Preface." 2002. *Alt/Dis: Alternative Discourses and the Academy*, ed. Christopher Schroeder, Helen Fox, and Patricia Bizzell, vii–x. Portsmouth, NH: Boynton/Cook Heinemann.

Quintilian. 1922. *The Institutio Oratoria of Quintilian*, trans. H. E. Butler. Loeb Classical Library, ed. G. P. Goold. Cambridge, MA: Harvard University Press.

Rama, Angel. 1996. *The Lettered City*. Ed. and trans. John Charles Chasteen. Latin America in Translation/En Traducción/Em Tradução. Post-Contemporary Interventions, ed. Stanley Fish and Frederic Jameson. Durham, NH: Duke University Press.

Ramose, Mogobe B. 2002a. "'African Renaissance': A Northbound Gaze." In *The African Philosophy Reader*, 2nd ed., ed. P. H. Coetzee and A.P.J. Roux, 600–610. London: Routledge.

Ramose, Mogobe. 2002b. "The Philosophy of Ubuntu and Ubuntu as a Philosophy." In *The African Philosophy Reader*. 2nd ed., ed. P. H. Coetzee and A.P.J. Roux, 230–38. London: Routledge.

Rasula, Jed. 1996. *The American Poetry Wax Museum*. Refiguring English Studies, ed. Stephen M. North. Urbana, IL: National Council of Teachers of English.

Ratcliffe, Krista. 2006. "Coming Out: Or, How Adrienne Rich's Feminist Theory Complicates Intersections of Rhetoric and Composition Studies, Cultural Studies, and Writing Program Administration." In *Teaching Rhetorica: Theory, Pedagogy, Practice*, ed. Kate Ronald and Joy Ritchie, 31–47. Portsmouth, NH: Boynton/Cook Heinemann.

Readings, Bill. 1997. *The University in Ruins*. Cambridge, MA: Harvard University Press.

Reich, Charles. 1970. *The Greening of America*. New York: Bantam.

Richards, I. A. 1936. *The Philosophy of Rhetoric*. New York: Oxford University Press. Originally quoted in "Discourse Theory: Implications for Research in Composing" by Charles Cooper, Lee Odell and Cynthia Courts, 1–12. In *Research on Composing: Points of Departure*, ed. Charles Cooper and Lee Odell. Urbana: National Council of Teachers of English, 1978.

Rice, Cora, and Monisha Pasupathi. 2010. "Reflecting on Self-Relevant Experiences: Adult Age Differences." *Developmental Psychology* 46 (2): 479–90. http://dx.doi.org/10.1037/a0018098.

Richardson, Elaine. 2003. *African American Literacies*. Literacies, ed. David Barton. New York: Routledge. http://dx.doi.org/10.4324/9780203166550.

Richardson, Elaine. 2010. "English-Only, African American Contributions to Standardized Communication Structures, and the Potential for Social Transformation." In *Cross-Language Relations in Composition*, ed. Bruce Horner, Min-Zhan Lu, and Paul Kei Matsuda, 97–112. Urbana: Southern Illinois University Press.

Rider, Janine. 1995. *The Writer's Book of Memory: An Interdisciplinary Study for Writing Teachers*. Mahwah, NJ: Lawrence Erlbaum.

Rijlaarsdam, Gert, ed. N.d. Studies in Writing Series. International Series on the Research of Learning and Instruction of Writing. Accessed January 28, 2012. http://www.emer-aldinsight.com/products/books/series.htm?id=1572-6304.

Ritchie, Joy, and Kate Ronald. 1998. "Riding Long Coattails, Subverting Tradition: The Tricky Business of Feminists Teaching Rhetoric(s)." In *Feminism and Composition Studies: In Other Words*, ed. Susan C. Jarratt and Lynn Worsham, 217–38. Research and Scholarship in Composition, ed. Lil Brannon et al. New York: Modern Language Association.

Ritzer, George. 2004. *The Globalization of Nothing*. Thousand Oaks, CA: Pine Forge Press/Sage.

Ritzer, George. 2007. *The Globalization of Nothing 2*. Thousand Oaks, CA: Pine Forge Press.

Romano, Tom. 2000. *Blending Genre, Alternate Style*. Portsmouth, NH: Boynton/Cook.

Romano, Susan. 2004. "Tlaltelolco: The Grammatical-Rhetorical Indios of Colonial Mexico." *College English* 66 (3): 257–77. http://dx.doi.org/10.2307/4140748.

Ronald, Kate, and Hephzibah Roskelly, eds. 1990. *Farther Along: Transforming Dichotomies in Rhetoric and Composition*. Portsmouth, NH: Boynton/Cook Heinemann.

Ronald, Kate, and Joy Ritchie. 2006. "Introduction." In *Teaching Rhetorica: Theory, Pedagogy, Practice*, ed. Kate Ronald and Joy Ritchie, 1–12. Portsmouth, NH: Boynton/Cook Heinemann.

Rorty, Richard. 1981. *Philosophy and the Mirror of Nature*. Princeton, NJ: Princeton University Press.

Roskelly, Hephzibah, and Kate Ronald. 1998. *Reason to Believe: Romanticism, Pragmatism, and the Teaching of Writing*. Albany: State University of New York Press.

Royster, Jacqueline Jones. 2000. *Traces of a Stream: Literacy and Social Change among African American Women*. Pittsburgh Series in Composition, Literacy and Culture, ed. David Bartholomae and Jean Ferguson Carr. Pittsburgh: University of Pittsburgh Press.

Russell, David R. 2002. *Writing in the Disciplines: A Curricular History*. 2nd ed. Carbondale: Southern Illinois University Press.

Russo, Richard. 1994. *Mohawk*. New York: Vintage.

Russo, Richard. 1994. *The Risk Pool*. New York: Vintage.

Russo, Richard. 1995. *Nobody's Fool*. New York: Vintage.

Russo, Richard. 2008. *Bridge of Sighs*. New York: Vintage.

San Juan, E., Jr. 2000. *After Postcolonialism: Remapping Philippines–United States Confrontations*. Pacific Formations, ed. Arif Dirlik. Lanham, MD: Rowman & Littlefield.

Sartre, Jean-Paul. N.d. *Being and Nothingness: An Essay on Phenomenological Ontology*, trans. Hazel E. Barnes. New York: Philosophical Library.

Sartre, Jean-Paul. 1965. "What Is Writing?" In *Essays in Existentialism*, ed. Wade Baskin, 301–31. Secaucus, NJ: Citadel Press.

Schaasfma, David, and Ruth Vinz, with Sara Brock, Randi Dickson, and Nick Sousanis. 2011. *Narrative Inquiry: Approaches to Language and Literacy Research*. Language and Literacy Series, ed. Celia Genishi and Donna E. Alvermann. NCRLL Series, ed. JoBeth Allen and Donna E. Alvermann. New York: Teachers College Press.

Schilb, John. 1996. *Between the Lines: Relating Composition Theory and Literary Theory*. Portsmouth, NH: Boynton/Cook Heinemann.

Schroeder, Christopher, Helen Fox, and Patricia Bizzell, eds. 2002. *Alt/Dis: Alternative Discourses and the Academy*. Portsmouth, NH: Boynton/Cook Heinemann.

Scott, Fred Newton, and Joseph Villiers Denney. 1897. *Composition-Rhetoric: Designed for Use in Secondary Schools*. Boston: Allyn and Bacon.

Scott, Fred Newton, and Joseph Villiers Denney. 1909. *Paragraph-Writing: A Rhetoric for Colleges*. Boston: Allyn and Bacon.

Schell, Eileen E., and K. J. Rawson. 2010. *Rhetroica in Motion: Feminist Rhetorical Methods and Methodologies*. Pittsburgh Series in Composition, Literacy, and Culture, ed. David Bartholomae and Jean Ferguson Carr. Pittsburgh: University of Pittsburgh Press.

Severino, Carol, Juan C. Guerra, and Johnnella E. Butler, eds. 1997. *Writing in Multicultural Settings*. Research and Scholarship in Composition. New York: Modern Language Association.

Shaker, Fatna. 1994. "I Practice Reading Secretly." In *Women and Words in Saudi Arabia: The Politics of Literary Discourse* by Saddeka Arebi, 210–11. New York: Columbia University Press. Excerpt originally from *Nabt Al-Ard (The Earth's Plant)*. Jeddah: Tihama, 1981.

Shames, Germaine W. 1997. *Transcultural Odysseys: The Evolving Global Consciousness*. Yarmouth, ME: Intercultural Press.

Shih, Shu-mei, and Francoise Lionnet. 2005. "Introduction: Thinking through the Minor, Transnationally." In *Minor Transnationalism*, ed. Shu-mei Shih and Francoise Lionnet, 1–23. Durham, NC: Duke University Press.

Shohat, Ella, and Robert Stam. 1994. *Unthinking Eurocentrism: Multiculturalism and the Media*. London: Routledge.

Shor, Ira. 1992. *Empowering Education: Critical Teaching for Social Change*. Chicago: University of Chicago Press.

Shum, Mark Shui-Kee, and Zhang De-lu, eds. 2010. *Teaching Writing in Chinese Speaking Areas*. Studies in Writing. vol. 16. New York: Springer.

Sieburth, Richard. 2003. *Introduction to The Pisan Cantos by Ezra Pound*. Ed. Richard Sieburth, ix–xliii. New York: New Directions.

Tu, Sikong. 1996. "The Twenty-Four Styles of Poetry." In *The Art of Writing: Teachings of the Chinese Masters*, ed. Tony Barnstone and Chou Ping, 21–39. Boston: Shambala Books.

Simmons, Jay, and Timothy McLaughlin. 2003. "Longer, Deeper, Better." *Teaching English in the Two-Year College* (May): 416–26.

Sipe, Rebecca Bowers. 2000. "Virtually Being There: Creating Authentic Experiences through Interactive Exchanges." *English Journal* 90 (2): 104–11. http://dx.doi.org/10.2307/821226.

Sirc, Geoffrey. 2002. *English Composition as a Happening*. Logan: Utah State University Press.

6th Conference on Intercultural Rhetoric and Discourse. 2011. Georgia State University, Atlanta, Georgia, June 11–12. Accessed January 27, 2012. http://www2.gsu. edu/~wwwesl/conference.html.

Skutnabb-Kangas, Tove. 2000. *Linguistic Genocide in Education, or Worldwide Diversity and Human Rights?* Mahwah, NJ: Lawrence Erlbaum.

Slaughter, Sheila, and Larry L. Leslie. 1999. *Academic Capitalism: Politics, Policies, and the Entrepreneurial University.* American Land Classics. Baltimore: Johns Hopkins University Press.

Slaughter, Sheila, and Gary Rhoades. 2009. *Academic Capitalism and the New Economy: Markets, State, and Higher Education.* Baltimore: Johns Hopkins University Press.

Sledd, James. 1996. *Eloquent Discourse: The Writings of James Sledd.* Ed. Richard D. Freed. Boynton/Cook Heinemann.

Smith, Anthony D. 1971. *Theories of Nationalism.* London: Gerald Duckworth and Co.

Smith, Anthony D. 1998. *Nationalism and Modernism: A Critical Survey of Recent Theories of Nations and Nationalism.* London: Routledge.

Smith, Michael Peter, and Luis Eduardo Guarnizo. 2008. "The Locations of Transnationalism." In *Transnationalism from Below,* ed. Michael Peter Smith and Luis Eduardo Guarnizo, 3–34. Comparative Urban and Community Research, Vol. 6. New Brunswick, NJ: Transaction.

Smitherman, Geneva. 1977. "'The Forms of Things Unknown': Black Modes of Discourse." In *Talkin and Testifyin: The Language of Black America,* by Geneva Smitherman, 101–66. Detroit: Wayne State University Press.

Smitherman, Geneva. 1994. "'The Blacker the Berry, the Sweeter the Juice': African American Student Writers." In *The Need for Story: Cultural Diversity in Classroom and Community,* ed. Anne Haas Dyson and Celia Genishi, 80–101. Urbana, IL: National Council of Teachers of English.

Smitherman, Geneva. 2004. "Meditations on Language, Pedagogy, and a Life of Struggle." In *Rhetoric and Ethnicity,* ed. Keith Gilyard and Vorris Nunley, 3–14. Portsmouth, NH: Boynton/Cook Heinemann.

Snyder, Ilana, ed. 2002. *Silicon Literacies: Communication, Innovation, and Education in the Electronic Age.* Literacies. New York: Routledge.

Spahr, Juliana. 2001. *Everybody's Autonomy: Connective Reading and Collective Identity.* Modern and Contemporary Poetics, ed. Charles Bernstein and Hank Lazer. Tuscaloosa: University of Alabama Press.

Spooner, Michael. 2002. "An Essay We're Learning To Read: Responding to Alt.Style." In *Alt/Dis: Alternative Discourses and the Academy,* ed. Christopher Schroeder, Helen Fox, and Patricia Bizzell, 155–77. Portsmouth, NH: Boynton/Cook Heinemann.

Stam, Robert. 1995. "Eurocentrism, Polycentrism, and Multicultural Pedagogy: Film and the Quincentennial." In *Late Imperial Culture,* ed. Román De La Campa, E. Ann Kaplan, and Michael Sprinker, 97–121. London: Verso.

Stein, Gertrude. 1975. *How to Write.* New York: Dover.

Stiver, Jan. 1996. "The Writing Partners Project." *Phi Delta Kappan* 77 (10): 694–5.

Stroud, Scott R. 2009. "Pragmatism and the Methodology of Comparative Rhetoric." *Rhetoric Society Quarterly* 39 (4): 353–79. http://dx.doi.org/10.1080/02773940903196614.

Stuckey, J. Elspeth. 1991. *The Violence of Literacy.* Portsmouth, NH: Boynton/Cook Heinemann.

Summerfield, Judith, and Geoffrey Summerfield. 1986. *Texts and Contexts: A Contribution to the Theory and Practice of Teaching Composition.* New York: Random House.

"Sustainable Writing Development: Approaches and Challenges." 2010. The Writing Development in Higher Education Conference, United Kingdom, June 28–30. Accessed January 28, 2012. http://www.writenow.ac.uk/wp-content/uploads/2010/01/wdhe-2010-detailed-programme.pdf.

Tarrow, Sidney. 2005. *The New Transnational Activism.* Cambridge Studies in Contentious Politics, ed. Jack A. Goldstone, Doug McAdam, Sidney Tarrow, Charles Tilly, and Elisabeth J. Wood. Cambridge: Cambridge University Press. http://dx.doi.org/10.1017/CBO9780511791055.

Thaiss, Chris, and Terry Myers Zawacki. 2006. *Engaged Writers and Dynamic Disciplines: Research on the Academic Life.* Portsmouth, NH: Boynton/Cook Heinemann.

Thumboo, Edwin. 2009. "Literary Creativity in World Englishes." In *The Handbook of World Englishes,* ed. Braj B. Kachru Yamuna Kachru and Cecil L. Nelson, 405–27. Malden, MA: Wiley-Blackwell.

"Toward an International Rhetoric." 2005. Indiana University of Pennsylvania. December. Accessed June 16, 2005. www.people.iup.edu/xxjm/rhetoric.htm.

Trimbur, John. 2004. "Keeping the World Safe for Class Struggle: Revolutionary Memory in a Post-Marxist Time." In *The Private, the Public and the Published: Reconciling Private Lives and Public Rhetoric,* ed. Barbara Couture and Thomas Kent, 47–58. Logan: Utah State University Press.

Tyrrell, Ian. 2007. *Transnational Nation: United States History in Global Perspective since 1789.* New York: Palmgrave Macmillan.

"University Literacies: Knowledge, Writing, Disciplines." 2010. Lille, France. September 2–4. Accessed April 9, 2010. http://evenements.univ-lille3.fr/litteracies-universitaires/en/.

Urban, Greg. 2001. *Metaculture: How Culture Moves through the World.* Public Worlds, vol. 8, ed. Dilip Gaonkar and Benjamin Lee. Minneapolis: University of Minnesota Press.

Vallejo, José F. 2004. "ESL Writing Center Conferencing: A Study of One-To-One Tutoring Dynamics and the Writing Process." PhD diss., Indiana University of Pennsylvania, Indiana.

Vandenburg, Peter. 2006. "Taming Multiculturalism: The Will to Literacy in Composition Studies." In *Relations, Locations, Positions: Composition Theory for Writing Teachers,* ed. Peter Vandenberg, Sue Hum, and Jennifer Clary-Lemon, 535–62. Urbana, IL: National Council of Teachers of English.

Varelas Christine Maria, C. Pappas, Sofia Kokkino, and Ibett Ortiz. 2010. "Students as Authors: Science and Children." National Science Teachers Association. February 28. Accessed May 7, 2011. http://cmapspublic2.ihmc.us/rid=1H0VWXN37-W4SDWY-KL2/NSTA_Students%20as%20Authors.pdf.

Vasilyuk, Fyodor. 1988. *The Psychology of Experience.* Moscow: Progress.

Villaneuva, Victor. 1993. *Bootstraps: From an American Academic of Color.* Urbana, IL: National Council of Teachers of English.

Ware, Paige Daniel, and Claire Kramsch. 2005. "Towards an Intercultural Stance: Teaching German and English through Telecollaboration." *Modern Language Journal* 89 (2): 190–205. http://dx.doi.org/10.1111/j.1540-4781.2005.00274.x.

Warner, Mary. 1995. "Writing Partners: Facilitating Learning and Fostering Mentorships across Course Levels." Annual Convention of the National Council of Teachers of English. San Diego, CA. November. (ERIC Document Reproduction Service No. ED 397441).

Warriner, John E., and Francis Griffith. 1957. *English Grammar and Composition.* New York: Harcourt, Brace and World. Quoted in Charles Cooper and Lee Odell. 1978. *Research on Composing: Points of Departure,* (Urbana: National Council of Teachers of English).

Warschauer, Mark, ed. 1996. *Telecollaboration in Foreign Language Learning: Proceedings of the Hawaii Symposium.* Second Language Teaching & Curriculum Center. Technical Report #12. Honolulu: University of Hawaii at Manoa.

Warschauer, Mark, ed. 1999. *Electronic Literaces: Language, Culture, and Power in Online Education.* Mahwah, NJ: Lawrence Erlbaum.

Warschauer, Mark, and Richard Kern. 2000. "Introduction: Theory and Practice of Network-Based Language Teaching." In *Network-Based Language Teaching: Concepts and Practice*, ed. Mark Warschauer and Richard Kern, 1–19. The Cambridge Applied Linguistics Series, ed. Michael H. Long and Jack C. Richards. New York: Cambridge University Press.

Watkins, Evan. 2003. "World Bank Literacy and the Culture of Jobs." In *World Bank Literature*, ed. Amitava Kumar, 12–25. Minneapolis: University of Minnesota Press.

Wei Qingzhi, ed. 1996. *Poets' Jade Splinters*. In *The Art of Writing: Teachings of the Chinese Masters*, 41–68. Boston: Shambala Books.

Weiler, Kathleen. 1988. *Women Teaching for Change: Gender, Class and Power*. Critical Studies in Education Series, ed. Paulo Freire and Henry A. Giroux. South Hadley, MA: Bergin and Garvery.

Weiler, Kathleen. 1992. "Teaching, Feminism, and Social Change." In *Social Issues in the English Classroom*, ed. C. Mark Hurlbert and Samuel Totten, 322–37. Urbana: National Council of Teachers of English.

Welch, Kathleen. 1999. *Electric Rhetoric: Classical Rhetoric, Oralism, and a New Literacy*. Digital Communication, ed. Edward Barrett. Cambridge, MA: MIT Press.

Welch, Nancy. 2008. *Living Room: Teaching Public Writing in a Privatized World*. Portsmouth, NH: Boynton/Cook Heinemann.

"What Should CCCC Do (and Not Do) to Support the Globalization of Writing Studies?" 2010. Panel at the annual meeting of the Conference on College Composition and Communication, Louisville, Kentucky, March 18–21.

Widodo, Handoyo Puji, Gloria Park, Terry Locke, and Lisya Seloni. 2004–2012. *The International Journal of Innovation in English Language Teaching and Research*. Accessed January 28, 2012. https://www.novapublishers.com/catalog/product_info. php?products_id=14903.

Williams, Tamara R. 1995. Introduction to *The Doubtful Straight* by Ernesto Cardenal, viii–xxxi. Trans. John Lyons. Bloomington: Indiana University Press.

Willis, Paul. 1977. *Learning to Labour: How Working-Class Kids Get Working-Class Jobs*. New York: Columbia University Press.

Wright, William. 1992. "Telecomputing and Social Action." In *Social Issues in the English Classroom*, ed. C. Mark Hurlbert and Samuel Totten, 122–33. Urbana, IL: National Council of Teachers of English.

"Writing Research Across Borders II." 2011. 4th International Conference on Writing Research. February 17–21. Accessed February 1, 2011. http://www.writing.ucsb.edu/wrconf11/.

Yancey, Kathleen Blake. 2006. *Delivering College Composition: The Fifth Canon*. Portsmouth, NH: Boynton/Cook Heinemann.

You, Xiaoye. 2010. *Writing in the Devil's Tongue: A History of English Composition in China*. Carbondale: Southern Illinois University Press.

Young, Morris. 2004. *Minor Re/Visions: Asian American Literacy Narratives as a Rhetoric of Citizenship*. Studies in Writing and Rhetoric. Carbondale: Southern Illinois University Press.

Zawacki, Terry Myers, and Anna Sophia Habib. 2010. "'Will Our Stories Help Teachers Understand?': Multilingual Students Talk about Identity, Voice, and Expectations across Academic Communities." In *Reinventing Identities in Second Language Writing*, ed. Michelle Cox, Jay Jordan, Chrisitina Ortmeier-Hooper, and Gwen Gray Schwartz, 54–74. Urbana, IL: National Council of Teachers of English.

Zebroski, James Thomas. 1999. "Textbook Advertisements in the Formation of Composition: 1969–1990." In *(Re)Visioning Composition Textbooks: Conflicts of Culture, Ideology and Pedagogy*, ed. Xin Liu Gale and Frederic Gale, 231–48. Albany: State University of New York Press.

INDEX